S0-CLC-685

Violence in the Americas

SECURITY IN THE AMERICAS IN THE TWENTY-FIRST CENTURY

Series Editor: Jonathan D. Rosen

Countries throughout the Americas face many challenges in the twenty-first century such as drug trafficking, organized crime, environmental degradation, guerrilla movements, and terrorism among many other major threats. In this series, titled Security in the Americas in the twenty-first century, we invite contributions on topics focusing on security issues in specific countries or regions within the Americas. We are interested in approaching this topic from a political science and international relations perspective. However, we invite manuscript submissions from other disciplines. The aim of this series is to highlight the major security challenges in the twenty-first century and contribute to the security studies literature. We invite both policy-oriented and theoretical submissions.

Recent Titles

Cooperation and Drug Policies in the Americas: Trends in the Twenty-First Century, edited by Roberto Zepeda and Jonathan D. Rosen
Reconceptualizing Security in the Americas in the Twenty-First Century, edited by Bruce M. Bagley, Jonathan D. Rosen, and Hanna S. Kassab
Prisons in the Americas in the 21st Century: Human Dumping Ground, edited by Jonathan D. Rosen and Marten W. Brienen
Decline of the U.S. Hegemony?: A Challenge of ALBA and a New Latin American Integration of the Twenty-First Century, edited by Bruce M. Bagley and Magdalena Defort
Colombia's Political Economy at the Outset of the 21st Century: From Uribe to Santos and Beyond, edited by Bruce M. Bagley and Jonathan D. Rosen
The Obama Doctrine in the Americas, edited by Hanna S. Kassab and Jonathan D. Rosen
Linking Political Violence and Crime in Latin America: Myths, Realities, and Complexities, edited by Kirsten Howarth and Jenny H. Peterson
Organized Crime, Drug Trafficking, and Violence in Mexico: The Transition from Felipe Calderón to Enrique Peña Nieto (2006-2015), by Jonathan D. Rosen and Roberto Zepeda
U.S.-Cuba Relations: Charting a New Path, by Jonathan D. Rosen and Hanna S. Kassab
Fragile States in the Americas edited by Jonathan D. Rosen and Hanna S. Kassab
Culture and National Security in the Americas edited by Brian Fonseca and Eduardo A. Gamarra
Energy Security and Environmental Sustainability in the Western Hemisphere, edited by Remi B. Piet, Bruce Bagley, and Marcelo Zorovich
Transnational Organized Crime in Latin America and the Caribbean: From Evolving Threats and Responses to Integrated, Adaptive Solutions, by R. Evan Ellis
Violence in the Americas, edited by Hanna S. Kassab and Jonathan D. Rosen

Violence in the Americas

Edited by
Hanna S. Kassab and Jonathan D. Rosen

LEXINGTON BOOKS
Lanham • Boulder • New York • London

Published by Lexington Books
An imprint of The Rowman &Littlefield Publishing Group, Inc.
4501 Forbes Boulevard, Suite 200, Lanham, Maryland 20706
www.rowman.com

Unit A, Whitacre Mews, 26-34 Stannary Street, London SE11 4AB

British Library Cataloguing in Publication Information Available

Library of Congress Cataloging-in-Publication Data

Names: Kassab, Hanna Samir, 1984– editor. | Rosen, Jonathan D., editor.
Title: Violence in the Americas / edited by Jonathan D. Rosen and Hanna S. Kassab.
Description: Lanham : Lexington Books, 2018. | Series: Security in the Americas in the twenty-first century | Includes bibliographical references and index.
Identifiers: LCCN 2018006654 (print) | LCCN 2018005678 (ebook) | ISBN 9781498567312 (Electronic) | ISBN 9781498567305 (cloth : alk. paper)
Subjects: LCSH: Violence—Latin America. | Violence—Americas.
Classification: LCC HN110.5.Z9 (print) | LCC HN110.5.Z9 V58175 2018 (ebook) | DDC 303.6098—dc23
LC record available at https://lccn.loc.gov/2018006654

∞™ The paper used in this publication meets the minimum requirements of American National Standard for Information Sciences—Permanence of Paper for Printed Library Materials, ANSI/NISO Z39.48-1992.

Printed in the United States of America

To Bradford R. McGuinn—
an outstanding teacher, scholar, and mentor

Contents

Introduction

Jonathan D. Rosen and Hanna S. Kassab

Countries in Latin America have made tremendous strides in recent decades. Between 2003 and 2013, more than 80 million people living in Latin America moved above the threshold of moderate poverty. Furthermore, fourteen countries in the region reduce income inequality as seen by decreases in the Gini coefficient. Latin American states also experienced an expanding middle class to 34 percent in 2012 from 20 percent in 2003.[1] In spite of such successes, the region faces various security challenges. Latin American and Caribbean countries account for 37 percent of homicides in the world despite the fact that the region only has 8 percent of the population.[2] Moreover, violence in Latin American countries has spiked by 12 percent over the past 10 years. During this past decade, over one million people have died due to criminal violence in Latin America and Caribbean countries.[3] In 2013, Latin America became the most violent region in the world.[4] According to the United Nation's *Global Study on Homicide 2013* report, the world recorded 437,000 intentional homicides in 2012. The Americas had 157,000 homicides based on 2012 data compared to Africa's 135,000 homicides.[5] In terms of homicide rates, the Americas registered a homicide rate of 16.3 per 100,000 in 2012 compared to Africa's 12.5 per 100,000. Furthermore, the Americas homicide rate was much higher than the global rate of 6.2 per 100,000 (see figure I.1).[6]

Latin America is home to the most violent countries in the world. Honduras was the most violent non-waring country in the world in 2012 with a homicide rate of 90.4 per 100,000. Venezuela recorded a homicide rate of 53.7 per 100,000 in the same year. In addition, El Salvador had a homicide rate of 41.2 per 100,000, while Mexico recorded 21.5 homicides per 100,000 in 2012. Meanwhile Colombia and Brazil had homicide rates of 30.8 and 25.2, respectively (see figure I.2).[7] As of 2016, the region on average had a homicide rate of approximately 22 per 100,000 inhabitants. Yet the alarming

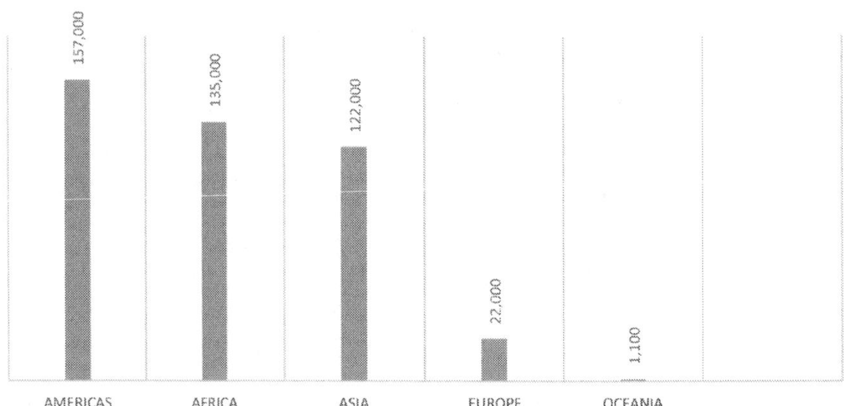

Figure I.1. Total Number of Homcides According to Region (2012)
Created by authors with data from UNODC, Global Study on Homicide: 2013.

data point is that the regional homicide average will spike to 35 per 100,000 inhabitants if the current trends in violence continue.[8]

In 2015, El Salvador became the most violent country on the planet with a homicide rate of 104 per 100,000 inhabitants. In 2016, El Salvador remained the most violent country with a homicide rate of 81.2 per 100,000, which is an improvement from the previous year. In the same year, Venezuela and Honduras recorded 59 homicides per 100,000. Violence also remained high in other countries throughout the region (see figure I.3). Laura Chioda contends,

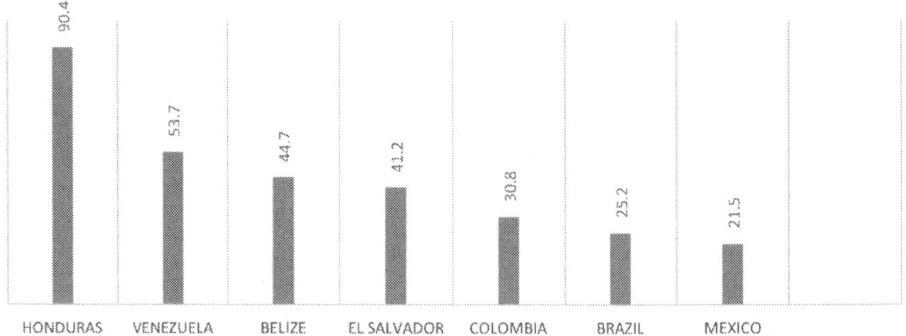

Figure I.2. Homicide Rate per 100,000 (2012 or latest year)
Created by authors with data from UNODC, Global Study on Homicide: 2013.

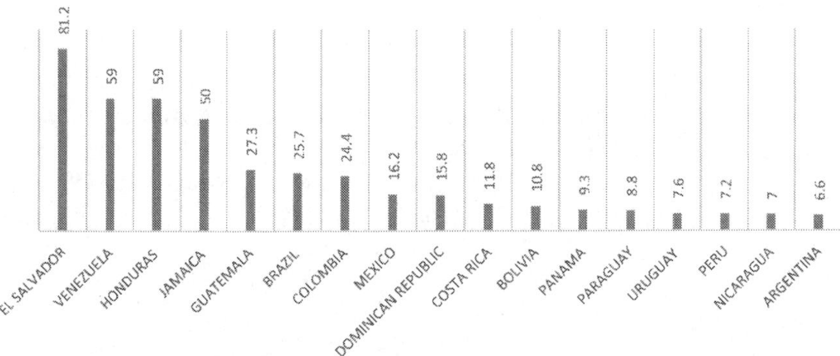

Figure I.3. 2016 Homicide Rates per 100,000
Created by authors with data from Insight Crime's 2016 Homicide Round-up.

"Over the last 15 years, the homicide rate has hovered stubbornly around 24 homicides per 100,000. The trend started to decline slightly in the first half of the 2000s, but with the deteriorating situation in Central America, any gain has been reversed."[9]

In addition to being home to the most violent countries in the world, the Americas has the most violence cities on the planet (see figure I.4). Research indicates that nearly around 86 percent of the most violent cities on the planet can be found in Latin America.[10] Ciudad Juárez, which is located in the state

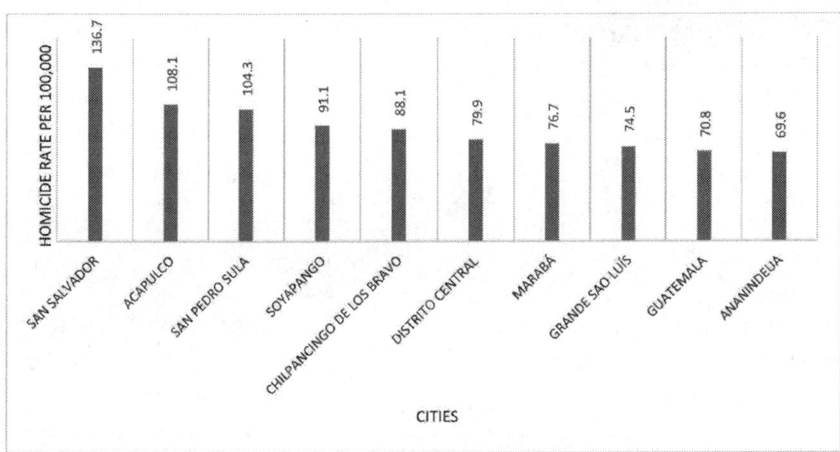

Figure I.4. Most Violent Cities In Latin America (Homicide Rate)
Created by authors with data from Robert Muggah and Ilona Szabó de Carvalho, "There's a cure for Latin America's murder epidemic—and it doesn't involve more police or prisons."

of Chihuahua, Mexico, ranked as the most violent city from 2008 to 2012.[11] In 2011, for example, Ciudad Juárez recorded a homicide rate of 148 per 100,000. By 2014, this city's homicide rate declined to 40 per 100,000 inhabitants.[12] In 2014, San Pedro Sula ranked as the most violent city in the world with a homicide rate of 171 per 100,000 inhabitants. In fact, the most violent cities on the list of the 50 most violent cities worldwide in 2014 are in Latin America. In 2014, Caracas, Venezuela ranked second with a homicide rate of 115 per 100,000.[13] Brazil had 19 cities on the list of the 50 most violent cities in the world in 2014.[14] The countries in Latin America with the most violent cities on the list, included Mexico (10 cities), Colombia (five cities), and Venezuela (four cities).[15] By 2016, San Salvador ranked as the most violent city on the planet with a homicide rate of 136.70 per 100,000 inhabitants. Acapulco ranked second with a homicide rate of 108.10 per 100,000 people followed by San Pedro Sula with a homicide rate of 104.30 per 100,000.[16]

The high levels of violence in Latin American and Caribbean countries present major challenges in terms of negative ramifications. The cost of violence is an estimated 3.5 percent of GDP for countries in the region, which is around $261 billion per year. According to 2015 data, Central America incurred a crime-related costs equivalent to 4.2 percent of GDP. Crime-related violence in Caribbean countries translate into 3.6 percent of GDP. Moreover, countries in the Andean region and the Southern Cone recorded crime-related costs of 3.1 and 3 percent, respectively.[17]

How can we explain the high levels of violence in the region? It is important to emphasize that the nature of violence is different in countries throughout the Americas. Countries, such as Colombia, have long histories of internal conflicts and political violence, which have contributed to the high levels of violence.[18] The Colombian Congress passed the peace accord in November 2016 ending the more than 50 year internal armed conflict with The Revolutionary Armed Forces of Colombia (Fuerzas Armadas Revolucionarias de Colombia—FARC).[19] More than 7 million people have been displaced as a result of the Colombian conflict. The number of forced internal displacements increased from 249,876 in 1999 to 711,315 in 2002. Forced internal displacements remained steady from 2003 (423,899) to 2008 (405,869). By 2014, this country had 204,473 forced internal displacements.[20] In addition, more than 200,000 deaths have occurred because of the internal armed conflict.[21]

Some countries, such as Mexico, Colombia, Brazil, and Guatemala—among others, have been plagued by high levels of drug trafficking, organized crime, and gangs.[22] Gangs, such as Mara Salvatrucha (MS-13) and the 18th Street gang present a security threat, particularly in the Northern Triangle countries (Guatemala, Honduras, and El Salvador). According to 2012 data, there are an estimated 22,000 MS-13 and 18th Street gang members in

Guatemala, 12,000 in Honduras, and 20,000 in El Salvador.[23] Gangs seek to increase territory and participate in a variety of illicit activities, such as drug trafficking and extortion. Street gangs use violence to intimidate rivals and civilians, which in turn generates a fear among the population, and has contributed to spikes in violence.[24] Adriana Beltrán of the Washington Office on Latin America (WOLA) contends that "[v]iolence and insecurity are also largely due to the proliferation of local street gangs or maras that impact every aspect of life in the neighborhoods and communities they control. While many well to do neighborhoods remain safe, in many poorer communities, gangs enforce curfews, control entry into their neighborhoods, and impose their own rules."[25] Young men as well as children often experience intense pressures to join such organizations. Sometimes these individuals are threatened to become members of the youth gangs. In addition, women have faced a variety of threats by gang members, including sexual assault.[26]

Latin America has seen a proliferation in the number of criminal organizations operating in the region, which presents a challenge for governments as they seek to combat such groups. Steven Dudley, an organized crime expert, argues that organized crime groups have some common traits that are important to analyze: 1) they increase their control of territory by taking advantage of weak state apparatuses; 2) they diversify their clandestine activities and flourish in areas where they are emerging criminal markets; and 3) they use violent tactics to obtain their objectives.[27] Thus, criminal organizations must adapt to survive in this clandestine world. Governments with weak institutions facilitate drug trafficking and organized crime. States that have high levels of corruption[28] and a lack of transparency and accountability create ripe conditions for drug traffickers and organized crime groups to thrive penetrating the state apparatus.[29] The high levels of corruption also impact the levels of violence in the region. Robert Muggah and Ilona Szabó de Carvalho argue that "[p]art of the reason for the persistently high rates of crime in Latin America is that homicides are seldom solved or result in a conviction. In North America and Europe, roughly 80 percent of all homicides are resolved. Yet in many Latin American countries, the percentage falls to roughly 20 percent. In Brazil, Colombia, Honduras and Venezuela, less than 10 percent of murders result in a conviction."[30] In sum, corruption and high levels of impunity create the necessary conditions for criminal organizations to operate unabated. Many countries in the region continue to face these institutional challenges that have not only impacted the levels of criminal activity within the state but also have contributed to the levels of violence.

The proliferation of criminal groups is in part due to the fragmentation of organized crime in Latin America. For example, Colombia and Mexico, with the support of the United States, sought to topple the leaders of the major drug trafficking organizations. The death of Pablo Escobar, the leader of the Medellín cartel, in 1993 as well as the collapse of the Cali cartel created a vacuum in the organized crime landscape. The collapse of the cartels led to the emergence of hundreds of smaller cartels.[31] On the other hand, Mexico had six major drug cartels in 2006. The number of cartels in the country increased to twelve in 2010.[32] In 2012, Mexico's Attorney General contended that the country had eighty drug cartels, demonstrating the proliferation in the number of organized crime groups operating in Mexico.[33]

Drug trafficking and criminal groups as well as government policies have contributed to the levels of violence in Latin America.[34] In Mexico, for example, President Felipe Calderón initiated a drug war to combat drug traffickers. During the six years of the Calderón administration more than 100,000 people died as a result of drug-related violence.[35] Violence has impacted many sectors of society, including journalists, government officials, and civilians. For example, the number of mayors and ex-mayors killed increased from one in 2006 to 17 in 2010.[36] Moreover, the number of journalists and media support workers killed increased from 11 in 2006 to 14 in 2010.[37] While violence decreased during the first year of the Enrique Peña Nieto government, homicides started to increase since late 2014. Violence has spiked in 2016: Mexico recorded 17,063 homicides during the first 10 months of 2016.[38]

Latin America has also seen high levels of violence against women. The region has some of the highest rates of female murders, known as femicides. Between 2010 and 2015, Mexico, for example, recorded 2,394 female homicide victims. During the same period, Brazil recorded 4,598 female homicide victims.[39] From 2005 to 2013, Honduras experienced a proliferation in the number of violent deaths of women by 263.4 percent, highlighting the levels of violence against women.[40] In 2012, El Salvador had a female homicide rate of 8.9 per 100,000 followed by Colombia with 6.3 per 100,000 in 2011, and Guatemala with 6.2 per 100,000 in 2012.[41] Thelma Aldana, the Attorney General of Guatemala, contended that half of the 854 people murdered in the country in 2015 died due to organized crime.[42]

VOLUME ORGANIZATION

This volume is an effort to understand the nature of violence in the Americas. The majority of chapters are divided into case studies that examine the general trends as well as the consequences of violence. The authors in this book analyze the various governments' responses to violence. Each country case study focuses on the following four questions: 1) What are the general trends and nature of violence in this country? 2) What are the causes of violence? (e.g., drug trafficking, organized crime, and armed conflict—among other threats)? 3) How has the government sought to combat violence? 4) What challenges do governments face implementing security policies? In addition to case studies, there are chapters that examine general trends as well as U.S. policy in the region.

The book begins with a chapter by Sebastián A. Cutrona on violence and security in Argentina. Cutrona examines the evolution of crime in Argentina, highlighting trends in robbery rates, victimization statistics, and homicide rates. He then turns to perceptions about fears of crime, citing the increasing sense of insecurity that Argentines have. Cutrona notes that in 2006 insecurity became the most important issue for people, surpassing other issues that previously dominated the agenda, particularly the economic situation in the country. He analyzes what regions have had higher levels of violence within the country, focusing specifically on homicide rates. The chapter then turns to an examination of Argentina's security policy by highlighting some recent trends with the Mauricio Macri administration. This government has discussed the need to combat organized crime in Argentina. The author provides a critical analysis of the current administration's policies, contending that the hardline approach to combat organized crime fails to address some of the major factors that contribute to violence in the country.

Chapter 2 explores Brazil and its experiences with violence within three areas: organized criminal networks, the militarization of the police force and within the prison system. Due to the escalation of crime associated with drug trafficking, the police force adopts strategies, tactics, and weapons more suited to fighting war. Civilians trying to make a living within the many slums of Brazil are caught in the crossfire. The authors highlight the enormous cost to Brazil's fragile democracy, given its legacy with racism and colonialism.

Marten Brienen in chapter 3 takes an in-depth look at public lynching in Bolivia. There is a long history of extrajudicial executions in Latin America with indigenous peoples of Bolivia serving as a case study. Using a sociocultural anthropological lens, Brienen deconstructs the phenomenon, taking the reader through a number of steps dictating ceremonial style killings as a common practice. Brienen underscores corrupt Bolivian institutions as one of the many reasons for communal style justice.

In chapter 4, Barnett S. Koven and Cynthia McClintock examine violence in Peru. The authors note that 2010 and 2012 survey data reveal that Peruvians had higher perceptions of insecurity than all other countries in the region.[43] One and three Peruvians were victims of crime each year in the 2010s. This perception of insecurity, however, is despite the fact that Peru had a much lower homicide rate per 100,000 inhabitants than other countries in Latin America. In order to explain this anomaly, the authors begin with an examination of the causes of violence in Peru. Koven and McClintock highlight how organized crime has penetrated the institutions that have been established to combat such activities. The authors delve into what they refer to as the long-standing threats in Peru, the Shining Path and drug trafficking. Koven and McClintock then turn to organized crime, which they classify as "the emergent threat." They note that criminal activity has evolved over time, contending: "Criminal activity now reaches into not only the unpaved streets of the remote villages near coca-growing areas but also into the luxury buildings in Peru's coastal ports where shipment routes are planned and money laundered. Concomitantly, organized crime exploded; a panoply of illegal businesses, including extortion and cell phone theft rings, emerged." Next, the chapter turns to how the government has responded to violence. The current government has stressed that Peru faces a major insecurity challenge. There has been a dissatisfaction among the people with the Central government and its response to the various security-related issues plaguing the country.

In chapter 5, Victor J. Hinojosa examines the case of violence in Colombia, which has a long history of internal armed conflict as well as drug trafficking and organized crime. He begins the chapter with an examination of political and criminal violence in the country. Colombia's two largest guerrilla organizations as well as the right-wing paramilitaries have contributed to the country's long history of violence. The author notes some of the trends in what he refers to as "battle-related deaths." However, Hinojosa explains that Colombia has also witnessed high levels of violence as a result of the drug trade. He analyzes the evolution of the drug trade, which has evolved from the days of Pablo Escobar's Medellín cartel, and its rival Cali cartel. The chapter also looks at the various initiatives, such as Plan Colombia, which was designed to combat drug trafficking and organized crime. Finally, the chapter turns to the peace accord between the FARC and the Colombian government. Despite the historic significance of this agreement, the author notes that there are various challenges ahead for this country.

In chapter 6, Bradford R. McGuinn examines violence in El Salvador, which is ranked as the most violent non-waring country in the world. McGuinn contends, "It is argued in this chapter that in the puzzling case of El Salvador, the problem is the problem. The antagonisms of this small country represent a class of social problems." The author begins the piece analyzing how the problem is framed. He explains El Salvador's troubled history of violence from the days of its bloody civil war. Much of the violence today is a result of gang-related violence. The chapter explains the key gangs operating in the country, such as MS-13, and how these organizations have contributed to the high levels of violence. The author also analyzes the responses of the Salvadoran government, focusing specifically on the *mano dura* policies designed to combat the gangs and gang-related violence.

Chapter 7 turns to the case of Guatemala. Adriana Beltrán describes how Guatemala is at a critical juncture in the fight against violence. She begins with an analysis of the main factors that are contributing to the levels of violence in the country. She contends that there is not a single cause of violence in the country, but rather there are multiple factors. She starts with an examination of the role of organized crime noting that the country has seen a rise in not only drug production but also drug trafficking. Due to its geographic location, Guatemala has become a transit country for cocaine trafficked to the United States. Another major factor is the role of gangs. Beltrán highlights the impact of the two major gangs, MS-13 and the 18th Street gang.

In chapter 8, Roberto Zepeda and Jonathan D. Rosen examine violence in Mexico. The chapter begins with an examination of trends in global violence in order to see where Mexico fits in the global and regional scenario. The authors highlight some of the underlying problems that have contributed to the high levels of violence. They note that Mexico is plagued by corruption and impunity and can be characterized as an imperfect democracy. These political and institutional factors have created the necessary conditions for organized crime groups to flourish in the country. Zepeda and Rosen argue that corruption in the country has increased over time despite the transition to democracy. Next, the authors stress various economic factors and trends that are important to analyze to understand drug-related violence in the country. Mexico has been plagued by high levels of poverty, inequality, and poor economic performance. Such conditions have contributed to the millions of disconnected youth operating in the country. In addition to these underlying factors, the authors note that violence in Mexico has occurred as a result of the drug war. President Felipe Calderón launched the drug war in 2006 in an effort to combat the drug cartels in the country. The chapter shows the high levels of bloodshed and violence that occurred as a result of the war on drugs as drug cartels not only fought among each other for control of territory and drug trafficking routes but also with the government. The authors examine the trends in violence during the Calderón administration, providing a thorough analysis of differences that exist between official sources and other databases. The chapter then turns to the initial successes that have occurred during the Enrique Peña Nieto government. However, the recent trends have been troubling as violence spiked in 2016.

Chapter 9 discusses the many problems plaguing Haiti, a country dealing with its own history of violence. Since its independence, Haiti has been dealt a difficult hand. Tyrants, earthquakes, hurricanes, rampant poverty, corrupted judicial systems, trafficking, gang violence, among other matters, have set the island state back many generations. While things look hopeful, the country still needs citizens to be confident in political institutions over vigilantism.

In chapter 10, R. Evan Ellis examines transnational organized crime and violence in the region. The chapter begins by explaining the causal relationship between transnational organized crime and violence. The chapter then turns to an examination of the major trends in organized crime that have impacted security in the region. He argues, "Throughout Latin America and the Caribbean, the activities of transnational criminal organizations threaten to expand violence and insecurity." Ellis highlights the different actors operating in the region that have contributed to drug-related violence and insecurity. The chapter also examines some of the potential solutions for solving this complex and evolving issue.

In chapter 11, Eric L. Golnick examines United States Security Policy in Latin America and the Caribbean. He begins with a brief history of security policy in the region. Moreover, the author provides insightful analysis into the national security and policy process. Next, Golnick analyzes U.S. policy toward the region, highlighting some of the major trends. He focuses on defense policy as well as important topics (e.g., counter-drug operations, counterterrorism, humanitarian assistance, and various other issues). The author also explains policy restrictions that exist in the region, focusing on human rights and shoot down laws. He concludes the chapter with an examination of the emergence of Russia and China in the region and highlights countries of vital importance.

CONCLUSION

Many countries throughout the region have experienced high levels of corruption, drug trafficking, and violence that have created elements of fragility. This volume is an effort to better understand the major trends in violence. The book is comprised of case studies that explore the nature of violence in countries throughout the region. Moreover, this work seeks to address some of the ways in which governments have sought to address violence. The cases examined in this volume are quite diverse in an effort to better understand the different types of violence as all of the countries in Latin America are not the same. Countries like Brazil, Colombia, El Salvador, Guatemala, and Mexico have high levels of drug trafficking and organized crime. Strategies designed to combat drug trafficking organizations, particularly in Colombia, Mexico, and Brazil, and counter-gang strategies in Central America have help foment violence as these various criminal organizations have responded to such government policies. Other countries, like Peru and Bolivia, have much lower levels of violence. However, the perception of insecurity is quite high despite the fact that Peru has one of the lower homicide rates in the region. On the other hand, the nature of violence in Bolivia is quite different. Bolivia does not have a homicide rate like El Salvador, but this country has witnessed public lynching's and other forms of violence.

Chapter One

Violence and Security in Argentina: Major Trends and Policy Responses

Sebastián A. Cutrona

Between 2000 and 2010, more than one million people died in Latin America and the Caribbean as a result of criminal violence. The murder rate in the region grew by 11 percent, registering more than 100,000 homicides per year.[1] Latin America and the Caribbean is home to eight of the top ten most violent countries and 40 of the world's 50 most dangerous cities. The region's average rate of 23.0 intentional homicides per 100,000 inhabitants is more than double the second highest regional average, held by Sub-Saharan Africa.[2] Brazil, Colombia, Mexico, and Venezuela account for one in four violent killings around the world each year.[3] Increasing homicide rates and the growth and dissemination of crime in many Latin American countries and the Caribbean has led to "an epidemic of violence," according to the World Health Organization (WHO).[4]

Not surprisingly, perceptions of insecurity are on the rise in Latin America and the Caribbean. Increasing from 37.6 on a 100-point scale in 2012 to 43.2 in 2014, insecurity is becoming a top concern among citizens. In 2014, for example, nearly one out of every three citizens identified security as the most important problem facing their country. The situation is even worse in the Latin American sub-region and the Caribbean, where the feeling of insecurity ranges from 36.0 to 65.0. Concerns about safety are especially high in Venezuela, Ecuador, and Bolivia, as the average country score on insecurity is above the mid-point of 50 on the 0–100 scale.[5]

Where does Argentina rank compared to other countries in Latin America? Is this South American country experiencing the same trends in terms of violence and insecurity as the rest of the region? How is the problem perceived by the population? And, most importantly, how is the relationship between fear and actual crime affecting the national government's policy-making alternatives? This chapter provides an assessment of the state of security in

Argentina. The first section addresses the South American country's levels of violence, focusing on its homicide and crime rates. Victimization statistics are also provided to untangle the problem of insecurity in Argentina. After examining the empirical data on crime, the second section assesses the population's growing fear of crime. The third and final section provides an evaluation of the national government's policy-making alternatives developed to tackle the problem of insecurity in Argentina, paying special attention to the main initiatives promoted by the Macri administration (December 2015 to 2019) The chapter closes by suggesting some policy-making recommendations to approach the South American country's increasing crime and victimization rates.

THE EVOLUTION OF CRIME IN ARGENTINA

Argentina's crime rates increased drastically during the 1990s, reaching historical levels in the 2001–2002 economic collapse and social crisis. While a total of 498,290 crimes of all types were registered in 1991, in 1999 the figures nearly doubled, accounting for a total of 1,062,241 illegal acts. Argentina's crime rates, in other words, shifted from 1,484 to 2,904 crimes per 100,000 inhabitants. After experiencing a peak in 2002, when the country recorded a high of 3,573 crimes per 100,000 inhabitants, the trend went downward thereafter.[6] Although the Fernández administration (2007 to 2015) stopped releasing official statistics in 2009, the evidence suggests that crime rates continued to increase after 2007, when Argentina registered 274,460 and 711,987 crimes against people and property, respectively. The figures in 2015, indeed, show a 10 percent increase with respect to 2008, corresponding to a rate of 3,636 crimes per 100,000 inhabitants (see figure 1.1).[7]

The United Nations Development Programme (UNDP) echoed this trend in Latin America. In 2013, for example, Argentina registered the region's highest robbery rate with 973.3 robberies per 100,000 inhabitants, followed by Mexico and Brazil with 688 and 572.7, respectively (see figure 1.2).[8] Scholars such as Gabriel Kessler, however, have raised concerns about the quality of crime reporting mechanisms. Kessler claims that "[t]he problem lays in the fact that the report considers theft attempt as theft." If the former category is not included, the scholar further contends that "Argentina could be indeed at the bottom of the Latin American ranking."[9] In addition to crime reporting mechanisms, others have casted doubts on the police recording strategy, the trust in the system of law enforcement, or even the structure and development of the insurance industry as relevant mechanisms determining the way in which crime and insecurity is measured in each country.[10]

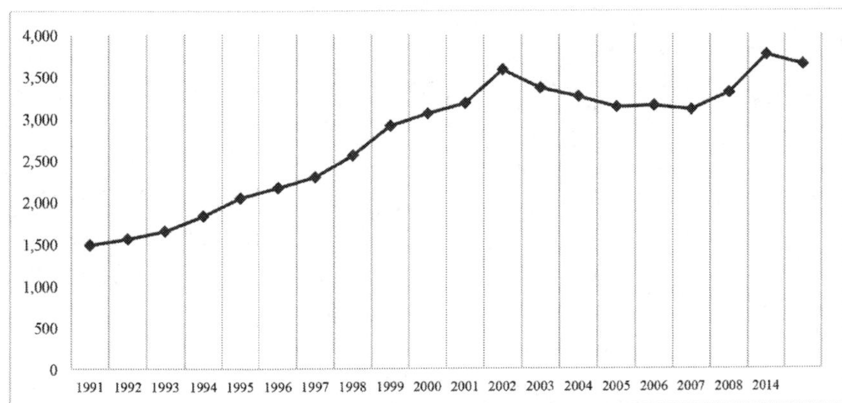

Figure 1.1. Crime Rates in Argentina, 1991–2008
Created by the author with data from Ministerio de Justicia y Derechos Humanos (2008) and Ministerio de Seguridad (2016).

Victimization statistics provide additional insights to the controversy over the ways in which crime is measured and defined. Perhaps surprisingly, the Latin American Public Opinion Project (LAPOP) confirms the trend depicted by the UNDP: 24.4 percent of Argentines have been victims of at least one crime in 2014 and the country ranks third in South America, only surpassed

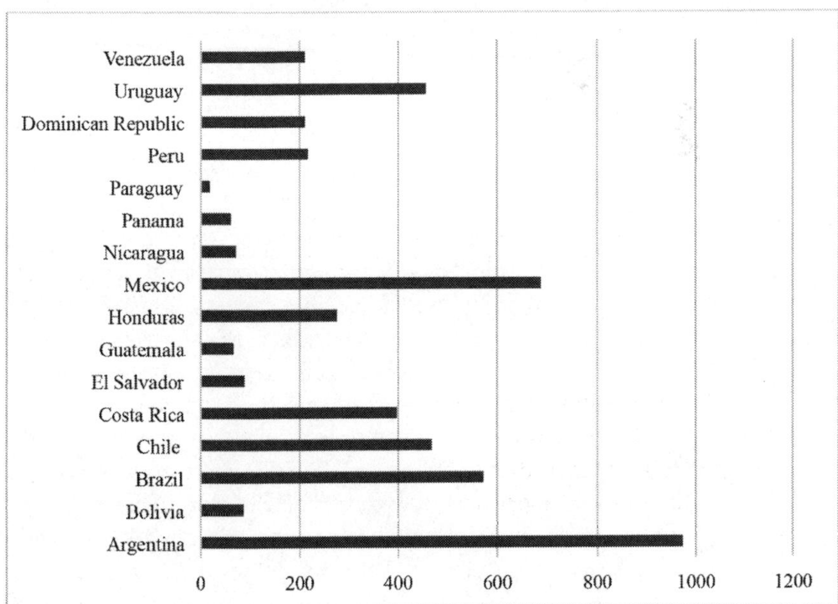

Figure 1.2. Robberies per 100,000 Inhabitants in the Americas
Created by the author with data from United Nations Development Programme (2014).

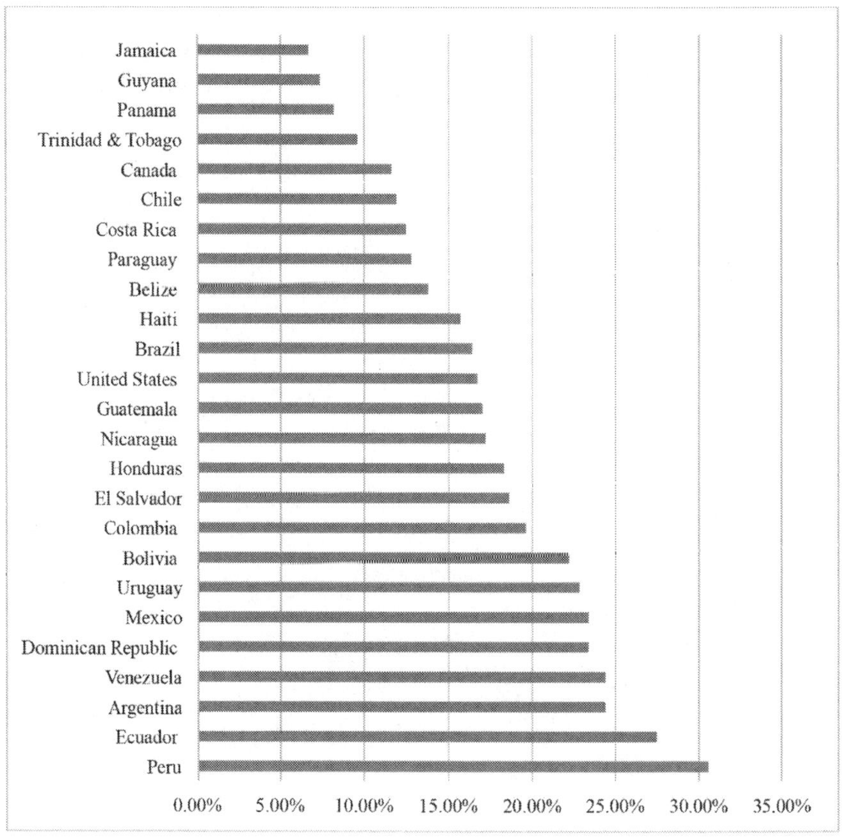

Figure 1.3. Crime Victimization Rates in the Americas, 2014
Created by the author with data from LAPOP (2014).

by Peru (30.6 percent) and Ecuador (27.5 percent) (see figure 1.3). Along the same lines, Argentina leads the ranking of countries whose citizens have experienced or heard of burglaries in their neighborhood with 71.8 percent, followed by the Dominican Republic and Venezuela with 71.5 percent and 69.9 percent, respectively.[11] Given the self-reporting nature of these data, the magnitude of robbery in Argentina is by no means negligible.

Data on homicides, in contrast, has been characterized by certain stability. While in 1991 there were 7.48 homicides per 100,000 inhabitants, by the end of the decade the country registered 7.29 homicides. Similar to the country's crime rates, a peak of 9.2 homicides was registered in 2002 when Argentina suffered its economic and social crisis.[12] The most recent figures suggest that homicide rates in Argentina remained stable, even in a context of economic recession. In 2015, for example, the country recorded 2,837 homicides, cor-

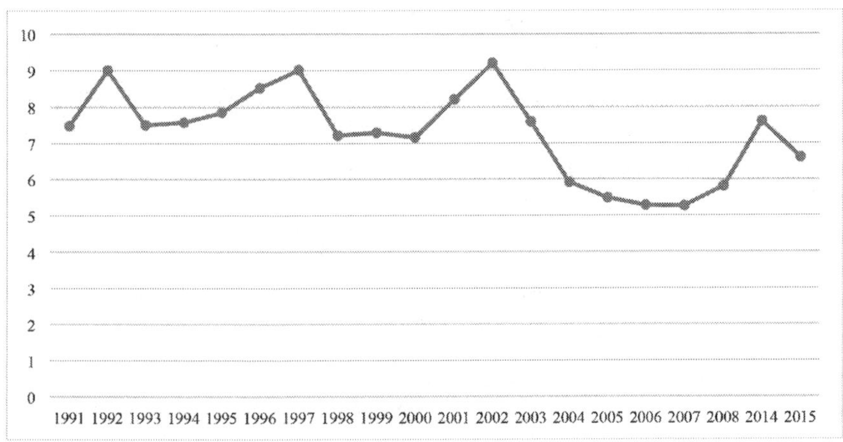

Figure 1.4. Homicide rates in Argentina, 1991–2008
Created by the author with data from Ministerio de Justicia y Derechos Humanos (2008) and Ministerio de Seguridad (2016).

responding to a homicide rate of 6.6 per 100,000 inhabitants. In other words, Argentina's murder rate decreased by 13 percent compared to 2003, when violence increased dramatically (see figure 1.4).[13] The South American country's map of violence is led by the province of Santa Fe with 12.2 homicides per 100,000 inhabitants, followed by Formosa (9.5), Mendoza (7.5), and Río Negro and Buenos Aires respectively (7.4).[14]

However, Argentina's homicide rates are relatively small compared to other countries in the region (see figure 1.5). In addition to Canada and the United States, only Chile (3.1) registers less homicides than Argentina in the Americas. The country's homicide profile is closer to those of Europe.[15] In Argentina, there are more lethal traffic accidents than homicides. Most important, the most frequent driving force behind homicides seems not to be connected to property crimes, as many pundits have suggested over the course of the years. In the city of Buenos Aires, for example, 39 percent of the homicides were committed as a result of quarrels, score settlings, or revenge, while theft followed by homicide accounts for only 17 percent of the killings.[16]

Thus, Argentina exhibits one of the lowest homicide rates in Latin America and the Caribbean sub-region but it ranks first in terms of robberies—the latter trend is not only confirmed by the South American country's robbery rates but also by its victimization statistics. Broadly speaking, crimes increased gradually since the 1990s, experiencing a peak with the 2001–2002 social and economic crisis. After a downward trend, both crimes against people and property proliferated. The murder rate, however, fluctuated over the course of the years, experiencing peaks in 1992, 1997, and 2002—the only moments in

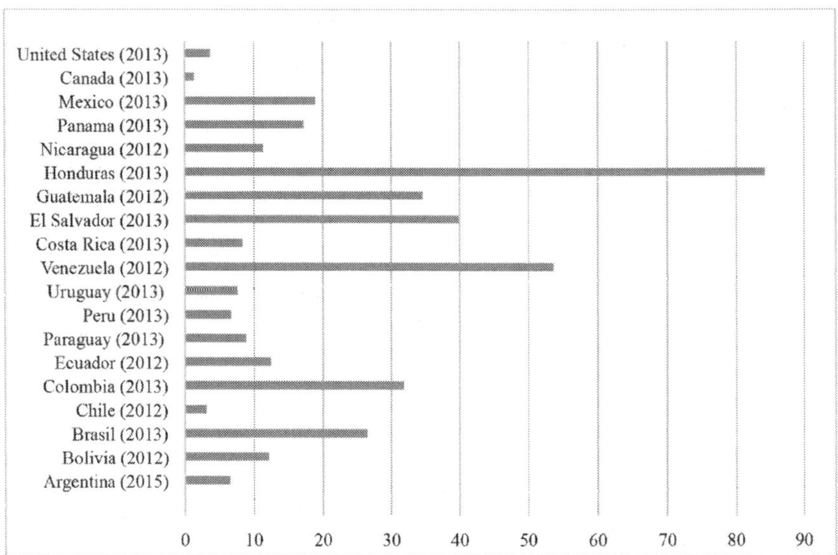

Figure 1.5. Homicides per 100,000 inhabitants in the Americas
Created by the author with data from Ministerio de Seguridad de la Nación (2016).

Argentina's recent history when the country came close to an epidemic level (10 homicides per 100,000 inhabitants).

FEAR OF CRIME

Since the first studies developed in the U.S. in the 1960s, research on the fear of crime has grown substantially over the past four decades, becoming a serious concern for criminologists, policy-makers, politicians, and the media.[17] Fear of crime also emerged from the convergence between technocratic debates and political disputes.[18] On the one hand, President Lyndon B. Johnson (1963 to 1969) brought the issue of crime into the public agenda by defining the problem of insecurity as a "public malady." In a short span of time, statistical information became available to support policy-making across different states in the U.S.[19] On the other hand, several methodological improvements in the field of criminology paved the way for new academic studies. Victimization polls, for example, provided additional insights about crime by considering data gathered from victims rather than police or other official records.

In Argentina, crime polls proliferated during the 1990s. First developed by the National Direction of Criminal Policy (Dirección Nacional de Política

Criminal—DNPC), surveys depicted different crime landscapes in Argentina, especially across the country's biggest metropolitan areas such as the city of Buenos Aires, Rosario, Cordoba, and Mendoza.[20] Over the course of the years, local surveys provided a fertile ground for the arrival of the first national crime polls, allowing data disaggregation at the district level. As Máximo Sozzo contends, Argentina's statistics, as it happened in other places in the world, were created to contemplate those crimes that were not included in official reports.[21] Most important, surveys and polls allowed scholarship to demonstrate that fear of crime has shown itself to be relatively autonomous from actual crime.[22]

In 2014, 33.7 percent of the population in Argentina rated citizen security as the biggest issue facing the country—a similar percentage to those reported in other Latin American countries such as Colombia, Mexico, or Venezuela. Perhaps not surprisingly, on a 0 to 100 scale, where high values represent negative evaluations of security, Argentina ranks ninth among other American countries with a score of 46.2, thereby surpassing the regional average of 43.2 points.[23] During some periods of time, indeed, fear of crime doubled victimization rates, suggesting that Argentina harbors a population highly concerned about the problem of insecurity (see figure 1.6).[24]

Between 2002 and 2005, security concerns continued to prosper even in a national context where crime rates decreased. As figure 1.6 shows, after 2006 insecurity ranked, for the first time in Argentina's recent history, as the most pressing issue facing the country. Unemployment and other economic prob-

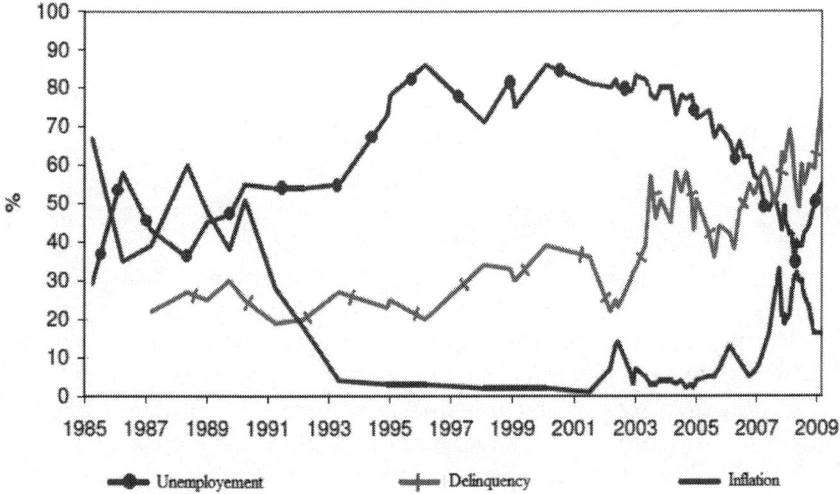

Figure 1.6. Fear of crime in Argentina

Created by the author with data from Gabriel Kessler, "Delito, Sentimiento de Inseguridad y Políticas Públicas," 2010.

lems such as inflation were relegated to second and third place, respectively. At the local level, this trend was also visible in major provinces such as Buenos Aires and Santa Fe. Under these circumstances, insecurity went from being recognized as the South American country's main problem by two percent of the population in 1995 to 35 percent in 2013. Simply put, insecurity always ranked first between 2006 and 2013, except in 2009, when unemployment reached the top of the public agenda for the first time in more than eight years.[25]

This trend was particularly evident after the assassination of Axel Blumberg, an Argentine college student kidnapped by a local gang in 2004. After the police confirmed the death of the young man, Axel became a symbol and his father, Juan Carlos Blumberg, led a crusade against insecurity that includes a series of public protests in the city and greater Buenos Aires. On April 1, 2004, for example, over 150,000 people mobilized into the National Congress, where Blumberg presented a formal petition accompanied by a dozen projects meant to toughen the South American country's sentences against crime. Although Blumberg's visibility eventually waned, the movement and the norms it left behind defined a salient peak in security (*seguridad*).[26]

Even though Argentina's increasing robbery and victimization rates may have influenced the population's concerns about insecurity over the last few years, fear of crime has also been connected to the country's socioeconomic situation. The empirical evidence suggests that when the economic situation is not a source of concern, crime anxiety tends to increase and vice versa.[27] According to Kessler, Argentina's fear of crime is extended among different social groups and sectors with diverse political ideologies. Unlike past experiences, indeed, it appears that insecurity is no longer linked to authoritarianism as it happened during Argentina's Dirty War (1976 to 1983).[28]

ARGENTINA'S SECURITY POLICY

Since December 2010, the Ministry of Security oversees Argentina's domestic security. Created as a consequence of the incidents that confronted the police and activists accused of inciting the occupation of Parque Indoamericano in Villa Soldati (Buenos Aires), the newly developed institution substituted the Minister of Justice and Human Rights.[29] The legal framework establishes that the responsibility of safeguarding the South American country's domestic security rests with federal law enforcement agencies, including the Federal Police (Policía Federal Argentina), Airport Security Police (Policía de Seguridad Aeroportuaria), National Gendarmerie (Gendarmería Nacional), the Coast Guard (Prefectura Naval Argentina), and local police forces. Unlike other Latin American countries, in Argentina the spheres of internal security and external defense are divided by law, thereby restricting the role of the military to foreign aggressions.[30]

Despite the formal organization of Argentina's domestic security, policymaking has been traditionally delegated to different law enforcement agencies, particularly since the recovery of democracy in 1983. In a context where the consequences of military repression remained fresh in the population's collective memory while the human rights agenda progressed rapidly, the executive power has virtually lost its policing prerogatives. According to Marcelo Sain, this process emerged as the consequence of a pact between the national government and police forces, where the executive power delegated the development and control of public security affairs to law-enforcement institutions in exchange for their political support and complicity.[31] Due to the *policialización* of Argentina's public security, the police forces have retained control over the South American country's security policy prerogatives vis-à-vis the national government.

In more than 30 years of democracy, and despite growing criticisms, changes to this scheme have been only superficial.[32] Law enforcement institutions have been in charge of designing and controlling Argentina's security policy. Moreover, none of the National Crime Prevention Plans promoted by civilian authorities since the 1990s have been completely implemented. According to Kessler, this is one of the country's most visible shortcomings in the management of security, which contributes to creating a sense of uncertainty and pessimism about the worsening of Argentina's problem of insecurity, as the bulk of the polls have indicated throughout the years.[33]

THE MACRI ADMINISTRATION

As it happened during the last 20 years, the relationship between crime and security concerns is having strong political implications in Argentina. Based on negative evaluations of the Fernández administration's (2007 to 2015) capacity for citizen security, the newly elected President, Mauricio Macri, defined insecurity as "one of the biggest debts of 30 years of democracy."[34] As a centerpiece of his administration's agenda, his government adopted measures to "reverse the situation of collective danger created by complex and organized crime."[35] The national government's new approach was confirmed only one month after taking office, when Macri issued a presidential decree declaring the state of "public security emergency" for one year, paving the way for the arrival of different hardline law-enforcement initiatives across Argentina, including the shoot-down policy, the deportation process of foreigners who have committed crimes, and lowering the age of criminal responsibility.

The starting-point of the security package approved in January 2016, was the implementation of the shoot-down policy. Launched without the formal intervention of the National Congress, this mechanism is intended to "identify, warn, intimidate, and use force" against planes suspected of carrying illegal drugs. Enforced by the South American country's armed forces, the initiative also promoted the installation of a radar system along Argentina's northern border while also revamping the security program known as "Operation Northern Shield."[36] The dynamics of the program favor the involvement of the armed forces in different counternarcotics operations, blurring the traditional distinctions between domestic security and external defense.[37] Most importantly, this initiative is in accordance with Macri's original request of "reviewing the role played by the armed forces in the fight against drug trafficking."[38]

The administration launched another hardline initiative to combat the population's growing demands for security in Argentina: a regulatory decree affecting the country's migration law. Based on opinion polls showing a widespread support for limiting immigration,[39] the measure aims at speeding up the deportation process of foreigners who have committed crimes while also curbing their chances of returning to Argentina.[40] As many high government officials confirmed, the president supported the decree by identifying foreigners, especially those from neighboring countries, as the source of insecurity. The national government's attempt to link immigration to crime was confirmed when Macri's security minister, Patricia Bullrich, declared that "Peruvian and Paraguayan citizens come here and end up killing for the control of the drug market."[41]

More recently, the Macri administration is also fueling a national debate aimed at lowering the age of criminal responsibility in the country. The national government's official proposal was spurred by an incident involving a 15 year old killer who avoided jail due to his legal age.[42] Promoted by the president himself, who already affirmed that the "age of criminal responsibility should be lowered,"[43] the initiative is under consideration of a commission appointed to work on a new juvenile criminal responsibility system. According to Macri's Justice Minister, Germán Garavano, the commission in charge of the official proposal should be "plural but not with partisan political representation."[44] Despite concerns raised by different human-rights organizations in Argentina, the bill pushed by the national government seems nonetheless to be moving forward rapidly.

Underlying the government's new approach, which by no means is limited to the declaration of the state of emergency, the shooting down of aircrafts, the deportation reform, or the attempt to lower the age of criminal responsibility,[45] there is a frequent procedure within Argentina's security cabinets: the creation of public policies based on a biased and unrepresentative diagnosis of the problem. The shoot-down policy, for example, proved to have limited success and appears to be a disproportionate response to the threat posed by organized crime. As in other Latin American countries, where about 20 percent of total narcotics smuggling is accomplished through aerial means,[46] the empirical evidence in Argentina suggests that drug trafficking is primarily terrestrial.[47] By the same token, approximately six percent of the country's total incarcerated population is not local, meaning that only 0.2 percent of the foreigners in Argentina are in prison.[48] Finally, statistics also confirm that age is not a relevant factor. According to UNICEF, there are 3,908 young offenders up to 17 years old detained in different establishments nationwide, representing only 0.14 percent of the total population between 14 and 17 years old in Argentina.[49] A report released by the Argentine Supreme Court shows similar results: in the City of Buenos Aires, only six percent of those accused of homicide are minors.[50]

In short, apart from being troubling from a human rights perspective, these hardline initiatives do not combat the underlying factors driving crime and violence in Argentina. Structural factors such as school dropout rates, income inequality, the familiarization with the use of violence, accelerated urban growth, and the dissolution of family contexts have been commonly ignored by government officials since the recovery of democracy in 1983. Instead, the focus has been regularly placed on the role of law enforcement agencies, the armed forces, and the penal system, thereby favoring the development of a punitive approach against crime and violence in Argentina. Based on a popular perception of a national outburst of violence, which so far is not supported by the empirical evidence available, this South American country is slowly yielding to the pressure of the masses.

CONCLUSION

Argentina's state of security presents contradictory trends. On the one hand, the country's robbery rates have increased gradually since the recovery of democracy in 1983, reaching historical levels in 2002 and 2015, respectively. Victimization surveys confirm this trend, particularly since the 1990s, when polls and survey information became available for the first time. On the other hand, Argentina's homicide rates have remained relatively stable and have never surpassed the limit of 10 killings per 100,000 inhabitants. This situation suggests that the country's homicide profile, unlike the experience with robberies, is closer to Europe than Latin America or the Caribbean sub-region.

Yet Argentines are highly concerned about crime. One out of three citizens rate insecurity as the most pressing issue facing the country. Under these circumstances, insecurity went from being recognized as Argentina's top concern by two percent of the population in 1995 to 35 percent in 2013. The population's growing fear of crime, however, has shown itself to be relatively autonomous from actual crime. During the last three decades, indeed, the country's homicide and robbery rates have varied but concerns nonetheless persisted or even increased. Away from the military threat characteristic of the Dirty War, Argentina's ongoing fear of crime is widely extended among different social groups and sectors with diverse political ideologies.

Notwithstanding the centrality of violence to the popular perception, police forces have been in charge of designing and controlling Argentina's security policy for the last three decades. In exchange for political support and complicity, law enforcement institutions have gradually increased their policing prerogatives vis-à-vis the national government. Despite growing criticisms and the lack of effectiveness in limiting the proliferation of crime, changes to this scheme have been only superficial. During the Macri administration, the focus has been regularly placed on the role of law enforcement agencies, the armed forces, and the penal system, thereby favoring the development of different hardline initiatives against crime. Apart from being troubling from a human rights perspective, this short-term and punitive approach, has not succeeded in tackling the foundations of violence in Argentina.

The question of how to bring solutions to Argentina's insecurity problems does not have an easy answer. Most of the country's crime determinants are rooted in structural factors that are not likely to be solved by hardline initiatives. The negative consequences of the neoliberal turn of the 1990s, including school dropout rates, income inequality, the familiarization with the use of violence, accelerated urban growth, and the dissolution of family contexts such as the family, school, and the neighborhood should be no longer ignored by government officials. An accurate diagnosis of the specific conditions under which crime and violence tend to prosper is crucial to avoid wrong interpretations and stigmatizations of Argentina's insecurity problem.

Calling into question a punitive approach against crime does not imply that short-term changes are not necessary. Major transformations need to be addressed within the domestic institutional setting, often characterized by the presence of weak institutions and corruption. Argentina needs to recover the political control over law enforcement agencies, favoring their professionalization and integration with the community. The prison system and the judiciary power also require major transformations. Rather than focusing on minor violations of the narcotics law, which are the cause of most of the incarcerations within Argentina's federal penitentiary system, the judiciary power needs to address complex investigations aimed at disrupting the growing presence of organized criminal networks involved in drug trafficking.

Chapter Two

Brazil: Violence and Public (un)Safety

Thiago Rodrigues, Mariana Kalil,
and Acácio Augusto

Amazing landscapes, boys and girls on white sand beaches, huge tropical forests, exotic cities, and a colorful gathering of many people participating in carnival festivities are some of the images that may come to mind when one thinks of Brazil. Such notions are based on the widespread myth of the supposed "cordiality" of the Brazilian people combined with another myth about the country being characterized as a "racial democracy." Since the nineteenth century—and especially during the authoritarian rule under Getúlio Vargas (1930–1945)—the combination of myths has become a type of official discourse in the Brazilian national identity that is based on the notion of a peaceful and perfectly integrated society. Young kids in public and private schools started learning about the allegedly cordial encounter among the three "constitutive races": the indigenous peoples, the white Portuguese, and the black Africans. The complex and tragic history of the Portuguese colonization of this immense part of South America was almost completely erased from textbooks. The vicious trajectory of the African slaves was pacified under an official valorization of their cultural legacy (e.g., the "samba" and food), while the history of the genocide of the indigenous peoples was silenced by civic holidays to hail the "indians from the forest" and the formation of state agencies for the tutelage of indigenous peoples. In Brazil, the Portuguese presence is always referred to as "colonization"—a word with positive and civilized connotations—which is different from other Latin American countries where the Spanish dominion is called by its name: *La Conquista* (the Conquest). Moreover, this Brazilian peaceful image is reflected in the National Hymn ("Peace in the Future, Glory in the Past"). It is also praised in the diplomatic rhetoric. The Baron of Rio Branco, the Minister of Foreign Affairs from 1902 to 1911, was responsible for the definition of the current 16,898 kilometers of the Brazilian border.

The myth of a "racial democracy" is so common among the Brazilian society that it persists as an aesthetic figure (in films, books, soap operas, TV shows) and in everyday life, when most of the Brazilians deny having any trace of racism against Afro-Brazilians. However, the reality is quite different. An examination of the patterns of violence also sheds light on the "tough on crime" policies of the government that have resulted in high levels of discrimination against many Brazilians, especially young black men and women who live in marginalized communities in the country.

This chapter aims to address violence in Brazil by focusing on government policies. In particular, this work examines the case of the two cities of Rio de Janeiro and Vitoria, which are the capital cities of two states and epitomize the high levels of social exclusion, geographic divides, militarization of public safety policies, and the role of the prison system in the repression and the production of "organized crime." This chapter will utilize the theoretical and methodological approaches developed by the French philosopher Michel Foucault,[1] notably his concepts of biopolitics. According to Michel Foucault,[2] the concentration of people in the new industrialized Western cities in the beginning of the nineteenth century, and the necessity to discipline them towards accepting hard work while diminishing their capacity to rebel, resulted in the production of a new set of government strategies. Foucault refers to this concept as a "new governmentality" understood as a set of governance practices that mobilize state policies, aiming to discipline individual bodies and to regulate the masses viewed as a "living collective body" or a "species body."[3] As a result, specific policies have been created to regulate the general level of health in order to produce an improvement in quality of life to maintain a controlled and pacified working class.

According to Foucault, such policies gave birth to "an era of biopower"[4] (i.e., the formulation of government policies aimed at offering an "additional element in life," *bios*) through urban, sanitary, and disciplinary interventions. Biopolitics can be understood in terms of producing healthy bodies, which are "useful and docile,"[5] while trying to control the political potential of these individuals. The biopolitical attention devoted to collective and to individual health constitutes one of the dimensions of the exercise of political power. The other dimension is the traditional use of coercive power to enforce the law and to maintain the internal political and social status quo. In other words, political power is not just a form of physical strength held by someone or some group entrenched in the state apparatus and used solely to oppress or abuse. On the contrary, political power also works to take care of the health of people to generate a useful and docile citizenry. For Foucault, *politics* means more than the traditional political institutions (the state, political institutions, and political parties). The complex set of human interaction constitute "the political" (i.e., every single aspect of human life is marked by confrontation, but is not necessarily violent). The Foucauldian perspective allows us to recognize that what we deem as "normal politics" is, in fact, a state of constant combat. In this environment, social, economic and political groups impose their values, scientific truths, laws, and prejudices.

The judicial and penal system (police forces, courts, and prisons) are some of the main resources to keep and reproduce a given way of life, combating people and ideas that oppose the hegemonic order. Seen as "enemies" of the state and society, the differential social groups are treated as threats to "peace" and "life." Their lives have become targets for disciplining techniques applied in several institutions (e.g., prisons, schools, hospitals, families, industries, and businesses) aiming to produce adaptable subjectivities. The ones who do not fit into the "pacified" categories are targeted by the repressive forces, mainly under the state's coordination (police and armed forces), but not exclusively by the state apparatus (militias, paramilitary, death squads, and private military companies). In sum, this is the analytical perspective through which we seek to examine contemporary Brazilian problems related to public safety and violence.

The chapter is divided into three parts. The first section examines recent data on violence in Brazil through an analysis of data on homicides, considering the use of firearms in sectors of society which are more victimized. The second section presents the current movement toward the militarization of the war on drugs and public safety in the country, focusing on the case of Rio de Janeiro. The third section of this chapter examines the militarization of the Brazilian State of Espírito Santo, which has been touted by some people as a success of the public safety policies. It also includes an account of trends in the Brazilian prison system and the relation between organized crime and prisons. Finally, the work concludes with an examination of the blurring distinction between "public safety" and "national security" regarding the "problem" of violence plaguing the country.

A NATIONAL TRAGEDY: WHO KILLS AND WHO IS BEING KILLED

During the first three months of 2017 more people were killed in Brazil than the number of individuals who died in all terrorist attacks around the world during the same period: 498 attacks with 3,314 fatal casualties. Moreover, the same number of deaths occurred during the first three weeks of January 2017.[6] Despite improvements in all social indicators since 2003 (i.e., life expectancy, illiteracy, access to sanitary services, and both basic and higher education), the homicide rates spiked, especially in the poorest states from the north and northeast regions. Although a considerable amount of the homicides in Brazil still occur in the country side, related to disputes between landowners and peasants, and among indigenous peoples, gold diggers, landowners and national and international lumberjack companies, lethal violence is concentrated in cities. This trend is because Brazil has been converted into a highly-urbanized country since the 1970s. The country is home to densely populated cities such as São Paulo (approximately 15 million inhabitants) and Rio de Janeiro (approximately 10 million people). Brazilian cities are divided between middle class and upper class neighborhoods, usually living in clusters and enclaves, and lower class populations that live in slums (*favelas*).

Using official data collected from the IBGE census and from the Ministry of Justice database on criminal justice, Daniel Cerqueira and his colleagues[7] analyze the number of deaths by violent means registered from 2005 until 2015. The data analysis show that Brazil is not a peaceful country. In fact, Brazil remains a very violent country despite the fact that it has not been involved in external military conflict since World War II. The authors also highlight that young black men with low levels of formal education are the main victims of violent death.

According to Cerqueira and Coelho, in 2014, five of every seven people killed in Brazil were black.[8] Moreover, certain members of society have been impacted more by the violence plaguing the country. There are two different trends that arise when studying the high levels of violence against Afro-Brazilians. The first group is known as the "racial democracy believers" who, supporting the idea that in Brazil the main source for violence is not "race" itself, but economic income and social strata. According to Cerqueira and Coelho,[9] other authors who examine this phenomenon disregard racism as a crucial variable to understand the prevalence of violence among black youth. Cerqueira and Coelho maintain that the following five factors impact levels of violence: 1) the economic income variable (or social inequality) with other variables; 2) the level of education; 3) access to high remunerable jobs; 4) the zone/neighborhood in which this demographic contingent live; and 5) the color of their skin. These variables are intrinsically related since Afro-Brazilians have historically had access to very poor-quality education, which in turn impacts one's ability to find a high paying job. In addition, Brazil has been plagued by racial prejudice. Higher levels of economic poverty increase the chances of this population living in poor and stigmatized neighborhoods. Cerqueira and Coelho highlight that the most homicide-prone age was 21 in 2014. However, the chance of a 21 year old black male being killed was 147 percent higher than a white, Asian or indigenous male of the same age.[10]

The case for the relationship between race and the homicide rate is a major issue in Rio de Janeiro. Afro-Brazilians account for nearly 50 percent of the city's total population. Blacks are overrepresented in terms of homicides as well as the prison population. However, Afro-Brazilians are underrepresented among the percentages of well-educated populations (primary and high school degrees).[11] Finally, in contemporary Rio, a young black male has a 23.7 percent higher probability of being killed than a young male who is not black.[12] The city is deadlier for Afro-Brazilians (including black women when compared to white and Asian women), even in the less violent urban areas. In sum, Afro-Brazilians are impacted more by violence in both violent and safer neighborhoods.

For Cerqueira and Coelho,[13] Rio de Janeiro is plagued by a "racism that kills." The "race/color of skin" variable has a crucial importance when analyzing levels of dangerousness. In other words, Afro-Brazilians are targeted at higher rates by police forces and are more exposed to the illegal market activities—primarily drug trafficking—that occur in town. Rio de Janeiro is an epicenter in the transnational flows of illegal drugs (cocaine toward Europe, via West Africa, and European methamphetamine en route to South American consumers), and a retail market for cocaine, crack cocaine, inhalants, and marijuana.[14] The criminal gangs which control Rio's favelas such as the Red Command (*Comando Vermelho*), the Third Commando (*Terceiro Comando*), and ADA (*Amigos dos Amigos*, acronym for Friends' Friend) began inside the state prison system. The Red Commando emerged first at the end of the 1970s. The group borrowed its name from the connection with leftist guerrilla members ("reds" or communists) who were inmates in supermax prisons during the authoritarian regime (1964–1985). The Commando's members learned from the guerrillas' tactics and organizational structure. In addition, they took advantage of the illegalities which connected the inmates inside the prison with people living in the favelas.[15]

During the 1980s, the boom of the cocaine economy in the United States and Europe helped Rio become a strategic position as a trampoline for Bolivian, Peruvian, and Colombian cocaine toward Europe. It did not take long for fights between drug gangs for control of territory. Meanwhile, representatives of European mafias, such as the Italian Cosanostra, started working with local drug gangs in Brazil. However, it is important to note that the Cosanostra did not depend on these local drug transportation gangs. Controlling territory is vital for gangs seeking to earn money in the drug trade. The competition for control in the favelas has resulted in increases in violence. Many of Rio's 763 favelas are located on hills, and controlling these favelas became a central goal for drug gangs which started conquering and defending their turf. Confrontations occurred near condos owned by the middle class and upper class, which are world-famous zones that attract thousands of foreign tourists per year. As Luis Fernando Sarmiento and Ciro Krauthausen note,[16] the zones of open competition among illegal actors tend to be violent areas because criminal gangs battle to capture strategic positions within neighborhoods.

The visibility and lethality of confrontation have increased the prejudice against favelas and their impoverished inhabitants, the majority of whom are black. The incursions of the Military Police (MP), including its deadly special squad called BOPE (Special Operations Battalion), have become common. Moreover, the country has witnessed extrajudicial massacres by police officers and "death squads," which consist of off duty police officers. Thus, the "drug trafficking problem" has assumed the position of the most dangerous menace to "social peace" in Rio, an opinion corroborated by the mass media. The response of the government reflects previous policies: the favelas' territories had been "spaces of fear" for the white and richer population since the beginning of the twentieth century when the first poor migrants coming from rural areas started occupying Rio's hills to sell their services for industry, commerce, and domestic work. Afro-Brazilians have been viewed since times of slavery (until 1888) as the personification of the inner enemy, the criminal, the morally decayed, or the racial inferior. After the abolition of slavery, the vast majority of the former slaves became favela inhabitants. Today, their great grandchildren live there. The illegal drug economy during the 1980s provoked the juxtaposition between

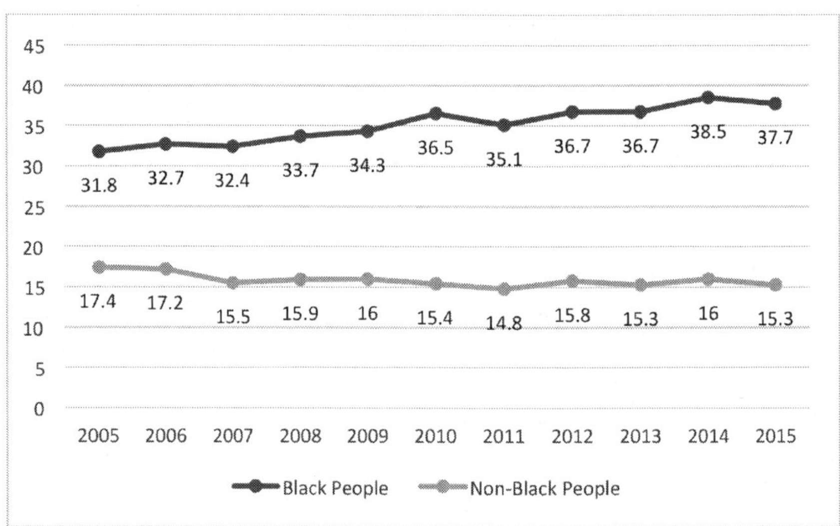

Figure 2.1. Evolution of Homicides among Black and Non-black People in Brazil
Created by the authors. IBGE/Diretoria de Pesquisas. Coordenação de População e Indicadores Sociais. Gerência de Estudos e Análises da Dinâmica Demográ ca e Sim/Dasis/SVS/MS. Elaboração: Diest/Ipea.

the "moral and social prejudice/fear" against the black population and the 'moral and social prejudice/fear' against the use and effects of psychoactive drugs such as marijuana and cocaine.[17]

Despite the overall decrease in the homicide rate in the south and southeast regions of Brazil, the north and northeast have registered a considerable increase in violent deaths from 2005 to 2015. In 2015, 71.9 percent of the homicides were committed with firearms[18]—this equates to a total of 41,817 people murdered. Moreover, men represented 92 percent of those individuals killed.[19] While the homicide rate for women is less than the rate of men, it remains high and might be underestimated since much of the violence against women can be classified as domestic violence and is not reported. In 2015, 4,621 women were killed, which is a rate of 4.3 women per 100,000 inhabitants.[20] There are significant discrepancies between the numbers for white and black women: while the homicide rate for white women has decreased by 7.4 percent from 2005 to 2015, the homicide rate for black women spiked by 22 percent during the same period reaching a rate of 5.2 per 100,000 women (see figure 2.1).[21] Thus, Afro-Brazilian women accounted for 65.3 percent of the women killed in Brazil in 2015. In summary, the high levels of violence against individuals, particularly black Brazilians sheds light on why Cerqueira and Coelho[22] identify a "racism that kills" as a current practice despite its illegality. In the next section, we examine the third level and its connection with the fourth level (*national security*).

PACIFICATION: WAR BY OTHER MEANS

In 2008, the state government of Rio de Janeiro launched a new innovative plan for public safety called the Pacifying Police Units Program (UPP). The UPP Program sought to occupy favelas using Military Police troops trained with community policing techniques to maintain a permanent presence in urban spaces controlled by drug gangs or "militias" (mafia-like armed groups composed of former policemen, firemen, and members of the military). During this period, the city of Rio de Janeiro underwent substantial transformation following Brazil's economic growth and social changes. That same year, Rio was chosen to host the 2016 Olympic Games. In addition, the "Wonder City" would be the main stage for the 2014 FIFA World Cup. Policymakers expected high levels of public and private investment for years to come. Both the national and the state governments were ready and willing to display a new wave of public safety policies that would secure the investors' interests in the region. It was necessary to change the image of danger and insecurity associated with this city.

Supported by public opinion and experts in security policy, the UPP Program has expanded, reaching 38 units in 2017. In November 2010, Rio de Janeiro's governor officially requested support from the national forces to occupy two sets of favelas known as *Complexo da Penha* and *Complexo do Alemão*. The mass media and government considered these favelas as "criminal fortresses" run by *Comando Vermelho* (Red Commando). In August 2010, President Lula da Silva signed a special Act (Additional Law 136/2010) that created the "Guarantee of Law and Order." The 1988 Brazilian constitution states in Article 142 that any of the legal powers can request support from National Forces (such as the military, federal police, and federal highway patrols) to enforce the law in cases of social and political turmoil.

However, the political climate in which this article was drafted can be characterized as tense. Political forces that opposed the dictatorship wanted to separate the state-level Military Police from the federal-level army central command (a definition established by the 1969 National Security Law). The connection between the Military Police and the army had its origins in the prior authoritarian rule as this body was used to fight, arrest, kill, and torture political opposition to the regime. During the years of the dictatorship, the armed forces commander in Brasilia held direct control over the states' Military Police. In 1988, conservative political forces wanted to maintain such policies in the new constitution. The solution reached was a compromise through which the Military Police would remain "militarized" and serve as the army's "back up force" in case of war or social upheaval. The ordinary command would be left in the hands of the democratically elected civilian state governors.[23] Yet Article 142 did not detail how the "power to guarantee law and order" would be enforced. There were some attempts to do this during the Fernando Henrique Cardoso administration in the 1990s, yet such efforts did not have success until August 2010 when President Lula da Silva signed the aforementioned law (AL 136/2010).

Soldiers with experience occupying and policing poor neighborhoods for the United Nations Stabilization Mission (MINUSTAH) in Haiti served with the "Pacification Force" (PF). Following their operations in Port-au-Prince's slums, the troops established bases in Alemão's and Penha's alleys and fought local gangs. Social movements, scholars, and local inhabitants have denounced the PF. The PF and UPP troops have been criticized as violent, authoritarian, and ruthless towards favela residents. Nonetheless, the PF stayed in the favelas until July 2012 until a gradual retreat followed by the installation of UPP's bases. It is important to note that this was the longest military occupation of the army in a Brazilian city. Despite the critiques, it was the inspiration for another version of PF operations which occupied another set of favelas known as the *Complexo da Maré* from April 2014 until

June 2015. The Complexo da Maré is a neighborhood plagued by crime and violence that is located next to Rio de Janeiro's International Airport and is the main gateway to Rio. Authorities deployed the second PF a month and a half prior to the inauguration of FIFA's World Cup at the Maracanã Arena, which is located in Rio.

By analyzing the geospatial distribution of UPP's bases and the PF occupied areas it is possible to grasp how they have followed a specific *rationale* aimed at securing the accesses to Rio (by road, air, and sea), as well as the downtown area (the city's financial and political heart) and the tourist neighborhoods of Rio's shore (e.g., Ipanema and Copacabana beaches). Authorities also paid attention to favelas nearby Olympic installations such as Cidade de Deus and Batam. The map below displays the geopolitics of Rio's Pacification process, showing how it has been developed as a means to control and restrain specific areas of the city to guarantee investments and the circulation of tourists (see figure 2.2).

The Army's Pacification Force had been exposed to "training modules and tactics and strategies specific to urban warfare . . . and high in-combat

Figure 2.2. Geopolitics of Rio's Pacification Process
Rio de Janeiro's Secretary of Public Safety, 2016.

interaction with local population."[24] The relationship between the specific training for MINUSTAH and its use in Brazilian favelas is a significant question worth analyzing to understand the intentions of the armed forces and the possible transformation of this institutions involvement in domestic affairs after its experience in Haiti. The modus operandi of the Pacification Force and the UPPs units are defined by three phases. The first is *invasion* when the military or the MP's special BOPE squad invades a favela to combat local gangs. The second phase is the *occupation* which is when the Military Police troops or the military take control of the situation by establishing bunkers and "strong-points" in strategic sites of the favela. Third, the favela is considered *pacified* when gang activities have ceased or decreased in intensity. The last phase is when traditional state public services that do not exist within the favela structures (such as public medical care, schools, postal services) are expected to arrive to these areas. Since its implementation, the UPP Program and the Army's Pacification Forces have been accused of establishing a type of "space of exception" where forces have been imposing a martial law governance style based on repression and authoritarianism.[25]

In addition, the "Pacification Program" has enabled the emergence of a more complex set of control and governance tactics and practices that do not focus exclusively on state violence. The so-called "pacified favelas" have received considerable private investment (e.g. shops, hotels, restaurants, discos, and banks) along with the presence of humanitarian and relief services run by businesses, foundations, churches, and national and foreign NGOs in association with local organizations. Hence, the illegal activities supposedly neutralized are reported to still be operating, but now with an undercover pattern and with new types of illegal agreements and renewed connections with public authorities, security agents, and private actors. The UPP and the Pacification Force operate beyond mere repression and apply a *biopolitical* approach of governance: a new mode of surveillance and control over individuals and collective bodies.

However, the term "pacification" itself is not a novelty in Brazilian history. The expression was used to describe the "conquest"—which is to say the enslavement, forcible baptism or simple slaughter—of indigenous people during colonial times (sixteen to the nineteenth centuries). After Brazil's independence from Portugal in 1822, the term became part of the ethos of the Brazilian army. Initially, it was linked to the military victories of the imperial central power based in Rio de Janeiro against rebel insurgencies. The Duke of Caxias, nicknamed "The Pacificator," served as one of the main leaders of the Brazilian army during these military campaigns. He is considered to be the patron of the army. Since the 1950s, one of the most distinguished medals offered by the army was named "The Pacificator Medal" as a tribute to Caxias.[26]

In the beginning of the twentieth century, the word "pacification" has been used to describe the process of "integration" of native groups from the Amazon forest by a military mission that connected isolated regions through the installation of telegraph lines and the establishment of new villages for indigenous peoples. The commander of this operation, Marshall Cândido Rondon, had a paternalistic approach to the native Brazilians belief that the state—and the Army in particular—had the duty to protect and "civilize" primitive people.[27] Rondon was the creator and first director of the Service for the Protection of Indigenous Peoples (SIP), which was established in 1910. This organization sought to promote the "acculturation" of indigenous groups. In sum, the notion of "pacification" is firmly intertwined with the army's vision of itself and its role in society.

It is remarkable that today the Military Police and the army have evoked an expression with such historical and military connotations. The new "savages" are the drug traffickers and gang members and, in a broader sense, the favela inhabitants. The armed forces' self-assumed role as "civilization keeper": in Brazil is illustrated by the long and hard experience of military rule in which the army—as occurred in many other Latin American countries—arrested, tortured, and killed fellow citizens labelled as criminals and "internal enemies." As a result, the presence of the army in long-term favela occupation missions is a delicate issue despite the efforts by the government and the army commanders who stress the legality and the exceptionalism of these operations. Ultimately, drug dealers operating in the country are Brazilians and the activities of the Pacification Forces created the possibility of seeing the armed forces arresting, controlling, or even killing Brazilians citizens.

Therefore, the "Pacification Process" by the Military Police and by the army has been part of an established repressive pattern in the poorest areas and populations of Rio de Janeiro. In the beginning of the twentieth century, Rio was the Brazilian capital city and a main reference for the country's political, social, and economic activities. Impoverished populations, composed mainly of black people (many of them former slaves), started occupying hills nearby the most well-off urban areas where they searched for work, usually in underpaid jobs. After World War II, Brazil passed through an accelerated process of urbanization and industrialization. Rio de Janeiro faced an unplanned and expansive increase of territorial occupation and demographic growth. The favelas expanded throughout hills, swamps, and suburban vacant lots, surrounding the urbanized areas. Seen as a space of transgression, criminality, and depravation, the favelas and their inhabitants have been historically targeted as a danger to the "formal city." Since the 1980s, the increasing feelings of threats associated with the favela's population increased with the increment of criminal practices associated with drug trafficking.[28]

Moreover, the emergence of the cocaine market in the late 1970s had it center of gravity in South America's Andean region. The first international division of cocaine's drug trafficking posed illegal groups based in Bolivia and Peru as the principal producers of coca leaf and coca paste. In Colombia, drug trafficking organizations (DTOs)—with national influence and international logistic connections—assumed the transformation of coca paste into pure powder to be smuggled into the North American and European markets. During the 1980s, Brazil was a "cocaine export corridor,"[29] connecting the Andean producing regions with the U.S. and Western Europe. Nevertheless, since the end of the 1990s, Brazil has assumed a different position as both a major consumer and producer of illegal drugs.[30] The 2016 United Nations World Drug Report[31] states that Brazil has reached second place in cocaine (powder and crack cocaine) consumption in the world after the United States. Although the situation regarding the production, trafficking, and consumption of illegal drugs in Brazil does not fit into a simple framework, the link between drug trafficking and poverty has been used as a justification for the implementation of public security programs that focus on repression as a means to address the illegal drug market.

Drug trafficking became an important issue for the public during the 1980s when rates of income concentration and the growth of urban poverty increased dramatically. This situation coincided with the rise of the international cocaine economy that established its influence and connections in Brazil, especially in Rio de Janeiro and São Paulo. Some of these cocaine-related actors benefited from the organizational skills of former bank robbers and kidnappers previously arrested during the military rule. In maximum-security prisons, people convicted of drug charges could learn from leftist guerrilla members. The "political prisoners" know-how about organizing clandestine cells and planning bank assaults and kidnappings were shared with "regular prisoners." After 1979, when the dictatorship relaxed its repressive policies, the former "regular prisoners" organized themselves in a new group, the Comando Vermelho (Red Commando). During the 1980s, the Comando Vermelho established units (or "cells") in many of Rio's favelas where they operated their business endeavors. The large amount of money produced by the illegal drug business, combined with the internal rivalries of the Comando, led to partitions and new factions such as the Terceiro Comando (Third Commando). The disputes for territories became violent. According to Krauthausen and Sarmiento,[32] violence is an unavoidable mechanism used by illegal gangs because the territorial base is crucial for a criminal group to maintain its activities.

Many of the main favelas in Rio de Janeiro controlled by the Commandos surrounded middle and upper-class neighborhoods. Therefore, territorial disputes generated a feeling of uneasiness and fear amongst Rio's citizenry. The Military Police, under the state governor's authority, started receiving special training and weaponry that included techniques of urban combat, armored vehicles, special equipment, and Fusil Automatique Léger 7.62mm rifles. However, unlike in countries such as Peru and Colombia, daily streets surveillance was not a military task. In fact, during the 1990s, the Brazilian army was required on certain occasions to occupy strategic areas of the city to secure international meetings such as the United Nations Conference on Environment and Development (ECO-92).

In 1994, the state government requested federal support to "fight criminality," responding to popular calls for a massive intervention to combat drug trafficking and other crimes in Rio.[33] This act created the legal framework to understand the militarization of public safety in Rio. The so-called "Operation Rio" performed "violent incursions into poor territories"[34] employing military troops. Today, the difference is the frequent recurrence of the military engagement to "secure" the city of Rio de Janeiro. After the experiences of the UPP Program and the Army's Pacification Forces, the presence of the military in Rio has emerged as a common public safety practice. In July 2017, President Michel Temer, who assumed office after a parliamentary coup against President Dilma Rousseff in 2016, authorized—based on the same AL 136/2010—the presence of military troops to patrol the city of Rio de Janeiro until the general elections in October 2018. The current presence of military troops in policing activities is justified by the alleged failure of Military Police capacity to enforce law and order in the metropolitan area. In summary, while Latin American countries that militarized their public safety policies (e.g., Mexico, Colombia, and Peru) are now in the process of reviewing these policies, Brazil is adopting such failed and violent strategies. In October 16, 2017, President Temer released an executive order which indicates that crimes committed by military personnel against civilians will be judged by military courts. This is an indication that the militarization of public safety is here to stay.

It is important to remember that the expression "pacification" does not mean "peace." Instead, it is a military term which expresses the imposition of a given order by a superior force. In other words, this is the evident expression of how politics is a "war by other means" as described by Michel Foucault.[35] According to Frédéric Gros,[36] politics is a continuum of different levels of "states of violence"—a diversity of violent practices which constitutes regular life in society.

PUBLIC SAFETY AND PRISONS IN BRAZIL: THE CASE OF ESPÍRITO SANTO

The main agent of violence in modern society is the state. The state defines itself and maintains its dominance by the exercise of violence. Violence in Brazil is directly linked to a police force characterized by a high degree of lethality, undoing another stereotype that violence would be exclusively connected to organized crime. According to official government data compiled by the Brazilian Forum on Public Security in 2016, 58,383 people were assassinated[37] in 2015, which translates into 160 people killed daily. Of these deaths, 3,345 are directly attributed to the police. However, several factors that link other deaths indirectly to police conduct must be considered (e.g., deaths recorded in confrontation or underreported). In general, this violence is applauded by the vast majority of the population, who have long rejoiced in a punitive populism boosted by the media and other sectors of society. In summary, institutionalized violence is a hallmark of a country that still faces strong colonization traits, the memory of a long period of slavery (Brazil was the last country in the Americas to abolish slavery), and the effects of 21 years of civil-military dictatorship.

When analyzing some current data of the state's violence in Brazil, it is important to understand the pertinence and urgency of the criminal abolitionist perspective. Two recent events illustrate this deadly violence: a series of decapitations in prisons in the north and northeast of the country and a police strike in the State of Espírito Santo. Both events occurred during a period of grave institutional instability. Such events have led to a series of cuts in public spending, putting austerity policy on the agenda.

The public debate on prisons and penalties is intense as there are many opinions, vast amounts of data, and many different prognoses. Criminal issues (e.g., riots in prisons or crimes that receive high levels of media attention) result in a flood of public commotion as debates ensue about what must be done to combat crime and increase security. The most emblematic of these debates is the reduction of the legal age of criminal responsibility. The ECA (Child and Adolescent Statute) was promulgated in 1990, Law 8.069. The PEC 171/1993 [Constitutional Amendment Project] occurred three years later and proposed the reduction of the legal age from 18 to 16. Debates regarding this issue have continued among Brazilian policymakers. Conservative sectors seek to pass their proposals for existing prisons for children and youth, while progressive sectors desire to stop the advance of conservatives defending "the achievements of ECA."

According to the 2016 *Mapa do Encarceramento* (Map of Incarceration), which provides data from 2005 to 2012, the majority of the country's prison population consists of young people between 18 and 24 years old. In 2005, 53,599 were between 18 and 24 years old and 42,689 between the ages of 25 and 29. In 2012 alone, 143,501 of the prison inmates were between the age of 18 and 24 years old, while 266,356 were between the ages of 25 and 29. In summary, the map reveals that in 2012, 54.8 percent of the population incarcerated in Brazil were young people under the age of 29.[38]

The beginning of 2017 witnessed decapitated bodies after the massacre in Manaus' main prison shocked the nation.[39] It is impossible to remain indifferent to the hundreds of beheaded bodies in penitentiaries located in the north and northeast of the country. Once again, the debate was accompanied by tactics to avoid the issue of the failure of the penal system. Some individuals in Brazil argue that the construction of more prisons and the implementation of tougher prison sentences are needed. On the other hand, liberals talk about improvements in prison conditions, reduction of criminalized acts (more specifically drug related), compliance with LEP 7,210/1984 (Law of Criminal Enforcement), alternative penalties, and various other policies. The answer to this symphony of virtuous prison specialists could be given with a straightforward, three-chord punk-style song: abolish jail for youth, stop incarceration, and cease punitive language.

Since 2001, the mafia-like organization called Primeiro Comando da Capital (Capital's First Commando—PCC) made its first public appearance in São Paulo. The PCC as a business organization is a result of the failed prison policies. The proposal of sharing prison management with state authorities has been characterized as a success culminating with the agreement established with São Paulo state government after the bloodbath that resulted in more than 500 bodies spread across São Paulo City in May 2006.[40] This odd "public-private partnership" has spread beyond prison and served as a peacemaker for favelas, ghettos, and peripheries with the monopoly on retail drugs in the State of São Paulo. More recently, there has been an expansion in such endeavors across the national territory and beyond Brazil's borders.

In January 2017, Alexandre Moraes, then Minister of Justice, announced the release of approximately U.S.$1.2 billion "for improvement of the prison system." It involves mobilizing U.S.$.500 million from the National Penitentiary Fund (Funpen) which would be complemented by other federal funds.[41] This shows the centrality of the issue of security in general, and the prison system specifically, as Brazil is facing various economic challenges. Funds destined for the construction of new prisons and computer-information control technology, such as the imprint of U.S.$40 million for the purchase of scanners and another U.S.$50 million for cell phone blockers to be used in prisons. Thus, the so-called "crime control industry" has received more resources. There will continue to be statements that justify new prisons, conservative reforms to the federal constitution, and the establishment of protocols for human rights guarantees.

Between 2006 and 2009, the Espírito Santo prison system made the headlines of the country's major newspapers as the representation of hell on Earth with 13 prison units in 2005 and a rising policy of mass incarceration. As a result of the inability of the facilities to meet the rising demand, authorities used metal containers nicknamed *microwaves* since they were made of zinc and displayed outdoors under the tropical sun. For the local government, the so-called problem of the "prison surplus" was solved. However, inmate decapitations occurred and pieces of bodies were found in the trash and/or buried beneath the containers. After a series of denunciations by human rights activists, including international organizations, interventions occurred. NGOs, the Federal Prosecutor's Office, and the National Penitentiary Criminal Policy Council (CNPCP) led such initiatives.[42] The denunciations went as far as Geneva, Switzerland, at the Office of the UN High Commissioner for Human Rights.

Today, after almost 10 years, the national press has written about Espírito Santo as a model for other prisons. Moreover, some people contend that this case provides a justification for the need to invest in the construction of new prisons. The then state's secretary of justice boasted about having controlled "prison chaos" in the state and reducing the number of deaths to zero. In an article for *BBC Brazil*, he states that his key word is "prison-architecture." Moreover, the state has gone from 13 to 35 prison units after investing more than U.S.$130 million.[43] Decentralized and inspired by U.S. prisons, they prevent communication between pavilions and prohibit the entrance of food and hygiene products brought by family members. These modern facilities replaced the so-called *cadeiões* ("big jails") based on the argument of efficiency. In summary, the experience of Espírito Santo is often viewed as a reference for solving what is happening in prisons in north and northeastern Brazilian states. This case promotes new prison reform proposals that aim to humanize the penitentiary system. However, such reforms do not address the problem of mass incarceration, the gangs' control over the prison facilities, and police brutality.

Fear overwhelmed the Espírito Santo complex between February 6 and 20, 2017. The blockades in the police battalions began two days earlier, but it took 24 hours of media, digital social networks and instant messaging applications for the panic to spread. Panic and fear become effective instruments of collective control when *crisis* becomes a permanent way of government and not an exceptional event to be overcome. Thus, this Brazilian state that had been touted as an example for public safety policy for pacifying its prisons, plunged into disorder precisely because of a problem in this area of public administration. Police officers' wives and family members have not backed down, showing they are well-organized. As a result of the warlike mentality deaths remained high with more than 200 people dying. People from the peripheral areas of Vitoria, the state's capital city, have contradicted official data by going straight to the state's morgue to count the bodies themselves.[44]

However, such events are not just a crisis of public safety, but rather are a consequence of budgetary austerity which indicates a curious tendency in the tug-of-war between state forces and events that can mobilize society. In a democracy that becomes more and more about security,[45] strikes by teachers or health workers are incapable of generating discomfort; such movements are repressed and ridiculed by government and society. Yet protests by the police—the people responsible for securing the social order and the defense of property—created an immediate state of alert and spread panic and despair among the population.

The aforementioned elements help us understand how a government that ended 2016 boasting about having the accounts in good order[46] is now at a dead end. There are several studies, based on Michel Foucault's[47] foundational reading of "The Birth of Biopolitics" which demonstrates how neoliberal government policies do not work without a contribution by "law enforcement" in a highly authoritarian fashion of security policies that produce mass incarceration and criminalization of poverty without forgoing the democratic form of institutional government, which includes attending the UN recommendations on human rights. One example is the Zero Tolerance policy, which was popular in New York City during the 1980s. This policy was later exported to countries governed both by right wing and leftist parties of the so-called Third Way.[48]

Furthermore, the arrival of army troops in cities such as Vitoria and Rio de Janeiro is often quite popular because the public is concerned about safety. However, these policies do not represent a reconfiguration of an authoritarian institutionalism. On the contrary, such policies show how authoritarianism works in contemporary Brazilian capitalism: it is perfectly capable of coexisting with democratic forms and international human rights protocols. When *crisis* becomes a governmental practice, any given instability justifies the use of security forces that are always ready to be utilized to combat insecurity.

Democratic authoritarianism is lethal. The synthesis of this violence introduced and practiced by the state can be found in news from February

11, 2017, about a young man assassinated by an army soldier who was part of the Espírito Santo's Joint Task Force—the troops that came to cover the Military Police. This young man was murdered in the neighborhood of São João Batista in the Vitoria metropolitan zone. The boy's cousin contends that this youth left a party at his aunt's house. After turning the corner, this young male was shot in the head. The army claimed that the death occurred amidst a confrontation with drug dealers.[49] The location and circumstances of this murder as well as the age and background of the young man who was killed demonstrate the kind of violence which has been intensified within the state.

Contrary to the Hobbesian idea of a "war of all against all," the situation in Espírito Santo can be characterized as the extermination by state forces and paramilitary support. In 1991, for example, a Civilian Police strike occurred that paved the way for the execution of 30 homeless children in Vitoria. The investigations pointed to the continuity of Scuderie Le Coq's action in Espírito Santo, a death squad created during the civil-military dictatorship in Brazil (1964–1985)—this group remained active even after the so-called "democratic opening."[50] Scuderie Le Coq was publicly displayed by its associates from the state, with a t-shirt and stickers glued to cars, and had affiliates that occupied posts in the judiciary and legislative, besides members of the Military and Civilian Police, and received financial contributions of businessmen and merchants.

In a securitized democracy, a police strike mobilizes the rest of society. Even when it creates a situation of momentary instability, its result is always the strengthening of order. The most immediate effect is the reinforcement of the daily conservative discourse: the inescapable necessity of the police, the Brazilian saying "good thief, dead thief,"[51] the cries for expanding firearm licenses for civilians, the praise of vigilantes and death squads, the expansion of punitive discourses and judicial solutions. Finally, the forces involved in such policies and their social effects remain rooted in conservative principles of law and order.

Moreover, Espírito Santo has been viewed as a possible reference for a national solution, but one that operates a complex combination between reformist and humanitarian discourses with military intervention, mass incarceration, and the presence of death squads. New massacres add to the violence that is said to be legitimate and tolerable (i.e., "rational violence" by the state carried out by the police and the army). The means to control, to surveil, and to punish has been amplified combining the renewed prison buildings, remote control engines, the increasing militarization of public safety, and the open deadliness of official and unofficial armed groups dedicated to maintaining law and order.

CONCLUSION

The increasing process of blurring functions between the police and armed forces is a phenomenon seen around the world by many authors from different perspectives.[52] By definition, police are used to maintain law and order, while the military protects the country against external enemies. Since the 1980s, the number of interstate conflicts has been decreasing. The blurring of the lines between these distinct forces creates concern among human rights activists and many policy analysts. The U.S. war on drugs, which began in 1971,[53] and the "war on terror" launched by the George W. Bush administration after the events of September 11, 2001, have many similarities when compared. They share the issue of being activated by the confrontation between non-state violent actors and a large array of state forces (e.g., the police and armed forces) and private security agencies, both legal (private military companies) and illegal (paramilitary groups, gangs, and self-defense militias).

Today, the common belief of a peaceful civil society, secured by the police and other state forces, are difficult to sustain when local, regional and global flows of transnational violent actors connect and operate despite the political borders and within distinctive legal environments. To fight those forces, repressive state apparatuses have been adapted, combining new technologies of control (e.g., electronic devices of remote surveillance) with updated forms of repression, imprisonment and extermination of specific groups. These groups can be refugees, illegal immigrants, or drug dealers; the most traditional targets are poor, young, and minority populations. In Brazil, the current trends of surveillance, control, and punishment is at pace with the global trend focused on renewed modes of produce "security" for the capital circulation and remuneration, as well as for the containment of dangerous populations, groups, ideas, regions and, sometimes, as in the case of Haiti and Somalia, entire countries.

In such a context, the military and police assume similar functions, which is reflected in their doctrines, weaponry, tactics, and outfits. The "Robocop" style is omnipresent as well as the legal reforms that empowers the military to act within national borders. This is not only the case for Latin American countries and the militarization of the drug war, but also a practice promoted among North Americans and Europeans in their fight against "terrorists" and immigrants. In Brazil, there is a combination of high-tech policing which utilizes electronic devices and up-to-date tactics of security[54] as well as the old-fashioned repression which uses over-populated prisons to incarcerate young men and women, who are mostly poor and black.

The data on homicides and prison populations, as well as the analysis about the militarization of public safety in Rio de Janeiro and Espírito Santo shown in this chapter are only two examples of the high levels of violence plaguing Brazil. The high levels of social inequality associated with the traditional practice of controlling poverty by a combination of private charity, public assistance and selective repression prevails in this large and diverse nation. The distinction between "national security" and "public safety" is increasingly disappearing under a continuum of militarized police forces.

Chapter Three

Spectacular (In) Justice: Impunity and Communal Violence in Bolivia

Marten Brienen

INTRODUCTION

On Monday, November 14, 2016, some three hundred people gathered at the *cancha* (soccer field) of Entre Ríos, Cochabamba, to witness a peculiar and macabre spectacle. While women and children filled the stands to capacity as one would when the home team is playing, several dozen adults, both male and female, engaged in an hours-long ritual of torture; kicking, hitting, and beating 20 year old Raúl Sandoval to within inches of his life. The event concluded with Sandoval, pleading for his life, being doused in gasoline and set ablaze. He thrashed about and screamed until he could no longer muster the strength, and then effectively lay down to die amid the flames. Sandoval had been the third victim of a three day long orgy of violence, and had only been seized and dragged to the scene of his terrifying demise when his name had been dropped by two other alleged delinquents, who had undergone two days of torture at the Fejuve (*Federación de Juntas Vecinales*) headquarters in the rural town, having been accused of the theft of a motorcycle, prior to naming the unfortunate Sandoval.[1]

Reactions to the lynching of Sandoval signaled outrage, but not necessarily at the brutality of burning a man to death on suspicion of theft. Rather, it was the presence of large groups of children in the audience that caused dismay among members of the press:

> The representative of the ombudsman, Marcelo Cox, condemned the "irresponsibility" of the parents and organizers in permitting that children watch the murder. Former assemblyman Henry Paredes affirmed: 'it is shameful that this is occurring.[2]

We know the details of the case because, in addition to having been burned to death in front of a large and diverse audience, his torture, pleading, and ultimate fate were recorded and made available on YouTube for the diversion of a global audience. Indeed, there are many such videos available of separate incidents from across Latin America.[3] What makes this event even more horrifying is that this public display of bloodlust is not an isolated case. Incidents of a similar nature have been taking place across Bolivia, which is currently ranked second in the region for lynchings of alleged delinquents, bested only by Guatemala.[4] Not only are unfortunate individuals beaten and murdered by enraged mobs with frightening regularity, but the violence is also exceptional in its very public nature and its extreme brutality.

One thing that is particularly interesting to make note of is the fact that even though this is a widespread phenomenon that is very much in the public eye—unlike U.S. and Western European media outlets, Latin American television channels often do not hesitate to show the graphic videos and images without much editing, save for the elimination of nudity[5]—is that there is relatively little literature that deals with violent vigilantism in modern Latin America. This is surprising given that there is an awful lot of attention to other forms of violence in the region: when it comes to gang violence, organized crime, and violence perpetrated by the state, there are myriad studies, articles, and books. Yet the violent wrath of the residents of marginal *barrios* (neighborhoods) is quite possibly another aspect of the profoundly broken nature of the Bolivian justice system and in its own right constitutes a branch of societal violence that merits both exploration and explanation. The most important question to be asked being: what drives this extreme violence?

THE UNCERTAIN SCOPE OF THE PROBLEM

It is unfortunate, given the often very public nature of the phenomenon and the widespread media coverage of individual incidents of what is referred to in Latin America as *linchamiento* (lynching) or *ajusticiamiento* (execution),[6] that only Guatemala officially tracks these incidents. In so far as the Bolivian criminal justice system is concerned, lynchings are counted as assault—when they do not result in the death of the victim—or as murder. This leaves researchers without good tools to make sense of the scope of the problem, given that official statistics do not allow us to distinguish between "regular" assault and incidences of *linchamiento*.

In the Bolivian case, the office of the national ombudsman—the *defensoría del pueblo*—does attempt to account for lynchings in its yearly report on the state of human rights in the country to the national assembly. However, the numbers it puts forward are gleaned from newspaper accounts from selected newspapers, producing an unreliable accounting of the problem. Given the nature of the phenomenon and a clear incentive among participants to keep these events within the *barrio* where they occur, there is little doubt that these occurrences are underreported, as both Donna Yates and Daniel M. Goldstein have noted.[7] Indeed, separate counts based on media reports have produced significantly higher numbers than the *defensoría*: whereas the *defensoría* counted 53 lynchings and attempted lynchings between 2005 and 2012, Goldstein and Fatima Williams Castro counted 42 incidents in 2005 alone.[8] Yhonny Mollericona counted 88 lynchings and attempted lynchings from 2001 to 2008, while Héctor Luna Acevedo counted 199 lynchings and attempted lynchings between 2005 and 2011, with a total of 373 victims.[9] However, this last account lists only 14 occurrences for 2005, when, as I noted above, Goldstein and Castro were able to identify 42 for that year alone, indicating that the numbers are likely significantly higher even than the highest count currently on offer.[10]

Further evidence of severe undercounting comes from the fact that in Goldstein's accounting, the vast majority of cases occurred in Cochabamba, whereas additional counting by Jorge-Carlos Derpic-Burgos appears to show that El Alto sees almost double the cases that Cochabamba does.[11] Moreover, *Asamblea Permanente de Derechos Humanos Regional El Alto* member David Inca estimated in 2014 that between 40 and 50 attempted and completed lynchings took place in El Alto alone,[12] which by itself exceeds the number provided by the *defensoría* for the country as a whole.[13] In effect, the only thing we can say with certainty is that these incidents are numerous and widespread, even though exact numbers will continue to escape us until the Bolivian state determines that it is necessary to create a separate category for the crime in the manner that Guatemala has done.[14] Any estimate of the frequency of *linchamiento* in Bolivia would, at this point, be rather speculative, other than to state that each of these complementary studies shows that they each severely undercount the total number. It is probably not an exaggeration to suggest that *linchamiento* may well occur at least on a weekly basis.

Moreover, given that it is clear that lynchings also occur with some frequency in rural areas, where it would be significantly easier to keep them from public view,[15] we must conclude that lynchings are surprisingly common occurrences that are very difficult indeed to track, especially in the absence of a specific category for such crimes. Interestingly, even the clearly undercounted reports of the *defensoría* have been considered enough to publicly declare that Bolivia is ranked second—after Guatemala—in lynchings in Latin America.[16] That said, since Guatemala is the only country in the region that tracks this particular form of violence, it is rather difficult to accept that notion at face value; not only is there great uncertainty with regard to the actual incidence in Bolivia itself, but there is equal uncertainty with regard to the frequency of *linchamiento* in other countries in the region. By way of example, we can note that it has also been suggested that Brazil may well have the highest incidence of lynchings in the region,[17] while an equally good case can be made for Venezuela, which has descended into virtual anarchy in recent years,[18] and Peru, where lynchings are also quite common.[19]

As much as it has proven nearly impossible to accurately assess the scope of the problem, there is also room to discuss its origins. There appears to be consensus among students of lynching in Bolivia that the phenomenon emerged in the 1990s, reflective perhaps of the overall violence that plagues many Latin American societies and of the tremendous frustration it has generated.[20] Indeed, Latin America is by far the most violent region in the world.[21] This view is certainly the one taken by Goldstein with regard to the emergence of the phenomenon in Bolivia.[22] In this sense, the phenomenon is generally linked to growing citizen insecurity in the region—and, indeed, in Bolivia—in the context of worsening economic conditions emerging in the 1990s. Increases in theft and robbery were followed, the argument goes, by angry communities along the periphery who, in the absence of effective policing, began to take the law into their own hands.[23]

It is interesting to note that newspaper reporting on these events tends to stress the marginality and "otherness" of the people involved in lynch-mobs, often describing them as *turbas enardecidas* (enraged mobs) that engage in acts of savagery.[24] Given that in the Bolivian case—as well as the Guatemalan and Mexican ones—the communities involved are generally of indigenous extraction, a link is very often made to the supposed innate savagery of the people themselves.[25] Indeed, many of the communities in which these incidents take place are relatively new settlements along the urban periphery, inhabited largely by relatively recent arrivals from rural areas, particularly in the Bolivian highlands, leading to a perception among the urban *gente decente* (bourgeoisie) that "their city is under siege by altiplano migrants . . . who are bringing disorder and lawlessness to the city."[26] This brings to the fore a very old theme in the Bolivian imaginary, in which urban elites feared the savage violence that the indigenous majority could inflict upon them. Perhaps the best example exists in the existential fear that Paceño elites harbored during the Federal War (1898–1899), when indigenous leader Pablo Zárate "El Temible" Willka was accused of engaging in "A devastating invasion of [these] populous cities, . . . the citizens of which suffer the painful anxiety of a possible attack."[27] In reading the newspaper reporting of *linchamientos* and *ajusticiamientos* in the urban periphery, one would get the sense that urban elites once again imagine themselves at the mercy of blood-thirsty savages who have arrived at their doorstep.

A HISTORY OF VIOLENCE

While the notion of lynchings as a new phenomenon seems to predominate among those who have studied lynchings in Bolivia and Guatemala, this question is effectively as difficult to answer as the question with regard to the prevalence of lynchings in most Latin American societies. While Snodgrass argues that traditional Mayan systems of community justice are focused on "restitution rather than retribution" and that lynchings did not appear until the 1990s, this seems like rather a facile position to take. As José de Souza Martins points out for the Brazilian case, the sensational press coverage that enthralls the public with this supposed savagery did not really take shape until the 1990s, in part as a result of the lack of freedom of the press in earlier years.[28] Moreover, in addition to showing the limitations to reporting on these events in Brazil, de Souza is able to demonstrate at least 515 lynchings in Brazil between 1970 and 1994, indicating that at least in that case, the history of lynchings certainly predates the 1990s, contradicting authors who regard the emergence of the phenomenon across Latin America as rooted in the 1990s (and its neoliberal reforms).[29] Likewise, Onken has demonstrated the practice of lynching in rural Peru quite extensively for the nineteenth and early twentieth centuries.[30] In yet another example of earlier lynching violence in the region, Orin Starn described the practice of lynching by the Peruvian *rondas campesinas* in the 1970s and 1980s.[31] Moreover, an argument can be made that since this violence appears to be largely relegated to marginal peri-urban communities transplanted from rural areas, it may be possible to imagine that such violence may have happened in earlier years in the communities of origin.[32] There, of course, no newspaper reporters were available to make note of them, nor was videographic evidence recorded for dissemination on YouTube.

In this context, it should be noted that indigenous communities in Bolivia have on a number of occasions wielded violence quite effectively to settle scores with perceived enemies and exploiters. We have ample historical evidence of indigenous communities engaging in violence—though this is usually pegged merely as "resistance"[33]—in order to make themselves heard and to extract concessions from political elites. The cycle of rebellion that marked the last twenty years of the nineteenth century is one such instance in which indigenous communities responded with violence to horrendously mismanaged land reforms, culminating in the participation of indigenous communities in the Federal War (1898–1899) which sowed an existential fear among the hearts of urban *criollos*.[34] The nineteenth century was pockmarked with occasional massacres committed by indigenous communities against those who had sought to harm them.

Some of the most memorable moments of the twentieth century are likewise marked by exceptional violence committed by indigenous communities: the 1927 Chayanta rebellion, in which landowners were murdered, cannibalized, and sacrificed to the mountains, stands as one example.[35] This experience was replicated on a much larger scale during the badly misnamed land reform of 1953: starting in the valley of Cochabamba, the "reform" consisted largely of a spontaneous movement in which armed *colonos*—the indigenous peasants belonging to a *hacienda*—murdered scores of landowners and overseers in what can best be described as a settling of scores of epic proportions. The reform enacted by the Bolivian state followed on the heels of this movement in an almost futile attempt to take charge of what was effectively a *fait accompli*.[36] Even lynchings themselves have been documented in Bolivian history, most notably with the lynching of President Gualberto Villarroel, who was hanged from a tree in front of the Palacio Quemado in 1946 by an enraged mob.[37]

Although (modern) literature rarely touches the subject of the indigenous capacity for violence[38]—due, in part, to an overwhelming desire still to paint indigenous communities as naïve, innocent, pure, proto-communist, harmonious, noble, and non-violent—there is plenty of evidence beyond the capacity for violence I described above. In fact, there is ample evidence that deadly violence is inherent to Bolivian indigenous communities and long has been, although I do not want to fall into the trap of what Painter described as 'telescoping' by suggesting that any behavior we observe in recent times must be rooted in ancient traditions.[39] It has been noted, for example, that violence against women is extremely widespread among large segments of the Bolivian population.[40] Harris, speaking of Northern Potosí, notes that wife-beating is expected behavior, considered both normal and socially acceptable.[41] There is also the *tinku*, a ritual of violence within moieties of indigenous communities where members of the communities engage in physical combat with each other to settle scores and disputes. These ritual events, often fueled by alcohol, can turn quite deadly, the blood spilt considered an offering to Pachamama (Mother Earth).[42]

Beyond the *tinku*, communities can devolve into *ch'axwa*—more aptly described as war, though not quite the same thing—in which communities, often in larger alliances, engage in widespread combat against each other, involving as many as tens of thousands of combatants and resulting in hundreds of deaths.[43] Generally related to territorial disputes, there are notable accounts of communities seeking to exterminate their neighbors in veritable orgies of violence. Indeed, historically, it is absolutely clear that different communities often sided with different factions in important political disputes, leading to very significant violence between them. Andrew Canessa describes one such *ch'axwa*, in which the *colonos* of Pocobaya exacted revenge upon the *colonos* of Thana—notably both moieties of the same community—by massacring them and cannibalizing some of the victims, while (allegedly) burying others alive.[44] Harris describes a similar *ch'axwa* between the Jukumani and Laymi communities in which hundreds died and in which "reported cases of cannibalism caused a national scandal."[45] Esteban Ticona Alejo and Xavier Albó Corrons describe yet more such conflicts between minor communities surrounding Jesús de Machaqa.[46] It should be noted that Canessa's study in particular makes reference to at least one instance of lynching, in which thieves "from beyond the mountains" were punished by the members of the community of Waychu by having (at least) one of them murdered and cannibalized by the *comunarios*.[47] Rumors of cannibalism are surprisingly common in these stories:[48] Olivia Harris notes that "[d]uring the *ch'axwa*, groups of men raid enemy villages, stealing their flocks, sometimes raping their women. Clearer still, they actually mimic the carnivorous predators in consuming the flesh of their enemies."[49]

While it is true that few of these instances prove that extrajudicial murder of accused delinquents occurred,[50] they do weaken the argument that this must be a new phenomenon rooted in migration to the urban periphery. Violence is specifically a part of Bolivian indigenous culture and has long been practiced with relish and ritual. In addition, it must be noted that for most of the country's history, national newspapers simply did not make it their business to describe events in the indigenous communities around the Bolivian countryside, leaving us largely in the dark with regard to the frequency and severity of communal justice. Likewise, while scholars like to describe "traditional" communal justice as different from western conceptions of justice in that it is to be understood as restorative rather than punitive, this is much too far-reaching a statement to accept in the face of the tremendous ethnic diversity that characterizes Bolivian society. There simply is no comparative study of traditional systems of communal justice that would allow anyone to legitimately draw that conclusion, relegating it rather to wishful thinking on the part of those who are intent upon describing indigenous peoples with a very broad and highly idealized brush.

VIOLENCE AS SPECTACLE

The *linchamientos* observed in the periphery of the larger urban areas—as well as in rural communities—are characterized primarily by several common themes. The first of these is the extensive communal and ritualistic nature of the violence, which includes large throngs of *vecinos*, either as spectators or as active participants.[51] In most of the cases for which written or videographic evidence exists, men tend to be the most active participants, while women are more likely to observe. Thus, there does appear to be a gendered aspect to the violence. At the same time, it should be noted that although there appears not to be a structural analysis of the gendered nature of the victims available at the current moment, my own observations, anecdotal though they may be, are that women are not spared. The communal nature of the violence is such that it has been noted that these are "routinized" events that appear to follow a script:[52] they are, in essence, ritualistic affairs in which certain steps are taken in a particular order. Those steps include a) the initial capture, usually under "suspicious circumstances," b) the alarm calling in other *vecinos*, c) the stripping of the victim, d) beating and torture, e) interrogation, f) when lucky, rescue by police, and g) the *ajusticiamiento* through fire, stoning, beating, or live burial.[53] These events are never short: they last from hours to days.[54]

The communal nature of these events is further illustrated by the culture of absolute non-cooperation with authorities in the aftermath of a lynching event.[55] Indeed, when police do arrive during the course of a lynching, they can expect to be greeted with great hostility by the community, which—when police attempt to intervene—may result in violence against police officers themselves. This occurred, for instance, in the rather early example described by Goldstein, which took place in Villa Pagador (Cochabamba) in 1995, and in which police were pelted with rocks and otherwise attacked sufficiently to necessitate the use of teargas and reinforcements to disperse the crowd.[56] In a more recent example, the police force of San Julián (Santa Cruz) were forced to abandon the town altogether when an "enraged mob" stormed the local jail in order to retrieve an inmate accused of murder and then proceeded to subject him to hours of torture prior to burning and then hanging him in the town square;[57] the situation in the town was considered sufficiently dangerous for police that the police station remained empty for a length of 16 days.[58]

Moreover, on several occasions members of the police themselves have been the explicit target of the *turba enardecida*: in Uncía (Potosí), members of two indigenous communities lynched four police officers in 2016, releasing the bodies after two weeks and only on the condition that no charges be filed.[59] Likewise, in El Alto two police officers were lynched after having been accused of theft and unable to prove that they were officers of the law.[60]

The second phenomenon worth noting is the exceptional nature of the violence employed and the terrifying ways in which *ajusticiamientos* are carried out. Victims can be tortured over periods of several days, often in some public place or square where they are beaten, often with sticks, kicked, and sometimes whipped, stoned, or caned.[61] Most victims have been disrobed, and genital mutilation is not altogether unheard of, while most of the victims are tied to a tree or a pole to prevent escape and self-defense.[62] There is tremendous creativity in the sheer cruelty of the punishments inflicted on alleged wrongdoers: in Caranavi, a 52 year old woman was tied, along with her two sons, to a *Palo Santo* tree (Triplaris) to be bitten to death by the mutualistic venomous fire ants (pseudomyrmex triplarinus) that inhabit the species.[63] Generally, *ajusticiamiento* is carried out by dousing a victim with gasoline and lighting them on fire, by live burial, or by mercilessly beating them until they die. That is to say that the purpose of these events is to inflict as much pain and suffering upon the victim as possible: they are intended to bring about humiliation, dehumanization, and profound suffering in the victim. Even in death, further mutilation of the bodies may occur to maximize the degradation. While it may sound like pure hyperbole, it can be argued that the biggest difference between the brutal and degrading executions performed by terrorist organizations such as the Islamic State (ISIS) and those carried out in Bolivian "street justice" lies in the production values of the videos that relay to the world what they have wrought.

The third phenomenon that marks these extrajudicial killings of supposed delinquents is that the exceptional cruelty is visited almost exclusively on outsiders:[64] individuals who are not members of the community itself, or in some cases, members of the community who for one reason or another are not recognized. The interrogation phase, as Risør points out, tends to focus on the origin of the alleged criminal: "where are they from?"[65] Indeed, there have been cases where victims were released because a *vecino* affirmed that they belonged to the community after all. This appears to be in line with the statements made by *vecinos* attempting to defend and explain this behavior to both the press and academic observers: a dominant theme in these is the protection of the community. This appears to be part and parcel of a national pathology of distrust toward outsiders. As Goldstein notes—and as the author himself has observed—Bolivians are quite eager to blame acts of criminal violence on Peruvians.[66]

A fourth characteristic worth noting is that in these events, which are both entirely spontaneous in that they occur immediately once an unknown individual is encountered engaging in "suspicious activities," and, as I described above when addressing the ritualistic nature of these *linchamientos*, "planned events" in the manner in which they are choreographed,[67] is that neither guilt nor the severity of the alleged crime appear to matter.[68] Although *vecinos*, when asked about these events, consistently speak of the lack of security in their *barrios*, the reality is that the vast majority of lynchings are precipitated by accusations of petty theft: based on his data, Luna Acevedo shows that 74.8 percent of lynchings involve allegations of simple theft, while more serious allegations such as murder and rape make up 4.0 percent and 3.5 percent, respectively.[69] In no traditional system of communal justice that we are aware of does the severity of the crime carry no weight at all in determining the sentence to be carried out, which in these cases is almost always death by burning, hanging, beating, or live burial. Once the process is set in motion, only forceful intervention by police seems to be able to interrupt the process sufficiently to let an alleged delinquent escape with his or her life.

Guilt appears immaterial in that the choreography does not include steps to determine whether a "suspicious" individual is, in fact, guilty of anything. Being in the wrong place is considered evidence enough, leading to a plethora of innocent people being burnt to death for crimes as varied as "being confused," "being drunk," "being schizophrenic," and "refusing to answer questions due to deafness."[70] In addition, scores have met an ugly fate simply for *looking* like a delinquent.[71]

FRUSTRATION, LAWLESSNESS, IMPUNITY, AND VIOLENCE

Explanations for the vigilante violence fall broadly into three categories: firstly, the argument has been widely made that the mob violence is the result of a dearth of law enforcement and the absence of faith in the justice system.[72] Secondly, it has been widely argued that these communities are responding to increases in criminal activity and a growing sense of public insecurity.[73] Lastly, and particularly in the case of Bolivia, the argument has been put forward—at times quite vociferously by perpetrators of these extrajudicial executions—that we can look at this phenomenon as an extension of *justicia comunitaria* (communal justice), the principle embedded in the 2009 constitution that holds that indigenous communities have the right to dispense traditional justice within their communities.[74]

It is indeed the case that organizers of this violence frequently invoke the absence of police forces as a reason for taking the law into their own hands. Then again, police officers themselves have been the target of lynching and when they attempt to interfere, they are frequently targeted for violence and abuse. In this sense, the *vecinos* tend to be slightly schizophrenic: they complain about the absence of police and in the same breath denounce the police as corrupt, complicit with criminals, and ineffective.[75] Indeed, Bolivia ranks lowest in the hemisphere when it comes to faith in the national police and in the justice system as a whole.[76] The explanation for this lack of faith lies in several related issues: for one, Bolivians report the highest incidence of having to pay bribes anywhere in the Americas, after Haiti, with some 30.2 percent of individuals reporting that they have personally had to pay a bribe;[77] most bribes are paid to police officers.[78] In rural areas, as Canessa points out, "the state is weak, particularly in small communities with little or no road access and where police presence is rare or non-existent. The community has to police itself, normally through fines or expulsion, but in extreme cases even through extra-judicial execution, such as burial alive."[79]

This creates a difficult situation: Bolivian police are hopelessly corrupt—demanding bribes even to investigate a crime[80]—and ineffective, leaving a correct impression of almost complete lawlessness and impunity.[81] At the same time, the primary concern among Bolivians is the notion of "citizen security," Bolivians ranking near the top (after Venezuela) in the hemisphere with regard for their sense of lacking personal safety,[82] thus creating a very specific demand for law enforcement. A further complicating factor in the relationship between *barrio* residents and law enforcement lies in the history of these communities. As Goldstein points out, many of these peri-urban communities are relative young settlements, often emerging illegally along the urban periphery, while residents hail from indigenous communities in rural areas.[83] Historically, of course, the role of both the military and the police was to control and subdue precisely these groups for the protection of *criollo* and *mestizo* townsfolk and landowners. There is, in that sense, no history of trust between law enforcement and the indigenous communities, which is reflected in the fact that confidence in the national police—already the lowest in the hemisphere—is lowest among indigenous Bolivians.[84] The atmosphere, then, is one of tremendous distrust.

With regard to the justice system, *vecinos* are correct that the system fails to adequately punish the guilty—or, indeed, protect the innocent. Beyond the corruption of the police, the judicial system is profoundly broken: there is widespread corruption among judges and prosecutors, which results in extortion of the accused, and impunity for the rich.[85] Moreover, the system is stretched incredibly thin: only slightly under half of Bolivian municipalities have a judge, about one quarter have a prosecutor, and no more than three percent have a public defender. This clearly puts justice beyond the reach of many Bolivians, and predictably, these shortages are felt most acutely along the periphery. The result has been an enormous backlog of cases for the roughly 750 judges that serve the population of over 10 million: some 396,482 cases still await a court date.[86] This also means that the wheels of justice turn excruciatingly slowly: more than 80 percent of inmates in the heavily overcrowded Bolivian prisons and jails are there in pre-trial detention, which can last—in extreme cases—up to 23 years.[87] It is perhaps not surprising, given the profound problems in the justice system, that tolerance for lynching is comparatively high.[88]

Ultimately, however, the entire argument falls down on the mere absurdness of the proposition: the notion that *vecinos*, mostly recent migrants from indigenous communities in the rural highlands and valleys, grew tired of the lack of policing and the absence of state services, and thus responded with extreme violence against trespassers, implies that in their communities of origin, law enforcement somehow had been present and had done a decent enough job of protecting these communities against criminals and delinquents, which is very clearly a nonsensical notion. The social structure of the Bolivian countryside has been the subject of intensive study, where there has long been a focus precisely on the profound and unrelenting injustice suffered by members of indigenous communities at the hands of rural elites and their enforcers. If the urban periphery is marked by lawlessness and impunity, then the rural areas—and ever more so the further we go back in recent history—are surely characterized by the complete absence of justice, especially for those who would go on to migrate to the urban periphery, and the active exploitation and abuse of the vulnerable by rural elites and their henchmen. Lawlessness and impunity, while real grievances of the *vecinos* of peri-urban settlements, are certainly not a new phenomenon, and indubitably not one that rural migrants would not have been accustomed to in their communities of origin.

With regard to citizen insecurity as a reason for lynchings,[89] there are several important points to bring to the fore. One of the most interesting aspects of this reasoning is that although Bolivians are near the very top in Latin America with regard to perceived insecurity,[90] it is in fact a relatively safe country with regionally low reported rates of murder and robbery.[91] There is, in that sense, a disconnect between Bolivian perceptions of insecurity and actual levels of crime. Likewise, while it is frequently reported that crime is on the rise, available statistics do not actually point in that direction: there has indeed been an uptick in crime from 2007, but that year counts as a year with some of the lowest reported crime figures in recent Bolivian history. Indeed, the amount of recorded homicides in 2014 (2,363 victims) remains lower than that of 2000 (3,169 victims).[92] Rising crime rates, then, appear not to offer an especially good explanation for the phenomenon. This is in line with an observation I made earlier in this chapter: one of the characteristics of the phenomenon of *linchamiento* is that there is a complete separation between the severity of the alleged transgression that prompts a lynching and the intended outcome—what Neil Whitehead might have described as "lingering death"[93]—of that lynching, which suggests that the phenomenon is not about crime *per sé*.[94]

LYNCHING AS COMMUNAL JUSTICE

The third of the frequently offered explanations, and the one most frequently offered by *vecinos* themselves, is that of *linchamiento* as a form of indigenous communal justice.[95] It should immediately be noted that most scholars reject this notion out of hand: Snodgrass argues that "there is no evidence to suggest that lynchings have their roots in traditional mechanisms of popular justice."[96]

Likewise, politicians have been very quick to point out that while the law explicitly permits communal justice, the death penalty is unconstitutional and communal justice is limited to minor offenses.[97]

Although this sentiment is in keeping with the notion that indigenous traditional justice is necessarily benevolent and restorative, the problem with this rejection of the notion of lynching as a form of communal justice rooted in indigenous tradition is that there is, in fact, ample evidence that this violence has its roots in indigenous communal practice and tradition: writing about the massacre at Thana, Andrew Canessa observes that "Burial alive is, in fact, a well-known form of communal justice in the area [of Achacachi]."[98] There is nothing restorative about burial alive. Moreover, as indicated above, indigenous communities in Bolivia have a long history of violence, including the settling of scores with those who had wronged them. On many occasions, this took place in the context of broader upheaval[99]—such as during the cycle of rebellion in the last quarter of the nineteenth century,[100] or the uprisings of the 1920s, or indeed following the Bolivian National Revolution of April 1952[101]—but there are also documented cases where such violence was directed against trespassers.[102]

We do not have a good understanding of the history of lynching in Bolivian indigenous communities and certainly not a good enough understanding to make any claim that this behavior emerged only in the 1990s in the periurban settlements of indigenous rural transplants. The notion that this is a new phenomenon, emerging in the 1990s as a result of neoliberalism, as has been suggested, is the result not of the fact that we know such behavior did not occur in indigenous communities in earlier times but of the fact that the national news media discovered only in the 1990s that an appeal to indigenous barbarism among frightened urban middle classes would be hugely profitable. It appears much more likely that the emergence of these new *barrios* populated by recent migrants along with the emergence of a (somewhat) free press created the circumstances for the phenomenon to become sensationalized: migration brought this violence to the very doorstep of "civilization" at just the right time. With regard to the brutality, we should take note of Harris's comments on violence in Andean indigenous culture: "A high value is placed on *losing control* [emphasis hers] in Andean cultures, which in this differ from the conception of civilization rooted in western culture. . . . And yet, there are no clear guidelines as to *how much* [emphasis hers] violence is good, and when it becomes too much."[103] It should also be noted that *vecinos* themselves consistently lay claim to their right to engage in *justicia comunitaria.* To reject the notion that this could be traditional justice is to ignore what they themselves think about the matter.

It is clear from Goldstein's description of what he considers one of the earliest examples, that the fixed pattern of the ritual is already clearly established and this pattern is precisely the one we observe in virtually every single case. This is suggestive of a pre-existing pattern. Moreover, it is strikingly typical of Bolivian indigenous migrants to bring their social structures and organizations right along with them: the *cocalero* communities of the Chapare, many of them transplants from the mining camps of the highlands, retained the high levels of political and social organization that had characterized the communities of origin, leading to the emergence of organized labor in the form of *sindicatos* and *federaciones* that took the mantle from the miners who preceded them—and, rather famously, brought Evo Morales to power.[104] Given that there is evidence for the existence of lynching as a practice among indigenous communities in the rural areas prior to the 1990s, there is an argument to be made that these, too, are traditions and forms of social organization that have travelled along with the migrants into their new settlements.

It is, moreover, a practice that the entire community shares in. On the one hand, this creates impunity, in that it would be difficult to prosecute and convict an entire community.[105] On the other hand, it also strengthens community bonds and mirrors the shared experience of both *tinku* and *ch'axwa*; the entire point, as Harris points out, of the *tinku* is to channel the violence in a community, by creating a specific and ritualized opportunity for scores to be settled and disputes to be resolved.[106] We see this reflected in the highly ritualized nature of the *linchamiento* and *ajusticiamiento*.

The final reasoning that is somewhat frequently employed to explain the violence of *linchamiento* without regarding it as *justicia comunitaria* has been to argue that the phenomenon is employed strategically in modern Bolivia to call attention to the plight of the community. As Snodgrass would have it, lynchings are yet another form of indigenous "resistance."[107] Likewise, Goldstein and Castro regard *linchamiento* as a form of "creative violence" that allows communities to call attention to their plight and to the absence of state services.[108] This is a weak argument: the fact that communities have discovered that they can use the sensationalism of the press to their advantage is not evidence of a preconceived strategy. When the press first began reporting on the phenomenon, as Goldstein describes, the reaction among *vecinos* was certainly not indicative of a community that was pleased with the attention or that felt "empowered."[109]

I am not a cultural relativist and it is with that in mind that I reject the notion of lynching, as it occurs in Bolivia today, as a form of *justicia comunitaria*: there is no justice in burning people alive for the crime of being alien to a *barrio* or for being deaf and therefore unable to respond satisfactorily to interrogations by *vecinos*. There is no justice in burning a person alive for the crime of petty theft. There is no justice in ignoring possible innocence prior to degrading, humiliating, and torturing an individual in the name of justice. Then again, as selfsame *vecinos* would agree: there is no justice in Bolivia.

Chapter Four

Violence in Peru

Barnett S. Koven and Cynthia McClintock

In the 2010s, despite the evisceration of armed insurgency and over a decade of rapid and sustained economic growth, perceptions of insecurity have increased in Peru.[1] Indeed, in 2010 and 2012, perceptions of insecurity were higher in Peru than in any other of the 14 countries surveyed by the Latin American Public Opinion Project (LAPOP).[2] Perceptions of insecurity in Peru was 56.6 on a 100 point scale (with higher numbers indicating more insecurity).[3] At first glance, this finding is perplexing, given that Peru has one of the lowest homicide rates in the hemisphere (7.2 homicides per 100,000 inhabitants in 2015).[4] By contrast, in El Salvador, perceptions of insecurity were nearly ten points less (46.9) than in Peru, despite a homicide rate many times greater (81.2 per 100,000).[5] What explains this seemingly paradoxical evidence?

In answering this question, this chapter proceeds in three sections. The first section seeks to understand the causes of violence in Peru. It examines two types of threats to citizen security: long-standing threats, namely the Shining Path insurgency and narcotrafficking, and also, the newer threat of organized crime, in particular extortion and cell phone theft. We explore the conditions that gave rise to these threats and how the threats have evolved in recent years. The second section of the chapter is devoted to responses to these threats. In particular, we analyze the responses of the most recent governments, under Presidents Ollanta Humala (2011–2016) and Pedro Pablo Kuczynski (often referred to by his initials, PPK; 2016–present). Unfortunately, most Peruvians were dissatisfied with the central government's responses and some developed their own coping mechanisms. We briefly examine these responses, which include vigilantism and the strengthening of the Serenazgo—unarmed patrols hired by municipalities. The third and final section concludes, noting that Peruvian perceptions of insecurity are well founded in the face of expanding criminality and limited abilities to combat organized criminal enterprises.

CAUSES OF VIOLENCE

A regarding Peruvian's heightened perceptions of insecurity, the first explanation is that, while homicide is rare in Peru by regional standards, it is becoming more prevalent; the 2015 homicide rate of 7.2 per 100,000 was considerably above the 2011 rate of 5.4.[6] Second, although terrorist attacks by the Shining Path (*Sendero Luminoso*) insurgency, which nearly toppled the Peruvian state in the early 1990s, have ended in almost all parts of the country, the narcotrafficking that originally fueled the insurgency expanded. Criminal activity now reaches into not only the unpaved streets of the remote villages near coca-growing areas but also into the luxury buildings in Peru's coastal ports where shipment routes are planned and money laundered. Concomitantly, organized crime exploded; a panoply of illegal businesses, including extortion and cell phone theft rings, emerged. As a result, of 23 Latin American countries for which data are available in the 2014 LAPOP survey, the rate at which citizens were the victim of a crime was higher in Peru than in any other country: 30.6 percent of Peruvians reported having been a victim of a crime in 2014 alone.[7] The 30.6 percent figure in Peru was nearly double the regional average (17 percent).[8] Over the last ten years, total crime increased by 88 percent and the number of victims by 70 percent.[9]

Moreover, organized crime corrupted the institutions that were expected to stop it; soldiers, police officers, politicians and judges were all enmeshed. At the same time, many other soldiers, police officers, politicians and judges remained honest and their colleagues' wrongdoings were revealed and prosecuted. Although of course these revelations were positive, the contamination of Peru's institutions by crime and corruption was broadcast persistently in Peru's media and Peruvians became ever more aware of the problem.

This section first examines long-standing menaces, namely insurgency and narcotrafficking; and, second, the newer threat of organized crime. Each subsection not only overviews the relevant types of wrongdoing but also describes their genesis. Although we discuss narcotrafficking and organized crime separately, the two are, of course, related; as in many Latin American countries, narcotraffickers in Peru diversified their businesses and expanded their criminal networks. The epicenter of crime in Peru in 2015 was its key drug transit port city, Callao (five percent of crimes and three percent of Peru's population) and its neighbor Lima (43 percent of crimes and 32 percent of the population). The highest rate of crime was in Tumbes, which recently became a key drug transit city.[10]

LONG-STANDING THREATS: THE SHINING PATH AND NARCOTRAFFICKING

Since the mid-1980s, the challenges of the Shining Path and narcotrafficking have been intertwined. At its armed onset in 1980, the Shining Path was a Maoist insurgency based in an impoverished highlands region. Then, in the mid-1980s, the Shining Path expanded into Peru's coca-growing areas and, in the twenty-first century, it was deeply enmeshed in the narcotics trade and operated only in Peru's major coca-growing areas.

For most of the last 40 years, Peru's major coca-growing areas have been the Upper Huallaga Valley (UHV) and the Valley of the Apurímac, Ene and Mantaro Rivers (VRAEM). The UHV and the VRAEM are located on the slopes between the Andes and the Amazon. The UHV stretches north from the Huánuco department [a state-like area] into the San Martín department; the VRAEM is located to the south of the UHV and includes parts of four different regions: Ayacucho, Cusco, Huancavelica, and Junín. Nevertheless, coca cultivation has been shifting from the UHV to the VRAEM, as well as a diverse array of new areas, as a result of forced eradication efforts. As of 2016, cultivation was occurring in more than half of Peru's 25 departments.[11] As cultivation spread across Peru, so too did narcotraffickers. Importantly, narcotrafficking has not just expanded geographically, but the number of illicit groups involved and the routes used have also increased.[12]

The Shining Path

The Maoist Shining Path insurgency was founded by Abimael Guzmán in the remote southern highlands of Ayacucho, Peru's most impoverished region.[13] In contrast to most Latin American insurgencies, the Shining Path was hierarchical, disciplined, sectarian, and often compared to a cult, with Guzmán as its deity. The Shining Path did not hesitate to use terrorism against the state and against civilians who opposed it; including civilians on the political left. After taking up arms in 1980, it seemed to expand inexorably, in part due to extremely adverse weather and severe economic crisis. As mentioned, in the mid-1980s, the Shining Path entered Peru's coca-producing areas, in particular the UHV, and gained financial resources for its fight. By the late 1980s and early 1990s, the Shining Path raged in most of the country, including Lima.

However, on September 12, 1992, the expansion of the Shining Path was halted when Guzmán was arrested along with seven other members of the Central Committee. During the capture, police recovered Guzmán's master files and, with this information, were able to identify and capture 90 percent of the Shining Path's leadership by the end of 1992.[14] Apparently, Guzmán had kept detailed records of his armed militants (including the types of weapons possessed by each unit).[15]

Soon, the insurgency was decimated.[16] Nonetheless, the Shining Path continued to exist, albeit dramatically reduced. In the twenty-first century, the number of armed Shining Path fighters was much smaller; at most 750 in 2011 versus approximately 10,000 in 1989.[17] Furthermore, the twenty-first century Shining Path controlled only a tiny percentage of municipalities, exclusively in Peru's coca-growing areas, versus roughly 28 percent of all municipalities in 1989.[18]

The twenty-first century Shining Path was different not only in its numbers and extension but also its character. Although the twenty-first century Shining Path proclaimed ideological goals, its ideological commitment was called into question by its zealous pursuit of financial gain through its deep involvement in narcotrafficking. Until about 2012, the Shining Path was divided between two factions, each of which was active only in one different coca-producing area. One faction—loyal to Guzmán—was active in the UHV and a second—not loyal to Guzmán—in the VRAEM. Both the UHV and the VRAEM factions levied taxes on coca producers in return for their provision of security against eradication units. In addition, the VRAEM faction pursued vertical integration with all aspects of the narcotics business, undertaking its own cultivation, processing and trafficking operations.[19] Revenues were immense. In 2012, one launderer was charged with laundering more than $100 million, and this launderer was one of several working for just this faction.[20] The proceeds were used to purchase advanced armaments and improve organizational practices.[21]

In the second decade of the twenty-first century, Peru's government achieved successes against both the Shining Path faction and coca production in the UHV (see subsequent sections). As of 2017, only the VRAEM faction of the Shining Path remained, and it was believed to number only between 120 to 150 armed fighters.[22] As of June 2017, the VRAEM faction's top leadership—the Quispe Palomino brothers—remain at large and are taking extra safety precautions. The VRAEM faction is still able to stage attacks and inflict casualties. The number of Shining Path terrorist actions in 2015 was 36 (versus 792 in 1996 and 161 in 2001) and the number of concomitant deaths was 11 in 2015 (versus 211 in 1996 and 35 in 2001).[23] Of the 36 terrorist attacks, 28 occurred in the VRAEM.[24] On April 9, 2016, Shining Path militants attacked a military convoy transporting polling materials to the VRAEM that were to be used on the following day in the first round of presidential elections. Eight soldiers and two civilians died in the attack.[25]

The VRAEM faction of the Shining Path posed a more serious challenge to Peru's government than the UHV faction for several reasons. First, even in the first decade of the 2000s, the VRAEM faction was stronger. It was better financed and consequently better armed.[26] Second, the UHV had much better road connections to provincial cities and was in general less remote than the VRAEM; alternative development was easier to achieve in the UHV than in the VRAEM. Third, the coca producers in the VRAEM are small-scale farmers who are poorly organized among themselves and consider the Shining Path to be their only source of protection.[27] Fourth, the VRAEM faction is cooperating to at least some degree with Colombian narcotraffickers (which in the twenty-first century, the UHV faction was not).[28]

Narcotrafficking

In the twenty-first century, coca cultivation and narcotrafficking expanded in Peru. In 2012, Peru overtook Colombia as the world's largest cultivator of coca (although Colombia re-gained this status in 2014). At the same time, the menaces associated with cultivation—trafficking (and rival trafficking gangs, which frequently evolved into international crime syndicates, as discussed below) and money-laundering escalated. As of 2016, the cost of a kilo of cocaine ranged from an estimated $600 to $1,100 (varying with the degree of refinement of the cocaine and the particularities of the site) and the cost of its transport to the United States or Europe perhaps $2,000 or $3,000; then, in Belgium, the price increased to approximately $40,000.[29] An average family clan in the UHV processed between 200 to 500 kilos per month. One top trafficker has been sending a ton of cocaine every month out of Callao for a decade.[30] Of course, total profits were immense.

From the 1970s through 1995, Peru was the world's top producer of coca. The UHV was the primary site. During this period, most of the coca or coca paste was transported from the eastern Andean slopes in Colombian traffickers' small planes to Colombia, where it was refined and then smuggled into the United States and Europe. Then, in 1994–95, the government of Alberto Fujimori (1990–2000) initiated aerial interdiction; supported by U.S. intelligence, Peru's air force shot down Colombian traffickers' planes.[31] As a result, coca production shifted to Colombia and traffickers established alternative routes through Peru's coastal cities.

As of 1999, Peru cultivated a record low of less than 40,000 hectares of coca (see table 4.1). Yet in 2001, amid the air interdiction policy, a U.S. plane was shot down by mistake and a U.S. missionary and her daughter died; the U.S. immediately cancelled the program. Successive Peruvian governments have requested the restoration of the program but to no avail regardless of improved safeguards. At the same time, the Colombian government was implementing draconian coca eradication policies and, as a result, pushing cultivation back to Peru. According to both the United Nations Office on Drugs and Crime (UNODC) and the U.S. Department of State's International Narcotics Control Strategy Reports (INCSR), which use different calculation methods, coca cultivation increased quite steadily between 1999 and 2011 (see table 4.1). The UNODC reported a peak of 62,500 hectares in 2011, while the INSCR documented a peak of 53,000 hectares in 2010.

As we discuss below, after 2011 the Humala government vigorously pursued eradication and alternative development. The UNODC reported significant success: a decline from 63,500 hectares in 2011 to 40,500 hectares in 2015 (see table 4.1). But the INCSR did not; by its calculation, cultivation remained steady at about 50,000 hectares between 2011 and 2015 (see table 4.1).[32] In 2017, anti-narcotics officials in the PPK government announced their view that the 53,000 figure reported by the INCSR was more accurate—or, indeed, that the figure could have been 55,000.[33]

Over the last 40 years, the vast majority of Peruvian coca has been produced in the UHV and the VRAEM. Beginning in the 1990s after the initiation of the air bridge denial program and continuing into the twenty-first century, the trend has been for production to shift from the UHV to the VRAEM. According to the UNODC, coca cultivation in the UHV plummeted from 17,080 hectares in 2006 to 1,099 hectares in 2015 (see table 4.2). For example, of the 23,800 hectares eradicated in 2013, the vast majority were in the UHV valleys of Pichis-Palcazu and Monzón.[34] Specifically, the Pichis-Palcazu Valley saw an 82 percent decline to 863 hectares and the Monzón Valley a 55 percent decrease to 863 hectares.[35] As of 2015, the VRAEM was by far the largest source of Peruvian coca, responsible for 18,333 hectares or 45 percent of Peru's cultivation (according to the UNODC figures).

Despite the Peruvian government's success in the battle against coca in the UHV, it is clear from tables 4.1 and 4.2 that the war was not won. Although the U.S. government reported that Peru eradicated 23,800 hectares of coca in 2013, it also reported that, overall, coca cultivation increased by 9,000 hectares (see table 4.1). The "balloon effect"—in which the eradication of coca in one area merely displaces cultivation to other areas—was very evident. As of 2016, coca was grown in parts of thirteen of Peru's twenty-five departments.[36] In particular, table 4.2 shows that, as coca cultivation declined in the UHV, it increased in the VRAEM. Indeed, in figures for 2016 that remain unofficial, cultivation in the VRAEM is reported to have risen by almost 5,000 hectares

Table 4.1. Coca Cultivation in Peru (Estimates, Thousands of Hectares)

Year	*1999*	*2000*	*2001*	*2002*	*2003*	*2004*	*2005*	*2006*	*2007*	*2008*	*2009*	*2010*	*2011*	*2012*	*2013*	*2014*	*2015*
UNODC	38.7	43.4	46.2	46.7	44.2	50.3	48.2	51.4	53.7	56.1	59.9	61.2	62.5	60.4	49.8	42.9	40.5
INCSR	34.7	31.7	32.1	34.7	29.3	27.5	34.0	42.0	36.0	41.0	40.0	53.0	49.5	50.5	59.5	46.5	53.0

Sources: Data is derived from the United Nations Office on Drugs and Crime, *Perú: Monitoreo de cultivos de coca 2012,* September 2013, Lima, Peru, p. 65; the United Nations Office on Drugs and Crime, *Perú: Monitoreo de cultivos de coca 2013,* June 2014, Lima, Peru, p. 7; the United Nations Office on Drugs and Crime, *Perú: Monitoreo de cultivos de coca 2015,* July 2016, Lima, Peru, p. 27; and the U.S. Department of State, Bureau of International Narcotics and Law Enforcement Affairs, *International Narcotics Control Strategy Report (INCSR),* from 2000–2017, Washington, DC; U.S. Department of State, Bureau of International Narcotics and Law Enforcement Affairs.

Table 4.2. Coca Cultivation in the VRAEM and UHV (Estimates, Hectares)

Year	*2006*	*2007*	*2008*	*2009*	*2010*	*2011*	*2012*	*2013*	*2014*	*2015*
VRAEM	15,813	16,019	16,719	17,486	19,723	19,925	19,965	19,167	18,845	18,333
UHV	17,080	17,217	17,848	17,497	13,025	12,421	9,509	4,302	1,555	1,099

Source: ConsultAndes, *Sector Report—February 2014: Next Steps in the War on Drugs,* February 2014, Lima, Peru, 2 and expanded based on data derived from the United Nations Office on Drugs and Crime, *Perú: Monitoreo de cultivos de coca 2015,* July 2016, Lima, Peru, p. 27.

to as much as 23,000 hectares—a roughly 25 percent jump. The problem is compounded by the fact that, due to climatic conditions, the coca yields per hectare are higher in the VRAEM than virtually anywhere else in Peru or in the entire coca-producing world.[37]

The "cockroach effect"—the displacement of coca cultivation and trafficking to the areas of weaker law enforcement and social and physical infrastructure—was also evident. Cultivation increased not only in the VRAEM, where to date the government has not attempted eradication (see below), but also in two other areas—Putumayo and the "triborder area"—that are not only remote but near international borders, complicating enforcement.[38] Putumayo abuts the border with Colombia to the north and the "triborder area" is in the northeastern Amazon lowlands where Peru, Colombia, and Brazil connect.

As cultivation spread, the number of illicit groups involved in narcotics expanded considerably.[39] Most of these organizations were family-based clans that usually cooperated but sometimes competed; even though the clans were small, they were often vertically integrated and at times collaborated with Colombian traffickers.[40] Even in the UHV, where despite rapidly declining levels of cultivation, an estimated 16 small clans operated towards the end of 2012.[41]

In contrast to the 1980s and early 1990s when coca from the UHV was transported out of Peru by air to Colombia and did not greatly affect the vast majority of Peruvians who lived in coastal cities, in the twenty-first century trafficking routes diversified. Most of the coca from the UHV was transported by land to Peru's coastal port cities.[42] As previously indicated, a great deal went to Callao and Lima, and some went to Peru's northern port cities, such as Barranca, Chimbote, Trujillo, and Tumbes, where the drug was shipped north by boat. By contrast, between approximately 2013 and 2016, most of the coca from the VRAEM was transported by air to western Bolivia or Brazil. As of 2014, roughly 79 illegal flights per month originated from just one of the many areas of these flights in the VRAEM.[43] It is estimated that on average, each flight carried about 325 kilos of product.[44]

As coca production in the VRAEM increased and the air route between the VRAEM and Bolivia and Brazil was more and more frequented, the Humala government debated its interdiction policy. The primary strategy was to destroy airstrips; but, these were usually quickly re-built. Increasingly, the government sought the resumption of aerial interdiction, but the U.S. opposed such strategies. Still, in August 2015, Peru's congress voted unanimously in favor of a new aerial interdiction law (*Ley de Interdicción Aérea*), which authorized the Peruvian military to shoot down traffickers.[45] The U.S. government continued its opposition but offered "some alternatives in terms of technological help" instead.[46] It appears that a compromise had been reached to facilitate the aerial pursuit but not the shoot down of traffickers' planes. Nevertheless, the new law frightened traffickers, and, as in the 1990s, they shifted transport methods. In particular, they began moving drugs in hidden compartments in the trucks and pickups used by mining and construction companies across the border with Brazil.[47] In addition, they returned to the land routes to Peru's coastal cities.[48]

As has been common elsewhere in Latin America, violence in Peru's transport cities surged as a result of competition among rival drug gangs. For example, in 2013 the murder rate in Barranca, 36.2 deaths per 100,000 inhabitants, was five and a half times greater than the national average that year; in Trujillo, the rate was 25.0 deaths per 100,000; and in Chimbote, 22.1 deaths per 100,000).[49] Peru's largest port city, Callao, located on Lima's western boundary, has also become increasingly violent. Its homicide rate was 15.2 per 100,000 inhabitants in 2015, more than double the national average that year and a large jump from 10.2 in 2011.[50]

Moreover, as has also been common elsewhere in Latin America, narcotraffickers' offer of "silver" and threat of "lead" have detonated corruption among Peruvian authorities. As is discussed further below, some military and police became directly involved in the drug trade. In one of many examples, a ring of former military officers operated a cocaine trafficking and storage enterprise out of a Lima hotel; the officers were arrested and the ring dismantled in early 2017.[51] Many politicians engaged in money-laundering. Indeed, the 2016 election turned in part on allegations of money-laundering against the head of the political party of PPK's rival, Keiko Fujimori. In the campaign, PPK raised the specter that Peru was becoming a "narco state"; analysts have charged that at least 20 legislators elected in 2016 were complicit with the drug trade.[52]

THE EMERGENT THREAT: ORGANIZED CRIME

While terrorism and narcotrafficking have threatened security in Peru for decades, organized crime is relatively new. This is not to say that organized crime did not exist previously, but its current prevalence is unprecedented. Organized crime in Peru spans numerous types of crime, including extortion, cell phone theft, bank heists, human trafficking, illegal mining, and illegal logging. The patterns and dynamics are particularly evident in extortion and cell phone theft and they are analyzed in depth below.

Organized crime is distinct from common crime in several respects. First, criminal enterprises are hierarchically organized into groups that perform specialized functions. For example, in cell phone theft rings, thieves steal phones; technicians erase, unblock and reprogram them; and traffickers ship the phones overseas. Second, like the drug trade, many of the criminal enterprises operate internationally.Third, criminal enterprises are enabled through extensive corruption, ranging from officials' acceptance of bribes in exchange for turning a blind eye to direct engagement in crime.[53] Soldiers' complicity with narcotrafficking in the VRAEM is indicated below.

Corruption extends to civilian authorities as well. As of July 2014, a staggering 1,699 of 1,841 mayors (92 percent) were under investigation by the Attorney General's anti-corruption office for corruption. In one example, in April 2017, a mayor in the department of Lima, Richard Ramos Ávalos, was arrested on charges of land trafficking, extortion and assassination; during the arrest, authorities found approximately $100,000 in cash in his home. Sadly, the vast majority of mayors subsequently stood for reelection; the mayor of Chiclayo stood for reelection despite accusations of 18 distinct crimes (and despite representing the Clean Hands Movement (*Movimiento Manos Limpias*)). In addition, as of July 2014, 19 of Peru's 25 governors were under investigation. The governor of Ancash, César Álvarez, was accused of running a criminal gang that spent $1 million a month on bribes and hired hitmen to assassinate those who did not yield to bribes.[54]

Further, every past president since 1985 has been subject to criminal investigation for corruption. This includes Alberto Fujimori, who is incarcerated on charges ranging from human rights abuses to fraud, embezzlement and misappropriation of funds.[55] Like many officials throughout Latin America, former presidents Alan García (2006–2011) and Alejandro Toledo (2001–2006) are under investigation for accepting bribes by the Brazilian construction giant Odebrecht. Toledo is residing in California and the Peruvian government has requested his extradition; the U.S. government has asked for stronger evidence. If Toledo is extradited, he might present material that implicates PPK, who served as Toledo's Minister of Finance and Prime Minister.

Organized crime increased not only in Peru but in most of Latin America for reasons that are manifold and controversial. Exact measurement of the weight of the various explanations is impossible. Clearly, however, in Peru a major factor was the diversification of drug mafias' businesses. From their roles in coca cultivation and trafficking, Peruvian and Colombian mafias were in place to expand and exploit new opportunities. Amid the immense revenues of the drug trade, both the temptations for and the pressures against countries' authorities increased and, as a result, corruption skyrocketed. Expansion into criminal activities such as cell phone theft was also attractive because controls were minimal and the risks far lower than in narcotrafficking.[56]

Ironically, another factor in the increase in organized crime was economic growth. Growth enabled new, lucrative targets of opportunity, such as smart phones; yet it did not end poverty.[57] Although poverty rates have declined, the World Bank estimated that in 2015 more than one fifth (21.8 percent) of the Peruvian population remained mired in poverty.[58] For a young Peruvian from a poor family, the possibilities for a quality education and well-paying employment remained small; but, as the example of Joaquín Ramírez (who started as a fare collector on buses but bought a luxurious condominium in Miami and became the head of Keiko Fujimori's party, allegedly through money laundering) illustrates, organized crime appeared to offer a way out.

The examination of Peru's north-coast city of Tumbes by Elohim Monard for Duke University offers a window into the causes of violence.[59] As Monard reports, the homicide rate in Tumbes in 2015 was almost six times Peru's national average and more than eight times the rate in Tumbes in 2011.[60] Most of the violence was perpetrated by criminal gangs that were engaged in drug trafficking, extortion and contraband. Why Tumbes? As pressure was placed on violence in the north-coast city of Trujillo, crime mafias sought new attractive locations and found Tumbes. First, while Tumbes recorded superior economic growth compared to Peru's average between 2001 and 2012, education and other basic services remained far from adequate; 30 percent of young people neither studied nor worked.[61] Second, Tumbes is located very near Ecuador, and the price of cocaine in Ecuador was more than twice the price in Peru; huge profits were available. Third, the authorities in Tumbes were corruptible. Both the governor and the mayor during this period were charged with corruption that netted them more than $25 million.

EXTORTION

Extortion constitutes a major threat. It is not only widespread, affecting over 500 major firms across all of Peru and an unknown number of small businesses, but it is also exceptionally violent.[62] In a less than three month period in early 2014, extortion in the construction industry alone was estimated to be responsible for 34 murders—or about nine percent of all homicides during that time.[63] This figure likely underestimates the number of homicides resulting from extortion insofar as these gangs also use their enforcers for contract killings.[64]

Major extortion rings began in the construction industry and they remain most prevalent in this sector. Construction has been a particularly attractive target as its growth has been astronomical. Comprising about five percent of Peru's GDP, the construction sector has consistently recorded expansion exceeding aggregate GDP growth; during its best year in recent history, 2012, the sector grew by 18.5 percent—more than triple the annual GDP growth rate.[65] Construction is an attractive target also because of permissive conditions. Construction projects are in fixed locations and involve large amounts of capitalization plus expensive tools and equipment onsite; attacks by extortion rings are especially costly. Moreover, these projects have many different types of employees (e.g. laborers versus electrical contractors), enabling extortion rings to mask illicit payments with less difficulty.

Extortion rings often target construction companies through the establishment of fake unions. It is estimated that as many as 80 percent of Peru's 72 informal construction unions are fronts for extortion.[66] The leaders of these fake unions demand either a cash contribution or the hiring of "ghost employees." "Ghost employees" exist on the books and draw a normal salary but are not present on the job sites and do not perform any work.[67] Alternatively, extortion rings demand that their own shell companies be hired by the construction firms and paid for goods or services that are never provided.[68] It is not just the construction companies that are victimized; the rings also dispatch armed "union leaders" to job sites on payday and demand that workers pay "union dues."[69]

It is estimated that Peru's construction companies pay about $32 million per annum to extortion gangs. As much as 90 percent of construction projects are afflicted by extortion rings.[70] The amount paid by a given company varies between one percent and as much as five percent, depending on the size of the job and the company's relationship with the extortion ring.[71] By one estimate, companies paid an average of $17,000 per month per project.[72]

Despite the high cost posed to the construction industry, non-payment can prove far more costly. As the aforementioned homicide statistics demonstrated, the death threats made by gangs to extract payment are not idle. Extortion rings often used improvised explosive devices and grenades, which are readily available on Lima's black market for less than $50, to frighten or kill victims.[73] In one recent incident, a bomb was thrown at the house of a businessman who had presumably refused to pay his extorters; in another, a grenade was detonated at a Lima construction site.[74]

To date, Peru's police have been unable to curb extortion. Said a former Peruvian National Police (Policía Nacional del Perú—PNP) commander: "extortion is growing for a simple reason: businessmen prefer to make the payments demanded because they know the police are ineffective. The situation is so serious that criminal organizations are replacing the state in the public function of security."[75] Worse yet, some police are complicit. In 2013, the chief of police in an area of northern Peru was arrested for working with the extortion gang, *El Nuevo Clan del Norte*.[76]

Given the success of extortion gangs in the construction industry, it is not surprising that they have expanded into other sectors of Peru's licit economy. In particular, extortion gangs have become common in the transportation sector and against small businesses.[77] In one case in Chiclayo, in northwest Peru, gangs extorting 33 transportation companies collected nearly a million dollars.[78] Following an example set in Colombia, gangs have begun targeting small businesses, such as florists and restaurants. While small businesses may each pay only a few thousand dollars, the micro extortion rings target hundreds of businesses and generate windfall profits. Unfortunately, it is estimated that 30 percent of the businesses targeted are forced to either close or relocate.[79]

As the types of businesses targeted have diversified, so too have the extortion gangs. In particular, the scope of the gangs is increasingly international. For the gangs, collaboration with similar networks in other countries is a means of expanding their market share. Internationalization is also a way to increase the specialization of the criminal workforce. For example, the Chiclayo-based *La Gran Familia* reportedly maintains connections with extortion rings in Ecuador, Bolivia, and Colombia; it uses predominantly Peruvian and Ecuadorian criminals to make extortion demands and collect payments but Colombian criminals to act as enforcers.[80]

Cell Phone Theft

By government estimates, over 6,000 mobile phones are stolen per day in Peru.[81] Other estimates are much higher: 14,000 thefts per day—one stolen phone per year for every six Peruvians.[82] While the exact value of stolen phones in Peru is unknown, the value region-wide is about $550,000 a day or more than $200 million per year.[83] Like extortion, cell phone theft can prove deadly. Reports of individuals murdered for their phones are common in Peru's newspapers and the lament "they kill you for a cell phone" is frequent. In April 2017, a 22 year old worker was killed during the robbery of his cell phone and back pack.[84] In December 2016, when a college student threw his phone over a fence rather than surrender it to a thief, the thief shot him three times in the head.[85]

Cell phone theft became a lucrative target of opportunity in Peru in part due to rapid economic growth and the emergence of a significant middle class that can afford cell phones. For the first time, everyday Peruvians are walking around with very valuable and easy to steal possessions. It is estimated that, between 2005 and 2014, the size of Peru's middle class increased from 25 percent of the population to 60 percent.[86] By 2015, 25 percent of Peruvians owned smart phones; although this percentage was small compared to the United States, where 72 percent owned smart phones, it is rapidly increasing.[87] Moreover, many Peruvians without smart phones had basic cell phones; more than 65 percent of Peruvians had at least basic cell phones.[88]

Still, Peru remains severely unequal and not rich (its per capita GDP was below $6,000 in 2015).[89] Cell phones are expensive and consequently attractive to thieves. For example, Saga Falabella, a major department store, is currently offering a Samsung Galaxy S7 (a 2016 model) for 2,499 soles or about $762.[90] The price of the latest model Samsung and Apple smart phones can easily exceed $1,000.[91]

Cell phone theft in Peru is just the tip of the iceberg of a highly specialized criminal enterprise. An investigation by the International Police Organization (INTERPOL) noted that cell phone theft rings incorporate five distinct specialties.[92] First, thieves acquire the phones. Second, computer technicians unlock and reprogram the phones. These technicians also change identifying information, such as the International Mobile Equipment Identity (IMEI), a unique identifier for each phone used by cell service providers to block network access and by law enforcement officers to trace the phones. Third, after the stolen phones have been "hacked," smugglers move the phones across international borders; it is much harder for authorities to trace stolen phones that have moved across borders. Most importantly, thieves exploit massive price differentials for the same phone in different countries (due to different tariffs). For example, a new iPhone may cost $1,000 in Peru and an astonishing $2,000 in Brazil. Fourth, sellers market the discounted stolen phones. And, finally, there are the customers.

As already noted, cell phone theft rings are international. The four countries in the region in which the rings are most active are Peru, Colombia, Bolivia, and Ecuador.[93] As with narcotrafficking, the ties between Peru and Colombia are particularly strong. In 2011, during the largest bust in Colombia to date, police dismantled a network that moved nearly 14,000 stolen phones in just three months from Colombia to Argentina and elsewhere; all the criminals handling the air freight logistics were Peruvian.[94] In another arrest in 2013 by Colombian police, a 16 person network had been operating in Colombia, Peru, Argentina and Venezuela; 850 phones, 125 motherboards and 60 sim cards were recovered.[95]

Even phones stolen in the United States have turned up in Peru. In one case, a phone was stolen from a San Francisco resident in a local bar; six days later she received an email, subsequently traced to Lima, demanding $5,000 and threatening to release compromising photos stored on the phone if she did not comply.[96] This incident speaks to the rapidity with which cell phones are trafficked a well as the sophistication of the rings. It also indicates another way in which thieves profit from stolen phones; they sell the troves of personal and business data on the phones back to the original owner or to unscrupulous rivals.

RESPONDING TO VIOLENCE

This section describes the responses by both Peru's governments and Peru's people to the country's increased violence. The first subsection examines the approaches by the central government, including the Humala and PPK administrations. The second subsection focuses on Peruvians' dissatisfaction with the central government's results and their search for remedies. It shows that Peruvians have increasingly taken matters into their own hands; vigilantism is on the rise. It also examines a strategy by municipal governments, the Serenazgo.

The Peruvian Government's Responses

Shortly before the second round of Peru's 2016 elections, PPK proclaimed that "the biggest challenge facing Peru today is security in the streets, homes, roads, everywhere."[97] Indeed, for many years, in poll after poll, insecurity has been Peruvians' number one concern.[98] PPK contended that "success can be measured in just one way, whether Peruvians feel safe on their streets, in their homes and at their businesses."[99] This subsection analyzes the responses of Peru's two most recent governments and Peruvians' dissatisfaction with the results as of 2016.

The Shining Path

In its counterinsurgency efforts, the Humala administration partnered closely with the U.S. government. The result was the demise of the Shining Path faction in the UHV; but, as mentioned above, the faction in the VRAEM endured, retaining about 120 to 150 armed fighters led by the Quispe Palomino brothers.

Especially valuable for Peru's counterinsurgency efforts was telephonic-interception equipment provided by the U.S. Drug Enforcement Administration (DEA).[100] The tracking of cellphone locations was judged key to the capture of insurgent leaders in Colombia and the drug kingpin Joaquín "El Chapo" Guzmán in Mexico, and it was crucial in important captures in Peru as well.[101]

The first major success in Peru occurred in February 2012 in the UHV; the police captured the Shining Path leader, "Artemio" (Florindo Flores), as well as his two replacements.[102] Subsequently, in February 2013, the Humala government recorded its first major success in the VRAEM: "Alipio" (Orlando Borda Casablanca, the military head of the VRAEM faction), "Gabriel" (Marco Antonio Quispe Palomino, the brother of the VRAEM faction's leaders) and "Alfonso" (Borda Casablanca's right-hand man) were ambushed and killed. It is speculated that the U.S. might have provided Peru with advanced armaments for this ambush. In Colombia, the U.S. supplied Precision Guided Munitions (PGMs)—Enhanced Paveway II bomb kits equipped with a GPS targeting kit—for the targeting of leaders of its insurgency.[103] Experts consider it possible, but not likely, that PGMs were used in the VRAEM as well.[104] However, the Humala government did not achieve further major successes against the VRAEM faction.

The PPK administration re-ignited efforts to capture high-profile Shining Path leaders and succeeded in August 2016. "Nelson" (Nelson Tiquillahuanca Parra), a former UHV leader who had participated in a 1993 ambush that killed seventeen police officers, was arrested following a 23 year pursuit.[105] "Amadeo" (Amadeo Reyes Rivero), a VRAEM leader culpable in many deadly ambushes, was captured by the Special VRAEM Command.[106]

Moreover, the PPK administration appeared to be planning a military offensive against the VRAEM faction. The administration and the U.S. agreed to augment bilateral military training. In 2017, U.S. military personnel will travel to Peru and train Peruvian special operations forces and intelligence officers operating in the VRAEM. Training locations were selected to mimic the difficult mountainous and dense jungle terrain of the VRAEM.[107] In addition, in late 2016, plans for a U.S. military base in the Amazonas department of Peru were announced.[108]

In August 2016, PPK's Minister of Defense visited the VRAEM and announced that nineteen new military bases would be established in the zone.[109] In October, when the government extended a state of emergency for the VRAEM for another 60 days, it modified the districts in question.[110] (The state of emergency provides security personnel enhanced legal authorities, such as the power to arrest subversives, and has been in place for several years.) At the same time, the administration returned responsibility for operations in the VRAEM to the military from the police (which had been put in charge in the last years of the Humala government).[111] Yet as of May 2017, a military offensive has not begun, and a long-term, comprehensive strategy has not been announced. The VRAEM faction remains strong; in the first five months of 2017, Shining Path snipers killed five police officers in the VRAEM.[112]

Narcotrafficking

To date, the narcotics control strategies of the Humala and PPK administrations have been similar. Indeed, both appointed Carmen Masías as the head of Peru's anti-drug agency, the National Commission for Drug-Free Life

(La Comisión Nacional para el Desarrollo y Vida Sin Drogas—DEVIDA), for extended periods (from January 2012 through mid-2014 under Humala and from September 2016 to the present under PPK). In previous positions at anti-drug NGOs, Masías had worked on U.S. Agency for International Development (USAID) programs for drug prevention and treatment and she was well-respected by U.S. officials—an important factor for both Presidents Humala and PPK.[113] Unfortunately, the results of the two administrations' strategies appear likely to be similar as well: success in specific localities after intense eradication and interdiction, which in turn shifts cultivation and trafficking to other areas of Peru or to other countries.

Only two months after her appointment by Humala in January 2012, Masías announced a new, hardline counternarcotics strategy. A cornerstone of the strategy was to drastically increase eradication. During the previous five years, about 11,000 hectares had been eradicated annually. The number of hectares eradicated jumped to 14,235 in 2012; 23,947 in 2013; 31,206 in 2014; and 35,868 in 2015. Each year, goals would be set—and then exceeded. At the same time, however, the eradication units often failed to follow up; it is estimated that well over half of the coca eradicated was replanted.[114]

In addition, the Humala government promoted alternative development. Indeed, the previous government had initiated alternative development in parts of the San Martín region in the UHV, and it facilitated the subsequent success in the valley. Peru's "Alternative Development Program III" ran from 2007 to 2012 in San Martín and helped 60,000 families across more than 700 communities embrace licit agriculture.[115] It was Peru's most successful alternative development initiative.[116]

After 2012, the Humala government continued to invest resources in alternative development projects.[117] One report noted the total investment in alternative development at 8 billion soles or about $2.5 billion.[118] As much as 5.9 billion soles or approximately $1.8 billion was allocated for alternative development in the VRAEM, but to little avail.[119] Especially in areas like the VRAEM where transportation is inadequate, licit crops remained much less profitable and less reliable than coca.

On May 28, 2014, Masías was fired. The cause was disagreement over forced eradication in the VRAEM. Masías wanted to pursue forced eradication. She argued that, in the UHV, eradication had been in tandem with counterinsurgency. As of 2016, about 45 bases with several thousand security personnel, as well as helicopters and military equipment, were located in the VRAEM.[120] However, many officials in the Humala government and in Peru's military opposed forced eradication. First, they pointed to the factors mentioned above that made forced eradication plus counterinsurgency much more challenging in the VRAEM than in the UHV. Second, they feared that a military offensive would drive the coca growers, who depend on the proceeds from coca for their meager subsistence, yet further into the open arms of the Shining Path.[121] An offensive was also likely to exact a high death toll, which in turn might provoke public backlash.

A third reason for the military's wariness was widely believed to be some officers' complicity with the drug trade.[122] One expert charged that cocaine was transported from the VRAEM to Callao in military helicopters.[123] In 2015, two PNP units competed to steal cocaine from narcotraffickers in the VRAEM.[124] Said one retired general, Wilson Barrantes: [assigning Peru's military to counternarcotics in the VRAEM was tantamount to assigning] "four street dogs to guard a plate of beefsteak."[125]

Under the PPK administration, Masías has retained her commitment to forced eradication. After considerable delay, in late May 2017 DEVIDA released its five-year plan (2017–2021), and massive forced eradication remained the plan's cornerstone. Indeed, the plan calls for eradicating 25,000 hectares in 2017; this figure is 3,000 hectares greater than the average annual target of the previous five-year plan.

However, to date under PPK, Masías has not argued for immediate forced eradication in the VRAEM. In May 2017, she announced that eradication would not occur in the VRAEM that year. It remained unclear if forced eradication in the VRAEM will be pursued subsequently. As previously indicated, as of 2016 the VRAEM cultivated an estimated 23,000 hectares of coca—almost equivalent to the entire eradication goal for 2017.

The PPK government is also continuing to stress the importance of economic development in coca-producing zones.[126] Like its predecessor, the PPK administration is planning funds for education and infrastructure, in particular farm-to-market infrastructure, in the VRAEM. It is also emphasizing greater access to credit and technical assistance for licit crops.[127]

One change in the 2017–2021 five-year plan is an increased focus on interdiction. To date, interdiction in Peru has been scant by regional standards. For example, in 2016, 19 tons of cocaine were interdicted in Peru versus 421 tons in Colombia.[128] In particular, scanners and similar equipment at Peru's ports have been lacking.[129] Beginning in 2019, the government is to seize 80 tons of cocaine HCL each year.[130]

To date, narcotics control has been a Sisyphean task. Coca grows readily in most Andean slopes; after a success in one place, the "balloon effect" is quickly evident in cultivation in another. The profits are huge—too huge for many subsistence farmers and poorly-paid security personnel to resist, especially when the alternative can be death. Some Peruvian experts had expressed frustration that the U.S. government opposed aerial interdiction after two deaths as the Peruvian military's entry into the VRAEM would almost certainly lead to scores of deaths. It is likely that many officials in the PPK government would prefer a very different narcotics policy, but debate has been scant.

Organized Crime

The focus of both the Humala and PPK governments has been on the improvement of the quantity and quality of Peru's police. While this improvement is important, and some indicators in PPK's first year are positive, major challenges remain, especially in Peru's prison system. As of 2006–2011, the number of police per capita in Peru was similar to the number in other Latin American countries wracked by violence: 330 per 100,000 in Peru versus 366 in Mexico, 335 in El Salvador, and 306 in Colombia.[131] The Humala government achieved the recruitment of more police officers and the improvement of equipment at police stations.[132] Between 2014 and 2016, the number of officers increased from one for every 938 inhabitants to one for every 755—approximately 20 percent. Similar increases were reported in the availability of essential services—internet access, telephone lines, electricity and water—at police stations. (Still, as of 2016, 40 percent of Peru's police stations did not have internet access.)

Further, the salaries for Peru's military and police jumped. For example, the salary of a petty officer increased by more than 50 percent in real terms (from 1,445 soles a month in 2011 to 2,826 soles a month in 2016 over a period of roughly 17 percent inflation); the 2016 salary was approximately $10,000 a year.[133] At the same time, however, the government ended what was called "24 by 24"—that officers work 24 hours for the PNP and then have 24 hours off. In their 24 hours off, most officers worked as security guards for private companies and many believed that the loss of these opportunities was not compensated by the government's salary increase. The issue festered. Despite campaign promises to the contrary, the PPK government again allowed officers to work as security guards on days off.

Under Interior Minister Carlos Basombrío (2016–present), the PPK government launched major initiatives. Almost immediately, the government announced a "reorganization" of Peru's police; a key goal was to purge corrupt officers[134] As already indicated, police corruption is a serious problem. In the first three quarters of 2016, 997 complaints were filed against PNP officers on the grounds of illicit activities; in the year 2016, nearly 50 PNP officers were arrested on charges of complicity in organized crime.[135] The highest-ranking officer arrested was a major who was involved in an extortion ring as well as a bank robbery that netted thieves over $1.1 million.[136] Within two months of PPK's inauguration, almost half of the generals in Peru's police force—39 of 86—were retired and 1,000 other officers were dismissed.[137] New officers were appointed to virtually all high-profile posts.

A second immediate effort was a major upgrade of a program called the "most-wanted" list that had begun under Humala. As the name suggests, Peru's most-wanted criminals are listed and publicized along with a secure telephone hotline that Peruvians can call to provide information; rewards, averaging about $5,000, are given for information that leads to a criminal's arrest. The Interior Ministry reported that, as of April 2017, the "most-wanted" list had 1,455 people and 280 criminals had been arrested thanks to the list.[138]

Like the Humala government, the PPK government is improving police equipment and technology. Since July 2016, the PNP has been received 2,846 new vehicles.[139] Many of these vehicles are high-technology sports utility vehicles (SUVs), which are equipped with a GPS system, three video cameras and a digital fingerprint scanner.[140] These SUVs are a huge improvement over past PNP vehicles, many of which lacked the necessary equipment even for officers' checking the background of a stopped driver. The GPS system and video cameras will allow tracking of PNP officers, in part to verify that they are where they are supposed to be. They will also help to curb abuses. In addition, the GPS system will enable PNP patrols to be distributed to high-crime areas and ensure that the closest units respond to crimes in progress, decreasing response times.[141]

Various additional initiatives for the improvement of technology are underway. First, an unspecified number of surveillance drones have been purchased and a new PNP unit for unmanned aircraft established. The drones complement four drones already in use by the PNP and an unknown number of additional drones in use by the Peruvian Air Force.[142] The drones will be employed primarily in Lima and other cities for citizen security but might also be employed against the Shining Path and narcotrafficking.[143] Second, the Division for High Technology Investigations (División de Investigación de Delitos de Alta Tecnologia—DIVINDAT) has been established within the PNP. As the name implies, this division is devoted to investigating crimes using technology.[144] Conferences and other events on the application of high technology to police operations are more frequent within the PNP.[145] Moreover, Peru is collaborating with Ecuador, Bolivia, and Colombia to build a database of stolen phones, called the "blacklist." It will help PNP officers recover stolen phones and prosecute the criminals even if the phones are stolen in one of the partner countries.[146]

Yet the arrest of criminals is far from enough. Neither the Humala government nor, to date, the PPK government has achieved significant reforms in patterns of imprisonment in Peru. It is notorious in Peru that wealthy criminals are able to bribe judges to annul their sentences or reduce jail time.[147]

One criminal who killed a police officer in 2017 had been jailed seven times in the previous five years.[148] In addition, many wealthy criminals retain cell phones and other equipment and continue to operate their businesses out of Peruvian prisons.[149]

Peru's Ministry of Justice is not oblivious to these problems. Between 2011 and 2016, the number of prisoners in Peru almost doubled.[150] While positive, the jump worsened over-crowding in prisons. Both the Humala and PPK governments have contracted for new prisons, but construction takes time. For low-level criminals, procedures for ankle bracelets with electronic tracking devices have been developed. Systems that block cell phone use and internet access are also under implementation. Very importantly too, given the internationalization of criminal networks, the Ministry of Justice is pursuing international cooperation, especially among Andean countries, for regularizing and streamlining extradition procedures.[151]

As in other countries with a flourishing drug trade as well as poverty, the imprisonment of one kingpin often merely creates a temporary vacuum that is quickly filled by rivals. This is especially the case in Peru, where as noted above most criminal gangs are small and disaggregated. Indeed, as Charles D. Brockett noted, "in the struggle to fill the vacuum left by the former leadership, it tends to be the most violent who succeed."[152] Between 2010 and mid-2014, 121 extortion rings were reported to have been disbanded in Peru; but the problem of extortion is worse.[153]

Still, as of April 2017, there were indications that the PPK government's reforms were having positive effects. The number of arrests of criminals complicit in organized crime increased a whopping 262 percent from August–December 2015 to August–December 2016.[154] And, most importantly, whereas 32.3 percent of the population had reported being a victim of some form of crime in the six-month period from November 2015 to April 2016, the figure was down to 26.3 percent for November 2016 to April 2017.[155]

Peruvians' Dissatisfaction and Their Localized Responses

It is not surprising, given the rise in violence in Peru through 2016, that Peruvians were dissatisfied with the central governments' responses. Most Peruvians want an "iron fist" by the central government. When Peruvians are asked about how to reduce crime, a common response is: "Lock the criminals up and throw away the key. And put the jails in the most miserable places in Peru, like frigid high-altitude Puno."[156]

Peruvians' preference for "an iron fist" was evident in the 2016 election campaign. Keiko Fujimori's major advantage against PPK was widely perceived to be that she was "tough on crime."[157] One of her proposals was to send the armed forces to Peru's streets; this proposal was endorsed by 85 percent of respondents in a December 2015 poll.[158] In the same poll, 95 percent favored life imprisonment for police murders and rape; more than 90 percent favored longer sentences for crime in general.

Frustrated Peruvians began taking security into their own hands. In a LAPOP poll in 2015, 40.6 percent of Peruvians favored vigilantism; this figure was the third highest among 24 countries, just a percentage point or two lower than in the Dominican Republic and Paraguay.[159] In another poll by a different organization in October 2015, 72 percent of Peruvians favored vigilantism.[160]

As Michael Fraiman reports, in this context, vigilantism became increasingly prevalent as well as increasingly vicious.[161] Vigilantism occurred in impoverished areas of Lima and other cities during the summer of 2015 and then spread to rural areas. Perhaps the most gruesome incident occurred in September 2015 in Andas, an isolated community in central Peru, where the nearest police outpost is two hours away. Andas residents captured two suspected murderers and proceeded to burn them alive. The mayor of Andas said that "their [the suspected killers'] death was the solution."[162]

Peru's vigilante movement has even adopted a name, *#ChapaTuChoro*, which is slang for "catch your thief." The name has been used in a myriad of social-media postings.[163] In one music video featuring a pop song entitled "Chapa tu Choro," the singer warns criminals to run because "the village is after you." The popular video has been viewed over 18,000 times on the YouTube platform alone.[164] In another emblematic YouTube video, local residents take turns whipping a young suspected burglar who is handcuffed, with his hands behind his back, standing in the middle of a circle. Just outside the circle is a PNP pickup truck; at various times in the video, police officers observe the mob violence and they eventually step in to take the suspect away. The officers do not appear to make any effort to halt the local residents' assaults.[165]

A more promising localized response to the rise in violence is what is called Serenazgo; the term is derived from the word *serenar*, which means to calm down. Specifically, Serenazgo refers to patrols and watchmen who are not armed and cannot intervene to stop a crime but can try to prevent it. Serenazgo dates back to the 1980s, when the police were stretched too thin as a result of the insurgencies and municipalities sought protection against crime. Subsequently, Serenazgo has been established by most municipalities in Lima and the patrols incorporate more than 1,000 men and women.[166]

Recently, Serenazgo initiatives have expanded beyond unarmed patrols. For example, Miraflores, a municipality in Lima that has been at the forefront of Serenazgo, constructed a fiber optic video surveillance system that includes 256 networked cameras that are controlled by operators in control rooms who can pan, tilt and zoom. The cameras are equipped with night vision capabilities and are strategically placed based on risk and previous incidents.[167] The municipality of Lima also recently debated arming its Serenazgo with less-than-lethal weapons such as pepper spray and stun guns.[168]

Serenazgo has been successful; Miraflores in particular became much safer. Serenazgo patrols provide a link between municipalities and the PNP and try to build social cohesion in the municipality and accordingly are in part an effort at community policing.[169] Indeed, during the 2016 election campaign, PPK promised to build on the Serenazgo model for a nation-wide community policing effort called *Barrio Seguro* (Secure Neighborhood).[170]

The challenge, however, is that Serenazgo is expensive and has worked well in the wealthiest municipalities of Lima, like Miraflores, which are able to invest heavily in it.[171] Currently, it is problematic that stronger vigilance in areas like Miraflores was likely to have displaced crime to poorer areas. To date, the PPK government has not advanced significantly toward the expansion of the Serenazgo model, but perhaps it will.

CONCLUSION

Peruvians' alarm about violence is well-founded. Despite the country's relatively low homicide rates, in the 2010s about one in three Peruvians were afflicted by a crime every year, suffering either violence or the fear of violence. Violence was detonated in the 1980s by the Shining Path and spread as the group became integrated with narcotrafficking. In the twenty-first century, despite government efforts, narcotrafficking expanded; the balloon effect and the cockroach effect were very evident. Also, in the VRAEM, the ties between the Shining Path and the drug trade were consolidated; further, the ties between Colombian and Peruvian drug mafias were solidified. Revenues from narcotrafficking were prodigious—much greater than the revenues from any previous illicit industry in Peru. These revenues enabled an explosion of corruption that infected both security personnel and civilian authorities and that went hand in hand with the escalation of organized crime. Unfortunately, as elsewhere in Latin America in the 2010s, to date in Peru this scourge of violence has been very difficult to combat effectively.

Chapter Five

Negotiating Peace and Strengthening the State: Reducing Violence in Colombia

Victor J. Hinojosa

Colombia has long been one of the most violent countries in one of the world's most violent regions. Home to one of the world's longest-running and most violent internal armed conflicts and the center of the global cocaine trade, Colombia's weak central state has struggled to protect its citizens from political and criminal violence. Yet in recent years, Colombia's homicide rate plummeted alongside dramatic reductions in combat deaths as Colombia successfully negotiated peace with its largest guerilla group and expanded state presence and the state security apparatus. This chapter first examines Colombia's history of violence and the state's recent successes. It then addresses the critical challenges that remain as Colombia seeks to fully implement the peace accords and continues to grapple with the ever-changing nature of the international narcotics business.

POLITICAL AND CRIMINAL VIOLENCE IN COLOMBIA

Much of Colombia's violence has been tied to Colombia's internal armed conflict. Guerrilla groups began to emerge in Colombia in the early 1960s and Colombia's two largest and most influential groups, the Revolutionary Armed Forces of Colombia (Fuerzas Armadas Revolucionarias de Colombia—FARC) and National Liberation Army (Ejército de Liberación Nacional—ELN) formed in 1964. At one point, FARC had a presence in half of the nation's municipalities and numbered more than 16,000 combatants with the capacity "to amass up to 1,500 fighters in one place to attack military installations and even a provincial capital."[1] The ELN has always been smaller, generally numbering between 3,000 and 5,000 soldiers, geographically centered in the Magdalena Medio region of the country.[2] The armed conflict intensified in significant ways with the emergence of paramilitary groups in the late 1980s and early 1990s. These groups, who operated independently of the state while sharing the state's antipathy for the guerillas, emerged simultaneously if independently from three main sources: peasant self-defense forces that emerged as a result of guerilla atrocities, the mercenary forces of large landowners who formed private militia forces to protect themselves from the guerillas and their extortion, and others emerged from Colombia's large narcotics syndicates.

With money from narcotics trafficking, both the FARC and Colombia's paramilitaries were able to grow wealthy and powerful and as a result the armed conflict escalated.[3] Sarah Zukerman Daly has noted that by 2002 "paramilitary brigades had expanded across nearly three quarters of Colombia's territory amassing significant power"[4] and that "the municipalities that escaped their violence were mostly in the depths of the jungles and other remote, unpopulated territories of Colombia."[5] Figure 5.1 demonstrates the trajectory of the Colombian armed conflict in terms of battlefield deaths. Here we see that conflict intensifies through the 1990s and peaks from about 2000–2005 when Colombia averages over 1,000 battlefield deaths per year.[6] This is particularly striking in that the rest of Latin America's armed conflicts had ended by the mid-1990s and only Peru continued to record battlefield deaths after 1999.[7]

Moreover, battlefield deaths tell only part of the story of the violence that resulted from the armed conflict. As Andreas E. Feldmann and Victor J. Hinojosa have argued, terrorism—the intentional targeting of civilians for political purposes—has been a central part of Colombia's armed conflict and a strategy

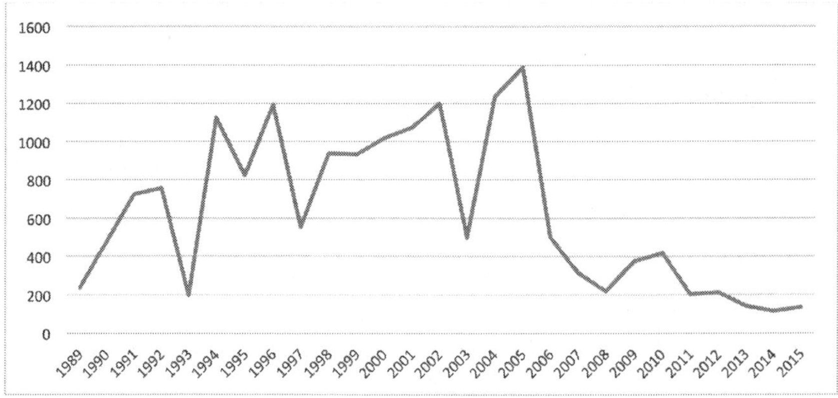

Figure 5.1. Battle-Related Deaths in Colombia, 1989–2015

Created by the author with data from Uppsala Conflict Data Program, pcr.uu.se/research/UCDP retrieved from the World Bank.

used by guerilla groups, paramilitary forces, and the state itself as the actors battled for control.[8] The global terrorism database lists Colombia as having the most terrorist incidents in the world between 1970 and 2004.[9] The conflict also led to the displacement of millions of Colombians. From 1985 through the end of 2016, the Colombian government's Victim's Registration Unit (Registro Único de Victimas—RUV) has registered 7.4 million[10] internally displaced peoples, making Colombia the country with the world's largest IDP population.[11] As the Internal Displacement Monitoring Center notes, "internally displaced women, children, adolescents and Afro-Colombian and indigenous peoples" are "particularly vulnerable to violence and sexual exploitation."[12] In addition to those internally displaced, the UNHCR counts some 311,100 refugees from Colombia's conflict as of the end of 2016.[13]

Violence in Colombia extends well beyond its armed conflict. Colombia has long been the center of the global cocaine trade. It began exporting cocaine to the United States in the 1970s, and traffickers in the cities of Medellín and Cali soon controlled most of the trade.[14] At first Colombian traffickers imported coca leaf or the slightly more processed coca base from Peru and Bolivia, refined the raw ingredients into processed cocaine, and exported the final product to markets in the United States and Europe. As the international narcotics business evolved, Colombia began to grow coca leaf and its traffickers soon controlled the entire production chain. The Colombian narcotics industry changed again in the mid-1990s as the Medellín and Cali syndicates were dismantled as a result of the death of Medellín chief Pablo Escobar in 1993 and the arrest of Cali leadership including brothers Gilberto and Miguel Rodríguez Orejuela in 1995. These syndicates were replaced by hundreds of smaller smuggling groups[15] who have shied away from direct access to U.S. markets, instead selling their products to Mexican crime syndicates who transport the final product to consumers in the United States.[16]

By its very nature, the narcotics industry is a violent enterprise. Unable to use the court system to resolve disputes or enforce contracts, and unable to call the authorities when products are stolen, drug traffickers resort to private forms of justice and rely on violence and threats of violence to ensure compliance and deter or punish defection. Figure 5.2 shows Colombia's homicide rate from 1995 to 2014. Even with its recent decline (discussed below), Colombia's rates are exceptionally high by global standards. Moreover, only a relatively small portion of the homicides are related to the armed conflict.[17] Instead, "a significant share of the country's homicides" are related to the drug trade, and the homicide rates of municipalities with high coca cultivation is significantly higher than the homicide rates of municipalities without significant coca cultivation.[18]

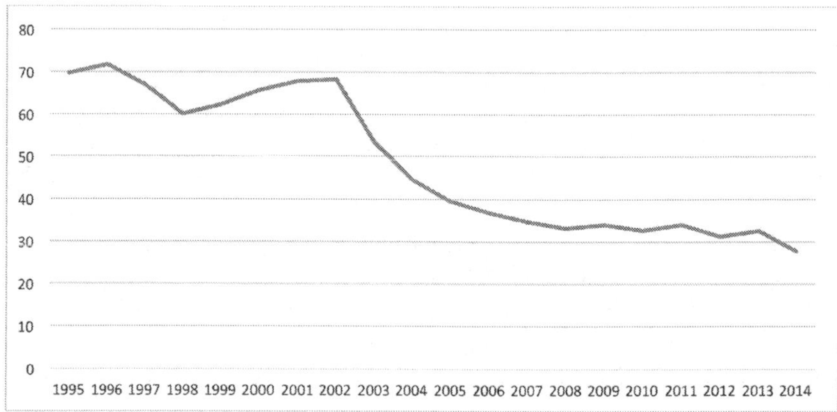

Figure 5.2. Intentional Homicides Per 100,000 People

Created by the author with data from UN Office on Drugs and Crime's International Homicide Statistics; database retrieved from the World Bank.

Colombia's high homicide rate and its history of armed conflict are of course related and political and economic forms of violence interact in complex ways. As noted above, non-state armed actors, both guerilla and paramilitary, use criminal violence in order to finance their political and military activities. For the FARC this has meant the extensive 'taxing' of coca cultivation in areas it controls and the extensive use of kidnapping for ransom as ways to raise funds.[19] The ELN has also used kidnapping, albeit to a lesser extent, and has relied heavily on extortion principally through bombing, or threatening to bomb, an oil pipeline in areas it controls. In the case of paramilitary groups, the links are even more complex. Paramilitary groups have extensive ties to drug trafficking and other forms of criminality (especially extortion) and many followed the pattern of guerillas in using criminal enterprises to fund political and military activities. However, many narcotics traffickers found in paramilitarism a way to gain political legitimacy and a way to negotiate with the state. Some narco-traffickers even purchased paramilitary franchises in order to do so. Indeed, Álvaro Camacho goes so far as to distinguish between what he terms "narco-paras," which are primarily narcotics trafficking groups engaged in paramilitary activities, and "para-narcos" who are first paramilitary groups engaged in extensive narcotics trafficking.[20]

Finally, it is important to note that Colombians have also been subject to extensive violence at the hands of the state itself. In prosecuting both its counter-narcotics and counter-insurgency campaigns, the Colombian state has engaged in extensive illicit violence. Figure 5.3 shows that from 1988 to 2012, the state committed a total of 1,975 massacres, abductions, and summary executions. As with the battle-related death and the homicide rate above,

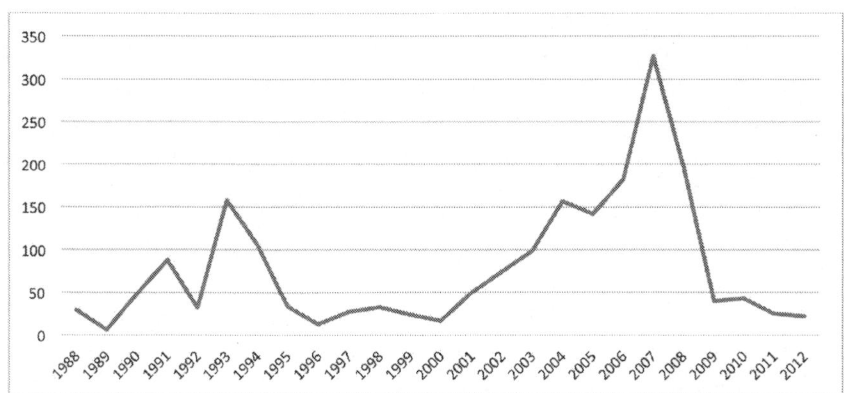

Figure 5.3. Massacres, Abductions, and Summary Executions by State Agents, 1988–2012. Note: The two organizations jointly produced the data in 1995.

Created by the author with data from 1988-1995 comes from Justicia y Paz and from 1995–2012 from CINEP's Noche y Niebla.

illicit state violence largely follows the trajectory of the counter-narcotics campaign and the armed conflict with a spike in the state's use of summary executions at the height of the war with Pablo Escobar's Medellín cartel in 1993, and another spike in state violence as the armed conflict intensified in the early 2000s. The vast majority of these atrocities, 1,421 of 1,975 acts (72 percent), were committed by the army with most of the remaining committed by the police. Figure 5.3 does not account for the "false positives" scandal wherein soldiers seeking promotions or financial rewards for guerillas killed in combat executed people from marginalized groups or communities and falsely claimed them as guerrilla kills (when in fact those killed were neither guerrillas nor killed in any combat operation). The Colombian Attorney General's office places the number of false positives at 2,997.[21]

Colombia's multifaceted violence points to a fundamental underlying cause: a state security apparatus in need of both strengthening and fundamental reform. Colombia's guerilla groups emerged in areas outside of effective state control, and some paramilitary forces emerged because of the state's inability to protect their patrons from guerilla abuses. Fundamentally, both paramilitarism and Colombia's plethora of guerilla groups stem from the state's inability to maintain a monopoly on the legitimate use of violence. In a similar way, organized crime groups gravitate to areas of weak state presence to avoid detection. Where such presence does exist, these criminal groups seek to weaken the state and reduce state effectiveness. Sometimes these efforts involve violence or threats of violence against state agents, a strategy exemplified in the unrelenting terror campaign against state judicial officials by the Medellín cartel. At other times, these efforts come through bribery and corruption, the preferred strategy of the Cali cartel and of paramilitary groups. Reducing Colombia's political and criminal violence then requires a strengthening of the state and an expansion of state presence throughout the entire nation and a fundamental reform to include a professionalization and respect for human rights and civil liberties by state security forces.

In short, Colombia has endured decades of violence as a result of the combined effects of a long-standing internal armed conflict, the centralization of the international cocaine trade in its territory, and the state itself using illicit violence in an attempt to grapple with these two realities. And yet, while Colombia's homicide rate is still high by global standards, violence has decreased dramatically in recent years as the dynamics of the armed conflict have changed and as Colombia has taken steps to strengthen and expand the state.

STRENGTHENING THE STATE: PLAN COLOMBIA AND BEYOND

In 1999, Colombian President Andrés Pastrana and his aides proposed a kind of "Marshall Plan for Colombia" to receptive officials in the U.S. government.[22] Originally designed as a $7.5 billion program to be funded by U.S. and European donors[23] along with the Colombian government, "the initial plan," Arlene Tickner argues, was not "conceived as a counternarcotics policy by the Colombian government" but instead had "the ultimate goal [of] state strengthening and particularly military strengthening."[24] The project quickly morphed into a counternarcotics program as the United States refused to engage in Colombia's internal conflict for fears of a Vietnam-style quagmire. Direct involvement in Colombia's armed conflict was so politically untenable that the State Department went so far as to release a fact sheet titled "Why Colombia is Not the 'Next Vietnam.'"[25] While the United States would not allow its funds to be used for counter-insurgency purposes, the U.S. was eager to help Colombia combat narcotics trafficking and in so doing reduce the funding of guerilla and paramilitary forces. In 2000, the United States Congress approved the first $1.6 billion in funds for Colombia[26] and would send some $9.5 billion in assistance for Plan Colombia and its successors from fiscal year 2000 through fiscal year 2014.[27]

With this aid from the United States and significant domestic funding, Colombia began to strengthen the state, especially its coercive apparatus. Initial Plan Colombia funding from the United States focused heavily on the "hard" components of the plan, with only 20 percent of U.S. assistance going to "soft" programs such as alternative economic development in coca-growing regions and human rights training and enforcement.[28] Colombia's 2002 presidential elections brought a new president with an even more militarized agenda. While President Pastrana had been elected on a platform of bringing peace with the FARC, his administration's efforts failed and his signature peace overture, the ceding of a Switzerland-sized demilitarized zone to the FARC for peace negotiations, ended in disaster.[29] Incoming President Álvaro Uribe campaigned on a *mano dura* (iron fist) platform, promising to take the fight to the guerillas. These efforts were aided by a receptive administration in Washington who saw President Uribe as its strongest ally in Latin America. Moreover, the 9/11 attacks in the United States opened the political space for the U.S. to allow its funding to be used in Colombia's counter-insurgency campaign since the FARC, ELN, and AUC (Autodefensas Unidas de Colombia—United Self Defense Forces of Colombia), the largest paramilitary umbrella group, were on the U.S. State Department's list of Foreign Terrorist Organizations. In 2002, the U.S. Congress approved language allowing for U.S. funds to be used in a "unified campaign to fight drug trafficking and terrorist organizations."[30]

President Uribe's Democratic Security and Defense Policy and his Plan Patriota (Patriot Plan) aimed to further strengthen the state's security apparatus and re-capture and control territory from Colombia's illegal armed actors. While highly criticized by human rights groups[31] on the grounds that the policies led to gross violations of human rights by state agents in the name of advancing security (including the atrocities described above), these programs doubled the size of both the military and the police and led to significant military operations against the illegal armed actors, especially the FARC. Table 5.1 shows the dramatic increase in combat incidents between the state and both guerrilla and paramilitary forces during this time period. In addition, in 2008 the Colombian government tricked the FARC into releasing fifteen of its most high-value political prisoners, including Colombian Senator and presidential candidate Íngrid Betancourt and three U.S. defense contractors in what was known as "Operation Checkmate." Together the military defeats, the humiliating loss of the hostages, and the killings of several key commanders significantly weakened the FARC. The ELN suffered similar losses on the battlefield. As a result, Jonathan D. Rosen argues that the number of FARC effectives declined from 17,000 in 2001 to 8,000 in 2008 and that the number of ELN effectives fell from 5,000 to between 2,000 and 3,000 in the same time period.[32]

With respect to Colombia's paramilitary groups, President Uribe's strategy included an additional dimension: dialogue and demobilization. At the peak of their power, in December of 2002, paramilitaries entered a dialogue with the government of Colombian President Álvaro Uribe.[33] Daly provides a compelling discussion of this process and of the paramilitary rationale

Table 5.1. Combat Incidents in Colombia, 1988–2009

Year	*State/Guerrilla*	*State/Paramilitary*
1988	193	0
1989	183	4
1990	390	2
1991	534	0
1992	578	3
1993	492	0
1994	469	1
1995	365	1
1996	462	2
1997	384	7
1998	315	6
1999	304	2
2000	484	6
2001	560	22
2002	827	35
2003	992	93
2004	907	117
2005	699	57
2006	622	6
2007	845	69
2008	285	43
2009	115	12

Note: The data for state/paramilitary combat include combat incidents with neo-paramilitary groups which emerged as the paramilitaries were demobilizing. This, along with those paramilitary groups that remobilized, explain the continued state/paramilitary combat incidents after 2006.

Source: Created by autor with data from BDCAC-CERAC: Base de Datos Sobre Conflicto Armado Colombiano-Centro de Recursos Para El Análisis de Conflictos

for it, arguing that "the paramilitaries entered peace talks with the Uribe administration because they were convinced of their power, but also of the forthcoming slow decline in that power, and they preferred to bargain from a position of strength."[34] She argues that "the paramilitaries also believed that they would be able to maintain cohesive units, control the peace process, and translate their power at war into power at peace."[35] Between 2003 and 2006, 37 of the 39 active paramilitary groups in Colombia were decommissioned,[36] resulting in 35,310 demobilized combatants.[37] Yet this demobilization process did not end paramilitarism as half of the demobilized fronts eventually remilitarized[38] and paramilitary successor groups like the criminal bands (*bandas criminales*), known as the BACRIM emerged to take their place. The demobilization did, however, fundamentally alter paramilitarism, ending the ideological battle between paramilitaries and guerrillas and ending the national political project of paramilitaries.

The combined effect of the state strengthening project, the weakening of Colombia's guerrilla groups, and the demobilization of Colombia's paramilitaries is a striking reduction in violence. As figure 5.1 shows, battle related deaths decline dramatically from 2005 to 2006, and maintain a much lower trajectory through 2015. Indeed, battle related deaths averaged 237 from 2007–2015, just 22 percent of the conflict's peak from 2000 to 2002. The homicide data in figure 5.2 tell a similar story. At the height of the armed conflict in 2002, Colombia's homicide rate per 100,000 stood at 68.3 and fell by slightly more than half to 32.7 at the end of President Uribe's second term in 2010.

PEACE AT LAST?

Colombia has continued to see a decline in homicides and combat deaths as it continues to strengthen the state and as it has embarked on a historic peace process with its largest and most dangerous guerrilla group, the FARC. In 2010, President Uribe was succeeded by his defense minister and protégé Juan Manuel Santos. Defense minister Santos had presided over some of the country's most significant military victories against the FARC and continued the military pressure early in his presidency. Yet in early 2012, the Santos administration and the FARC began a series of secret conversations in Havana, Cuba that would lead to the September 2012 announcement of formal peace negotiations between the two sides. The parties embarked on a difficult and complex set of negotiations focusing on five substantive areas: internal agricultural development, political rights of the opposition (especially the participation of former FARC guerrillas), ending the armed conflict and reintegration into civilian life for former combatants as well as transitional justice, illicit crops and drug trafficking, and reparations for victims of the conflict. In August 2016, the Colombian government and FARC announced the completion of the peace accords and a signing ceremony was held in Cartagena, Colombia the following month. This accord was narrowly rejected by Colombian voters in a national plebiscite in October and a revised accord was signed in November and ratified by the Colombian Congress on December 1, 2016. Under the terms of the accord, as many as 14,000 FARC combatants and militias[39] moved into rural hamlets the size of a village which served as demobilization zones where they surrendered their weapons and began the transition to civilian life.

The last of the FARC's arms were turned over in June 2017 and the coordinates of remaining arms caches given to U.N. officials who declared the disarmament process "essentially complete."[40] Many of the weapons will be melted down and remade into a monument for peace.[41] In the final disarmament ceremony on June 27, 2017, FARC Commander Rodrigo Londoño (who is known by the nom de guerre Timochenko) declared "Farewell to arms, farewell to war, welcome to peace," and in an acknowledgment of the FARC's intention to form a political party and enter the political process, "Today doesn't end the existence of the FARC, it ends our armed struggle."[42] President Santos, who received the 2016 Nobel Peace Prize for the peace accords, declared: "Today we see the end of this absurd war." He called the final disarmament "the best news for Colombia in 50 years—this is great news of peace" and said the country could now finally unify as a democracy.[43] He added, "I can say from the bottom of my heart that to live this day, to achieve this day, has made worthwhile being president of Colombia," because "our peace is real, and it's irreversible."[44]

The peace accords provide Colombia with its greatest opportunity to reduce violence throughout the country, and the accords are paying dividends. According to Colombian defense minister Luis Carlos Villegas, Colombia's homicide rate in 2016 fell to 24.4 per 100,000, Colombia's lowest rate in 42 years.[45] Yet important challenges remain. Even a weakened FARC continued to provide security and a kind of para-state apparatus in areas it controlled. With their disarmament and movement out of those areas and into these transition zones, a power vacuum has emerged. Other armed actors, especially paramilitary successor groups, have stepped into that void and as a result "attacks against civil society activists have increased at an alarming rate," generating condemnation and concern from leading Colombian and international human rights groups.[46] In November 2016, the Inter-American Commission of Human Rights condemned what it termed the "grave situation of violence against human rights defenders," noting the increased assassinations in late 2016 and the special vulnerability of peasant, indigenous, and Afro-Colombian community leaders.[47]

This power vacuum and the resulting violence is especially true in Colombia's coca-growing regions. As Adam Isacson has written, "Colombia is in the midst of a coca boom, perhaps its largest ever."[48] The United Nations estimates that coca cultivation increased 52 percent or 123,000 acres from 2015 to 2016.[49] This continues a trend that has been developing in recent years. In 2016, Colombia "shatter[ed]" its previous records for cocaine seizures "more than doubling the annual haul between 2010 and 2014."[50] One of the most significant questions about the implementation of the peace process was whether or not the FARC would fully abandon its participation in the coca trade. It appears that they are, which further exacerbates the security vacuum. As the FARC abandons the trade, this opens the industry to new participants, which introduces uncertainty to the market and increases violence. As Isacson argues, "with the FARC truly out of the drug trade, and Colombia's state dithering in filling the governance vacuum in most previously FARC-dominated areas, several regions of the country may soon see a very violent competition to determine who will be the next dominant coca-base buyer and processor" and, as a result, "this could get ugly."[51] Indeed, not only is there potential for new violence from new criminal organizations which move in, there is also the possibility that dissident FARC members who refuse to demobilize or that leave the reintegration zones and remobilize might join forces with the BACRIM and create a particularly strong and dangerous trafficking alliance.

Internal displacement remains a significant challenge as well. Even as the peace process was being implemented, the Internal Displacement Monitoring Center estimated 171,000 new internally displaced peoples as a result of the armed conflict in 2016.[52] The situation is especially difficult along Colombia's Pacific Coasts where the UNHCR recorded 11,363 people (3,068 families) displaced by violence. William Spindler, the UNHCR spokesman, noted that as of March 10, "fighting for territorial control in the Colombian Pacific Coast region among irregular armed groups has displaced 3,549 people (913 families) since the beginning of 2017."[53] Spindler further noted that, "Since the signing of the peace agreement, increased violence by new armed groups has resulted in killings, forced recruitment—including children—gender-based violence and limited access to education, water, and sanitation, as well as movement restrictions and forced displacement of the civilian population."[54] Group displacement increased significantly through the first half of 2017, and human rights groups accuse these new armed actors of "a range of offenses, including forced recruitment and displacement, planting mines, and preventing people in parts of the northwest from earning a livelihood on their farms."[55] Once again, minority populations are disproportionately victimized with the Norwegian Refugee Council (NRC) noting that indigenous and Afro-Colombians accounted for "over 70 percent" of those displaced in 2016 and 94 percent of those displaced in the first quarter of 2017.[56] The NRC further estimates that 60 percent of the forced displacements in 2017 have been caused by the ELN.[57] Reducing internal displacement is thus another critical challenge facing Colombia today. Central to that effort will be the successful completion of the peace dialogues with the ELN, which began in February 2017 but are stalled as of August 2017.

CONCLUSION

Colombia has made significant gains with violence at recent record lows and the FARC disbanded as an armed movement. Yet ending the FARC and their participation in illicit enterprises like drug trafficking does not end the enterprises themselves. New actors, especially the dangerous BACRIM and paramilitary successor groups, will attempt to take their place. And so much hinges on the successful implementation of the peace accords and the provision of security and development in marginalized areas left behind by the FARC. Implementing the peace accords will take more than a decade and cost billions of dollars. In an era of tight budgets and low oil prices this will be a difficult task for Colombia. U.S. funding of the Colombian peace process, which the Obama administration was committed to, is very much uncertain in the early days of the Trump administration. Colombia itself faces a political choice with executive and legislative elections in 2018 which will set the course for Colombia's future.

Fundamentally this chapter points to the continued need to strengthen the Colombian state and expand it especially to the approximately 20 percent of the country's municipalities where the FARC had a strong presence and where "one can travel for hours without seeing evidence of the Colombian state."[58] Colombia's illegal armed actors no longer control large swaths of territory. And yet, as Rosen has rightly observed, "a weak state will not be able to control the land within Colombia even after such territory has been reclaimed."[59] The state must not only provide security but infrastructure and basic services in these areas. The challenge for Colombia is to effectively govern its territory and provide its citizens with the safety and security they desire and deserve. Providing it will require not only more resources and state security forces that respect civil and political rights, but a political will to serve marginalized communities and provide effective citizenship throughout the country.

Chapter Six

Violence: El Salvador's "Ill-Structured" Problem

Bradford R. McGuinn

As 2017 began it was reported that El Salvador had experienced its first full day without a killing since 2015.[1] That such notice was taken of a victimless day is a reminder that Salvador is among the world's deadliest lands.[2] 6,657 people were killed in 2015,[3] a year in which homicide rates reached 104 per 100,000 residents.[4] The rate of killing declined by nearly 20 percent in 2016, leaving the country with a murder rate of 81.2.[5] The rise of gang-related violence had been attributed to the breakdown of the truce between the government and the gangs in 2012.[6] Yet the recent decline in killing has been credited to the latter's crackdown, its policy of *mano dura*, or "iron fist."[7] That strategies of accommodation and confrontation can both be claimed as ameliorative, with neither providing a demonstrable remedy for El Salvador's problem of violence, suggests they might be considered not as solutions but as symptoms of an intractable problem.

Why El Salvador should find itself caught in a storm of protracted violence is not self-evident. Its violent past is not a condition sufficient to obviate a passive present: the country's painful history does not yield a source of discord ostentatious for its singularity. It cannot be said that Salvador is governed by a violent authoritarian regime, as it is a leftist government of revolutionary pedigree, the Farabundo Martí National Liberation Front (Frente Farabundo Martí para la Liberación Nacional—FMLN) that has held power amidst these oscillations in violence. A country neither at war nor in the thrall of revolution, neither the center of the Western Hemisphere's narcotics trade or even its most important area for illicit transport, why it is that Salvador should be associated with such violence remains a puzzle.

It is argued in this chapter that in the puzzling case of El Salvador, the problem *is* the problem. The antagonisms of this small country represent a class of social problems that frustrate attempts to make causally intelligible what Claribel Alegria called El Salvador's "map of deep mystery."[8] Emphasis here will be placed upon the *ill-structured* nature of El Salvador's travails. Considered first will be the nature of the conceptual conundrum posed by Salvador's extreme violence. The chapter then explores three levels of theory capturing aspects of the crisis as well as the policy implications issuing from a domain of social vexations that have come to be called "wicked."

FRAMING

With Horst W. J. Rittel and Melvin M. Webber, a distinction can be observed between problems that are "well-structured" or "ill-structured," "tame" or "wicked."[9] Classification in such terms has renewed salience in an era in which the erosion of state authority and societal fragmentation inform conflict environments framed not in terms of a "single, integrated system," but as a "disunited, fragmented accumulation of disparate elements and events."[10] The ill-structured nature of such an "accumulation," denies to it the "clarifying traits" of a "single, integrated" problem. "Clarity," in this paradoxical telling, must await the unification of elements disunited, permitting visualization only upon the problem's "resolution."[11] With the problem itself amorphous, the definition of *causality,* the diagnosis of which is essential to policy-making, risks "taming," or "structuring," a condition in which causation is evanescent.

Absent causal clarity, a "wicked problem" is destined never to be "solved," but "re-solved—over and over again."[12] Without a logical point of termination, or a clear standard by which a "solution" can be judged as "true or false," the problem resists objective testing or experimentation, rendering unreliable the experience gained addressing "similar" problems. Limited too are the number of "known" options available by way of policy, as each aspect of the problem is both cause and symptom of another. In El Salvador's case, the cascade of troubles, from income and educational disparities to matters of institutional development and political culture, neighborhood and family breakdown, regional instability and the complex relationship with the United States, come in endless stream with variable intensity. In contrast to the types of policy problems that might be termed "structured" or "tame," El Salvador's are, then, ontologically unstable, epistemologically frustrating and devoid of teleological promise: contested at the level of *being*, inaccessible to our familiar ways of *knowing* and denied the *going* implicit in productive policy development.

FAILING

El Salvador's history tells of a place that "knows nothing about peace."[13] A country "free, sovereign, and independent"[14] since 1821,[15] yet burdened by institutional failure. With "the most rigid class structure and worst income inequality in all of Latin America,"[16] the political system has been administered in ways "populist, personalistic, and clientelistic."[17] Political hegemony has been held by the famous *Los Catorce familias,* the "fourteen families," dominating the country's economy,[18] its "coffee monoculture,"[19] with the aid of a security apparatus, employed in a manner that was often as violent as it was arbitrary in its actions.[20] *La Matanza*, the "peasant massacre" of 1932, was, perhaps, the event most emblematic of this condition.[21] What was said of the Philippines, another realm of the *familias*, might apply to the historical overlords of Salvador's "predatory state" who would "use corruption to barricade themselves in power," casting about "the crumbs of corruption to maintain their clientist support groups."[22]

In 1979, reformist military officers launched a putsch against El Salvador's authoritarian government.[23] The junta spoke of "deep divisions" and the "historical concentration of power, wealth and social prestige by small groups."[24] But the reformers were pushed aside by ardent spirits of left and right,[25] whose exertions would drive the country to civil war. The United States would engage the conflict with counter-insurgency assistance, designed to keep the FMLN at bay while encouraging the Christian Democrats with a view toward the marginalization of the far-right party known as Nationalist Republican Alliance (Alianza Republicana Nacionalista—ARENA).[26] Taken as a whole, the war's harvest was staggering: 80,000 people killed,[27] 7,000 missing,[28] and one million among the displaced.[29] The legacies of "death squads," the extreme and "intimate" violence known to civil wars could not but rend Salvador's social fabric.

The story of the 1990s begins with El Salvador's search for a democratic center upon the civil war's termination. The formation of criminal gangs, embryonic then,[30] would find stimulation in social traumas experienced in the United States at the end of its long Cold War. It would be among the Salvadoran refugees in the United States,[31] those who exchanged civil war for the gang wars of California[32] that would emerge Mara Salvatrucha (MS-13). Many would then find themselves "returned" to El Salvador, bringing with them their violent intensities.[33]

The years of neo-liberalism's ascendency would, indeed, see criminalization as pluralism's companion in El Salvador. It is now estimated that MS-13 has grown to an organization of some 70,000 people,[34] with nearly a half million individuals in some form of affiliation.[35] El Salvador's gangs have come to represent something of a "counter-society," challenging the authority of the leftist government, forcing it to declare a "war on crime" and "state of emergency."[36] Disparaging the erosion of the FMLN's ideological commitment, a regional leader of the 18th Street gang, or Barrio 18, observed that it "once meant to represent the interests of the poor,"[37] but is "no longer there for them."[38] Perhaps, seen in broader terms, it is amidst "failure of the left" in El Salvador, and elsewhere, that Salvador Sánchez Cerén and Donald Trump's administration have been conjoined in a strategy of "dual securitization," an attempt to structure an ill-structured social problem, to "tame" a "wicked problem" through the practice of hard security.

BEING

"A culture of extreme fear," Christian Krohn-Hansen argued, "implies that ontological thought is an everyday activity for the crowd."[39] What, then, is ontic in Salvador? It might be suggested, as Viridiana Rios said of the complexities associated with Mexico's escalating violence, that what obtains in El Salvador is a "self-reinforcing violent equilibrium."[40] A "mainstay of social and ecological systems,"[41] competition drives fragmentation and internal power struggles,[42] among both Salvador's political classes and the gangs.[43] "Shaped and shoved,"[44] then, have been El Salvador's antagonists into an ill-structured assemblage of agitation.[45] Absent mechanisms of liberal amelioration for its social conflicts, an oligarchic impulse dominates, with actors willing to assume risk for "market share." In his discussion of organized crime, Thomas Schelling argued that the criminal enterprise will "not merely extend itself broadly, but brooks no competition."[46] "It seeks," he continued, "not merely influence, but exclusive influence,"[47] as might be expected within an ontology of "deep uncertainty."[48]

One aspect of escalating violence can be seen in the *confrontations* between government forces and the gangs.[49] Between 2013 and 2015 they increased from 142 incidents to 676, "an increase of more than 370 percent."[50] In 2013, 39 gang members were killed in confrontations with police,[51] while 49 were killed the following year.[52] By 2015, 320 gang members were killed, rising to 560 in 2016,[53] amidst concerns that the National Civil Police was "becoming increasingly lethal over time."[54]

Still, law enforcement personnel have "become direct targets" for the gangs,[55] as MS-13 began assassinating police in April 2015.[56] It is thought that criminal groups were responsible for nearly 65 percent of the killings of "Salvadoran security forces between 2011 and 2016."[57] "When there is armed aggression against our officers," Howard Cotto, Director of the National Civil Police, remarked of this condition, "they cannot let themselves be killed."[58] "The police," an unidentified officer observed still more forcefully, "now go around in a state of psychosis, and at times it is natural that they say: 'better to shoot first.'"[59] In such an environment are risks compounded for security officials, human rights and unconstrained escalation.

In the retaliatory violence of gangs can be seen the wages of their "enforcement" operations, the normative center of which is "reputation," a gang's most critical "resource."[60] At "the heart" of what Elijah Anderson called "the code of the street," is the matter of "respect" or "deference."[61] The calculations of vengeance and revenge balancing are the mechanisms by which the arbitrage of minor or mortal "slights" are continually "priced."[62] To "respect your area," as a clique leader of the 18th Street gang put it,[63] in an imperative with no organic limit to the application of violence. Cliques (*clicas*), "programs" and "tribes,"[64] compete for hegemony in illicit markets and extortion rackets–effecting seventy percent of businesses, from stores to buses–in "247 of El Salvador's 262 municipalities."[65] The process by which $600,852 was "collected" in April 2016 was, as the *New York Times* reported, informed by an unstable dialectic of ambition and anxiety.[66] "It's a matter of survival," a bus company owner told the newspaper, "[w]hen they tell you they are going to kill you, you don't have a choice."[67]

El Salvador's *expressive* violence has run to extremes. "You want to prove to people, policemen and the members of your gang, that you are the best and you are the craziest," a gang member remarked, having admitted to "killing 26 people, 10 of whom he chopped up himself."[68] "[Y]ou think if you don't kill," he concluded, "they're going to kill you."[69] "Give me $400 by the end of the week," another gang member said with menaces, "or I'll kill you and your family."[70] "Do you understand me?" he continued in starkly escalatory terms, "[w]e can cut you into pieces."[71] And so the lurid rituals have commenced, with "pickaxes, machetes and guns," with victims "cut at the knees, at the hips, at the elbows, the arms, the neck."[72]

In the mantra "*mata, viola, controla*," or "kill, rape, control,"[73] is a warrant to femicide. Having risen 750 percent in the five years before 2017,[74] with "2,521 women murdered since 2009,"[75] mothers and sisters and daughters have become a "medium" of gang warfare,[76] sometimes pressed into marriages in order for gangs to collect insurance money upon the husband's assassination,[77] other times mutilated in a manner that causes language to break. Children have been weaponized.[78] In recent decades, the cohort of gang victims has migrated from the ages 30 to 20 toward the early teen-aged years.[79] The format of killings has also become extreme, with a trend toward "multiple homicides."[80] Ninety-four reported massacres occurred between 2012 and 2014, with 106 multiple killings in 2015 alone.[81]

Among the characteristics of this assemblage is also its propensity for *contagion*. From the displacement in El Salvador of some 324,000 people owing to "crime and violence,"[82] to the concatenation of gangs and terror that characterize the sub-region in which El Salvador seeks to manage its turbulence,[83] is added the weight of the powerful Mexican narcotics cartels.[84] These factors shape Salvador's connection with the United States, a relationship defined by the remittance payments of two million Salvadorans living in America,[85] totaling $4.48 billion in 2016,[86] representing 17.1 percent of El Salvador's economy.[87] But in the past, and again more recently, it is defined too by a series of homicides attributed to MS-13 members within the United States.[88] News accounts, for example, spoke of "*El programa de Maryland*,[89] featuring "[i]ncarcerated clique leaders based in El Salvador" directing "Maryland-based cliques through phones into Salvadoran prisons."[90] Such reports speak to the "double burden" carried by many Salvadorans in the United States: the risk of their youth becoming prey to gangs at one level and being essentialized, as a "threat within," amidst sharpened debates over immigration policy at another.

KNOWING

The "wicked problem" is one of both ontological diffusion and epistemological confusion. "Violent behavior," Jessica Yakeley and J. Reid Meloy argued along these lines, "is not a generic, homogeneous phenomenon.[91] What causal claims we might make for the violence of El Salvador carries with it the risk of imposing of conceptual "solids" onto the "liquids" of an ill-structured condition in the service of pragmatic "sense-making" or even partisan pleading.

What causal clarity we do possess might be suggested within three levels of theoretical exertion. One considers Salvador's problem of violence from the standpoint of *structural* factors. In the analysis of neoliberalism and its hegemonic "market civilization,"[92] issuing from the tradition of critical theory, is a sensitivity to the systemic socio-economic pressures occasioned by consumer capitalism,[93] ones, in it argued, that sharpen class differences while contributing to societal disintegration.[94] Neoliberalism's normative stress on individual consumption, its legitimation of socio-economic hierarchy has, in this view, contributed to the decay of the "social state."[95] In the vacuum have emerged patterns of "criminalization," a condition that stimulated the rise of the "security state," reinforcing further the "politics of exclusion"[96] in which poverty itself is "criminalized."[97] With considerations of class, so too with gender: structural theory might emphasize "misogynistic, macho and homophobic,"[98] aspects of Salvadoran culture, highlighting "linkages" between "the home and violence in the street,"[99] forces that serve to legitimate aggression[100] and fashion permissive space for "the abuse of women."[101]

At another structural register, social "disequilibrium" is said to exist when sanctioned "cultural goals" cannot be realized through available "institutionalized means."[102] The pressures a social structure might impose upon individuals, the "anomie" they occasion, provide ways to assess the disruptions El Salvador has experienced through forces as varied as civil war and neoliberalism.[103] In the more specific "strain theory," is an understanding of "delinquency" in terms of systemic pressures placed upon an individual "social relationships,"[104] preventing, in this rendition, the Salvadoran youth from achieving "positively valued" goals, threatening, instead to visit upon them conditions of a negative nature.[105] Causal theories of a structural nature risk "taming" El Salvador's problem of violence in the name of elegance. But they rightly direct us toward the broadest level of analysis and help make intelligible the problem's protracted nature.

With the inter-subjective processes implicit in "social learning theory," where aggression is assimilated through an "observational learning processes"[106] or with the "script theory," which emphasizes the ease with which young people are vulnerable to "aggressive scripts," shaping behavior through "well-rehearsed, highly associated concepts in memory,"[107] are constructs moving us from a structural, top-down image, to *associational* levels of theory. In this domain are the forces of "social disorganization." Communities unable to manage "commonly experienced problems,"[108] regimes of poor "tension management," yield, in this view, systems of weak social control, with lowered "costs associated with deviation."[109] A consequent "subculture of violence," a place of gangs or "dirty wars," is an ecosystem of aggression,[110] where violent action is, in fact, the "prescribed" norm.[111]

The process by which an individual integrates such norms into their personality[112] is, by its nature, a complex interaction between social experiences and what Lonnie Athens has called "soliloquies," or the internal conversations rehearsed by a young person caught in spaces of violence.[113] These "elliptical communications"[114] constitute an ensemble of discourses in a social construction Athens called a "phantom community." One version of which could be termed "civil," characterized by orderly material features and generally nonviolent "self-talk." Another is a "malignant" community, characterized by an acutely disordered tangible state and a phantom community populated by dire and violent ideations. In between is the "turbulent" community, a space liminal between the civil and the malignant, characterized by significant disorder and the anxious, antagonistic, soliloquies that follow.

Phantoms materialize in the "dominative engagement,"[115] the "dominance encounter," arising from "conflictive social acts."[116] In places of malignancy or turbulence, mechanisms for the negotiation of "status disputes"[117] or "revenge balancing,"[118] often assume violent form, making dangerous soliloquies of passivity. In this fashion, interpersonal conflict might assume the form of a "gaming move," in which an actor unconstrained by "legitimate" norms or attachments[119] engages in "a series of amoral, deliberate, highly individualistic, and engrossing behaviors."[120] Or, as Manni Crone has demonstrated in his studies on terrorist organizations, these behaviors may issue from "*aesthetic assemblages*," representations "that juxtapose linguistics, sound, images and matter,"[121] as is the case with the tattoos of gang-members meant to signify community, loyalty, commitment, a common "culture of the street" and, of course, threat.[122]

"An individual gang member is not just poor," Roberto Lovato argued at still another theoretical level, he is "also walking, talking trauma that's unresolved."[123] The "psychosocial trauma" induced by El Salvador's civil war could not help but alienate social relations,[124] attenuating what, in another context, Reinhold Niebuhr called the "social tissue" meant to adhere a social order.[125] The weakening or destruction of that tissue, the fracturing of civil society, poses a "social threat" to individuals, making acute the need to safeguard "honor" and locate new forms of social attachment.

For a community of turmoil, personal devaluation, a "loss of status, rank, or relational value,"[126] is especially associated with shame.[127] In the absence of "legitimate" institutional order, a person's sense of "self-worth" is invested with "sacred value," the loss of which "is equated with the loss of life,"[128] even the death of the self.[129] For some criminologists, shame is seen as the primary driver of violence.[130] The affect warns of the potential for "social exclusion,"[131] a threat of sufficient "pain"[132] to "diminish self-regulation, increasing anger and aggression."[133] Made "lonely in a crowd" owing to socially disintegrative structural and associational factors, the young Salvadoran can find only an anxious solace in the gang. But ontological centering it is still. "The main reasons why people continue joining the gang," an important study of El Salvador's *maras* argued, "still revolve around the excitement from hanging out with peers and the development of social respect and public recognition."[134]

When "excitement" itself, the "sensation seeking,[135] of violent action becomes its own reward, killing becomes "a source of pleasure."[136] "Flow theories" speak of the "transfer" of excitation from an initial to "subsequent arousal,"[137] offering insight into the dynamic of "overkill." The "forward panic," the "emotional entrainment" of aggressors "in their own release of adrenaline,"[138] directs us also toward the "hot rush," "the one-sided attack of the many against the few"[139] or the subtle shifts within "the emotional balance between two opponents," the micro-sociology of vehement inter-subjectivities.[140] Violent actors "beyond reason" or deadened to killing's consequence represent a class of erratic variables still more difficult to neatly categorize.

Theoretical insights with overt explanatory intention are difficult to connect to the ill-structured problem. It might be suggested that the pressure of structural strain—shaped by forces of class and gender—can be conjoined to the social disorganization—issuing from the rending of social tissue at national, neighborhood and household levels—from which malignant and violent sub-cultures are fashioned, within which pathologies of an idiopathic nature—from shame to sensation-seeking—associate themselves. Such a cascade might, however, be too smooth an epistemological exit from the wicked problem. Worse still, the unreliability of such causal constructs risks making arbitrary the process of policy.

GOING

It is among the features of the "ill-defined problem" to have about it an "ill-definable solution." El Salvador's responses to the problem of violence, under both right and left-wing governments, have oscillated between confrontation and accommodation, motifs of state power and societal engagement. The latter attracts critics viewing conciliation as weakness, while the former is inveighed against by those seeing in *mano dura* only a crisis perpetuated. Viewed, however, from the perspective of the ill-structured problem, the crisis is defined by its perpetuation. And, the movement back-and-forth between methods "hard and soft," may represent the extent of the options available to the Salvadoran government and its enemies.

For all that, policy problem has about it an especial urgency. El Salvador's homicide rates are among the world's highest. It has been estimated that the cost of violence approaches 16 percent of the country's gross domestic product, with gangs extorting vast sums from businesses, equivalent to three percent of GDP.[141] It has also been the case the levels of violence have fluctuated during El Salvador's recent history. In the first half of the 1990s, the homicide rate "reached 139 per 100,000 inhabitants."[142] By 2000 it had decreased to 44.[143] The number of killings dropped again in the months after the 2012 truce,[144] as they have amidst the techniques of confrontation undertaken since 2015, as the number of homicides decreased by 1,378 from 2016 "to 5,278, a decline of 20.7 percent."[145]

President Sánchez Cerén has pledged to "guarantee" El Salvador "the indispensible environment for a safe life."[146] The "shoot-to-kill policy,"[147] the "green-light to use deadly force against suspected gang members,"[148] is said to have resulted in the killing of nearly seven hundred alleged gang members during over a thousand "armed confrontations" through 2015 and 2016.[149] Yet civil liberties have been placed at risk with the "state of emergency."[150] The specter of extrajudicial killings,[151] the "return" of the "death squads,"[152] the paramilitary elements, "feeling ready to exterminate,"[153] speak less to "solutions" than to symptoms of the trap in which El Salvador finds itself.

Prison presents another paradox of policy. In 2000, there were 7,745 prisoners in El Salvador. By 2016 the number reached 35,879.[154] The government's decision in 2004 to "have exclusive prisons for the country's two principle gangs"[155] meant that the criminal groups had "won their segregation from the 'civilian' prisoners," with Quezaltepeque and Ciudad Barrios becoming the domains of MS-13 and Chalatenango and Cojutepeque controlled by Barrio 18.[156] The policy may have reduced violence in these facilities, but it conferred onto the gangs "a headquarters from which to recruit, and to expand their influence."[157] So too "zero-tolerance" sentencing strategies, with terms of 40 to 60 years for "a range of offenses,"[158] have sent a message of resolve at the cost of increasing Salvador's prison population. The surge in ex-convicts sent to El Salvador by the United States, from roughly 2000 in the late-1990s to nearly 9,000 by 2014, totaling 81,000, might have eased America's burdens, but they have placed strain on Salvador's society and prison system,[159] as might the proposals by the Trump administration to sharply increase gang deportations.[160]

In March 2017, when some thirty people, mostly "gang members," were killed in a single day, the country's Justice Minister reminded Salvadorans that the problem of security remains "complex and difficult."[161] "[I]ncreasingly tense" and "full of labyrinths," were also phrases apposite to describe Salvador's condition early in 2017.[162] Into this complexity, El Salvador's government has deployed a formidable force into the streets and the countryside, resulting in the killing of an extraordinary number of gang members. But impunity rates remain high and rates of conviction through orderly judicial processes are low.[163] The "solutions," the lines of policy—"green lights" here, incarceration strategies, there, peace overtures, America's "shifting risk" back to El Salvador[164]—all have about them the frustration of unintended consequence. About how to expand governing capacity, enhance the integrity of institutions and foster non-violent pluralism, the logic of the ill-structured problem can offer little guidance.

CONCLUSION

One approach to the governance of this *assemblage agité* might begin, to evoke the idiom of the old American progressive tradition, by highlighting the baleful effect of "capitalistic democracy" as the mechanism "for betraying the poor and the downtrodden into the hands of the rich.[165] Another, after the fashion of John Rawls, would suggest that with "the success of liberal constitutionalism" has emerged "a new social possibility: the possibility of a reasonably harmonious and stable pluralist society.[166] What exists between marxian and liberal remedy, neither of which seems within El Salvador's immediate reach, are the more familiar methods of "getting by."

The old American urban political machine offers a rough approximation of such a governing without *telos*. "A machine politician is essentially a broker between the claims of competing groups and classes," a writer for *Fortune Magazine* wrote of the violent land of Chicago in 1936, "and he must, if he is to maintain his broker's position, shift ground as the strength of awareness of the competing groups changes."[167] "He can be true to no faction or class or group," the argument continued.[168] "But to know the precise moment when to shift ground, when to alter the stress of your loyalty," the writer averred, "is not a matter in which the political scientist can be very helpful." "The moment must be felt," the article concluded, "it is something for an artist's intuition.[169]

Has Salvador Sánchez Cerén the intuition of the political artist? It is not unlikely that he, and his successors, will shift ground as circumstances change, from confrontation to accommodation and back again. It is also possible that such alterations might be affected more with a view to frustrating political opponents than to the combat of gangs. In the political warfare between the FMLN and ARENA is, after all, a sectarian struggle that has weakened El Salvador's institutions and attenuated trust between state and society. Political combat provides too "permissive space" for gangs and their violence. Without an authoritarian regime, regional war or exogenous intervention to "structure" El Salvador's system, the country is left to live in the causally complex truth of its ill-structured violence.

Might not, however, for whatever abstract utility might be associated with the "wicked problem" construct, it risks treating the matter of El Salvador's violence in terms both arid and unacceptable for its fatalistic implications regarding the prospect of ameliorative policy? "Well," Isabel Alvarez Mejia said with the vividness that makes an indulgence of fatalism, "we can't protect our children."[170] As "a single mother," she told a reporter from her mountain village in 2017, "I can't protect them against all this violence we have here in El Salvador."[171]

The complexity of the dilemma in which Ms. Mejia finds herself induces humility. Perhaps it is a governor to our vanities that the concept of the problem "ill-structured" has its greatest value. To govern a "wicked problem" is, after all, to be unsure of the ground upon which to operate, anxious about the true cause of the troubles, wary of the "illusion of solution," while knowing, as Luigi Barzini said years ago of turmoil in his native Italy, that "unsolved problems pile up and inevitably produce catastrophes at regular intervals."[172] As one season of violence gives way to yet another in El Salvador, Barzini's warning reminds us that the play of time upon pathology can only deepen a crisis and contribute to intractability of social problems.

Chapter Seven

At a Crossroads: Can Guatemala Prevail in Fight against Violence?

Adriana Beltrán

In May 2011, 27 farm workers were found massacred on the Los Cocos farm in Guatemala's remote, northeastern Petén department, 600 miles north of Guatemala City along the border with Mexico.[1] The incident is renowned for its brutality: the victims were decapitated, some with their legs and arms dismembered, which were used to write a warning message in blood on a wall of the estate. The workers had the unlucky fortune of being at the house of their employer, Otto Salguero, when a group identifying itself as "Z-200," a branch of the Zetas cartel, came looking for him.[2] Salguero, a landowner with links to drug trafficking networks, had allegedly stolen a cocaine shipment from the Zetas. Members of the criminal group arrived at his farm seeking revenge, and upon not finding him there, slaughtered his employees instead.[3] Ten days later, the mutilated body of an assistant prosecutor who had been involved in a seizure of cocaine from the Zetas was found in the department of Alta Verapaz, just one day after he had been abducted. A note left by his remains read "Z-200."[4]

The slayings demonstrated the lawlessness that persists in the country after three decades of civil war. After the 1996 peace accords, many Guatemalans thought the country was embarking on a new era. However, after a few years of declining murder rates, the country began to experience an explosion of criminal violence. Homicides more than doubled between 2000 and 2009, when the murder rate reached a peak of 46 homicides per 100,000 people, 270 percent higher than that of neighboring Mexico (17 per 100,000 people), and 920 percent higher than that of the United States (5 per 100,000 people) (see figure 7.1).[5] Failure to address the root causes of the conflict had allowed organized crime and urban gangs to flourish and insecurity to skyrocket. On a daily basis, Guatemalan citizens from all walks of life faced threats of extortion,

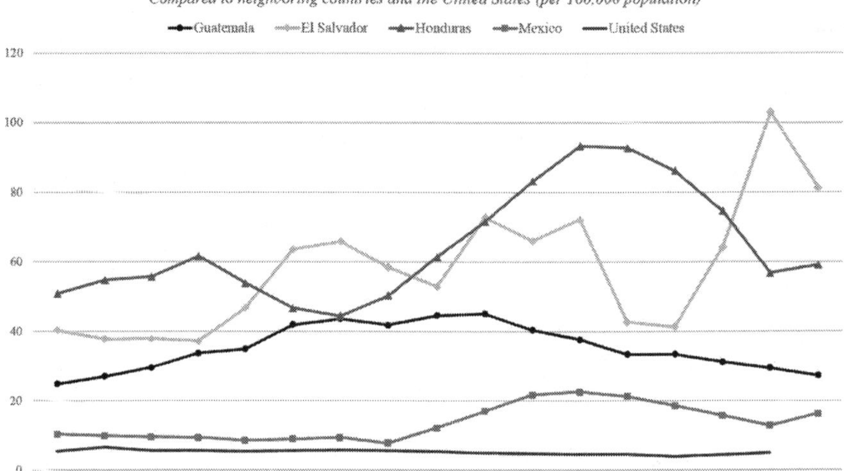

Figure 7.1. Homicide Rates in Guatemala, 2000–2016

Created by the author. "Homicide Counts and Rates," United Nations Office of Drugs and Crime; "InSight Crime's 2015 Latin America Homicide Round-up," InSight Crime, January 14, 2016; "InSight Crime's 2016 Homicide Round-up," InSight Crime, January 16, 2017; "Crime in the U.S.," Federal Bureau of Investigations, last accessed July 12, 2017, https://ucr.fbi.gov/crime-in-the-u.s. 2016 homicide rates for the United States unavailable as of July 14, 2017.

murder, and gang-related violence, while the country became a key corridor for illegal goods. In the face of high-profile killings and widespread violence, many lost trust in the state and took matters of protection into their own hands, resorting to security companies for protection or vigilantism, lynching, and assassins for hire.[6]

Beginning in 2010, the murder rate steadily begun to decline, hitting its lowest point in the past 15 years in 2016 (see figure 7.1). To a large extent, the drop is the result of a new wave of qualified and committed individuals determined to rein in the violence and break the wall of impunity that has existed for so many years. The decline offers a sign of hope, and illustrates the difference political resolve and solid investigative capacities can make. Today, Guatemala has the opportunity to build on this progress. However, the country still remains among the most violent in the world, and within the country regional discrepancies remain high. As Guatemala continues to tackle endemic impunity and deep-seated corruption, it is still unclear whether it will be able to muster the resources and political commitment needed to build the solid and accountable institutions vital to the security of its citizens.

MAIN DRIVERS OF VIOLENCE

There is no one clear cause of violence in Guatemala, nor one set of perpetrators. Behind the extraordinary crime and violence levels are a variety of criminal groups, including urban gangs, drug cartels, and criminal networks that stretch back decades. Insecurity has also been driven by the widespread availability of firearms.

Organized Crime

Sandwiched between the coca-producing nations of the Andes and the last stop before the world's largest consumer of cocaine, Guatemala has become an important transit country for drugs and other contraband traveling northbound from South America to Mexico and the United States. Transnational criminal organizations take advantage of more than 1,000 miles of porous borders and coastlines, at least 1,200 "blind" border crossings, and ill-equipped—and often absent—law enforcement presence in many areas of the country to smuggle illicit goods.

Recent years have seen an increase in both drug production and trafficking in the country. In 2016, the U.S. Department of State estimated that 90 percent of cocaine destined for the United States transited through Central America during the previous year.[7] In 2017, the Department estimated that every year 1,000 metric tons (MT) of cocaine are smuggled through the country, the majority headed for the U.S. market.[8] The manufacturing of methamphetamine and other synthetic drugs has been cited as another major problem, with large quantities of precursor chemicals entering and transiting the country.[9] In 2016, Guatemalan authorities estimated that an average of 4,500 hectares in the western part of the country were under poppy cultivation, a dramatic increase compared to previous years.[10]

Drug and other contraband trafficking has long afflicted Guatemala. For decades, homegrown criminal networks organized through family connections, known as *transportista* groups, have dominated the drug trade and smuggling of other illicit goods. Families such as the Lorenzana, Mendoza, and Leon clans accumulated prominence and territorial control by filling power vacuums in areas with little state presence, employing local citizens, providing social services, and corrupting local authorities in order to run their illegal businesses.[11] Most have enjoyed close ties to government officials.[12]

As the drug war in Mexico made it increasingly difficult for Colombian cartels to directly ship product to the country, traffickers shifted their routes overland, to Central America. As these groups expanded into Guatemala, they took advantage of the already existing criminal networks and allied with these groups to further establish themselves.[13] This shift transformed Guatemala from a mere "refueling stop" into a major link in the drug trade.[14]

Drugs are not the only things that move across Guatemala's borders with ease. The country has become an origin, transit, and destination country for transnational human trafficking. In 2015, Guatemalan authorities identified 673 victims of trafficking, a significant increase from the 287 victims identified in 2014. Of these, 68 percent were women and girls.[15] Quantifying the actual number of trafficking victims is difficult. Using the United Nations Office on Drugs and Crime (UNODC) parameter that thirty unreported cases exist for every identified victim, and including other cases of sexual exploitation as well as identified victims outside the criminal system, a 2016 report estimates there could be 48,617 sexual trafficking victims in Guatemala.[16]

Engaging with both the domestic criminal groups and transnational drug cartels are Guatemala's Illegal Clandestine Security Apparatuses (*Cuerpos Ilegales y Aparatos Clandestinos de Seguridad*—CIACS). Also referred to as "Hidden Powers," these groups formed as part of the military intelligence and counterinsurgency apparatus during the armed conflict. Utilizing its unchecked power and control, the Guatemalan military was able to develop close relationships with organized criminal groups. These illegal security structures were not fully dismantled after the peace accords—to the contrary, they transformed and became increasingly entrenched in a number of criminal activities including drug trafficking, arms smuggling, and contraband.[17] Since then, the CIACS have used their relationships to infiltrate nearly all government institutions, enabling them to profit from embezzlement schemes, kickbacks from public works contracts, customs fraud, and illegal contracting practices.[18]

The various organized criminal groups operating in Guatemala have managed to infiltrate law enforcement and justice institutions, customs agencies, local politics and businesses, and national political parties.[19] These connections have granted them privilege, access, and protection, which they repay through the financing of public works projects and political campaigns, for example.[20] According to a 2015 report by the International Commission against Impunity in Guatemala (Comisión Internacional contra la Impunidad en Guatemala—CICIG), political parties in Guatemala receive approximately 50 percent of their financing through corruption: 25 percent from criminal organizations and another 25 percent from wealthy elites.[21] In some areas of the country, these groups have become the guarantors of public order, with more control and power than state institutions. It has been estimated that 40 percent of Guatemalan territory is under the control of organized crime.[22]

Gangs

While violence along Guatemala's border and trafficking routes can be attributed to drug trafficking groups, criminal gangs are behind the high rates of violence and insecurity affecting urban neighborhoods. The MS-13 (*Mara Salvatrucha*) and 18th Street (*Barrio 18*) gangs are the two most dominant groups throughout Central America. Both originated in the 1980s in Los Angeles' immigrant communities. In the mid-1990s, the United States deported tens of thousands of Central American immigrants with criminal convictions back to their countries of origin, sending nearly 31,000 convicted criminals to Central America between 1996 and 2002.[23] Met with a lack of educational and economic opportunities, weak institutions, poverty, and social exclusion, gang members exported Los Angeles gang culture, assert dominance over the population, and expand their numbers.[24]

The exact number of gang members operating in Guatemala is unknown. In 2012, the UNODC estimated that there were approximately 54,000 gang members in Central America's Northern Triangle: 22,000 in Guatemala, 20,000 in El Salvador, and 12,000 in Honduras.[25] That same year, the State Department estimated that there were roughly 85,000 members of the MS-13 and 18th Street in the Northern Triangle.[26] In a 2014 interview, however, the director of the National Civil Police's (*Policía Nacional Civil*—PNC) anti-gang unit estimated the figure much lower, at around 5,000.[27] What is clear is the grave impact that criminal gangs have had, particularly in marginalized, urban areas in Guatemala City and the surrounding metropolitan area.[28] Citizens in gang-controlled neighborhoods live in a heightened state of insecurity and fear. Criminal gangs engage in various illicit activities, including street-level drug sales, hired assassination, extortion, and the trafficking of undocumented migrants.[29] They are responsible for violence through territorial disputes, confrontations with law enforcement, or retaliation against those who witness a crime or fail to obey orders. Gangs impose their own perception of order, setting curfews and controlling points of entry into neighborhoods under their jurisdiction.[30] They recruit members—often forcibly—from vulnerable youth in poor neighborhoods and prisons.[31] Women are targeted for sexual violence and often forced into relationships with gang members.

The majority of gang income is generated through running extortion rings—primarily targeting small businesses, street vendors, and the public transportation system—in which failure to pay results in violence and even death. Local law enforcement claims extortion brings in an estimated annual U.S.$61 million to gangs and other criminal organizations.[32] During the first half of 2014, 700 people—the majority of whom were small business owners, agricultural workers, and transportation workers—were murdered after reportedly refusing to pay extortion fees to criminal gangs.[33] Impunity for these cases is rampant: according to a local NGO, only 3,464 arrests had been made out of 35,524 extortion cases between 2008 and 2014.[34]

Guns

The availability of firearms is a major factor contributing to violence in the country. According to police statistics, of the 4,778 homicides that occurred in 2015, 3,899—or 82 percent—were carried out with a firearm.[35] Lax U.S. gun controls, outdated firearm laws in Guatemala, failure to enforce existing laws, porous borders and corruption, especially within the security forces, make it relatively easy for criminals to access weapons. Guns flowing to drug trafficking groups, gangs, private security, and corrupt elements of security forces all circulate the black market, as do weapons remaining from the armed conflict and demobilization process.[36]

Guatemala's black market for arms is well-stocked by weapons that have made their way illicitly by plane, ship, or car from the United States and other countries, as well as by police and military officers who have sold or rented their guns to criminals, and private security firms whose weapons, acquired both legally and illegally, have been known to end up in criminal hands. While citizens may purchase weapons, it is difficult for authorities to monitor compliance with the gun code. The General Directorate of Arms and Ammunition Control (*Dirección General de Control de Armas y Municiones*, DIGECAM), military entity responsible for regulating guns in the country, has in its registry several individuals with over 50 arms, including one family whose arms cache is valued above its annual income.[37] Weak government controls exacerbate the problem—UNODC 2012 estimates suggest that there were around one million unregistered firearms in the country.[38]

According to the ATF about 35 percent of firearms in Guatemala that are found at crime scenes and then traced are U.S. sourced.[39] This is very much an estimate however, because many arms are never put into the tracing database. Arms, grenades, and other weapons left over from the armed conflict and the demobilization process also circulate the black market.[40]

AN INSTITUTIONAL VACUUM

A critical factor to understanding Guatemala's epidemic levels of violence and insecurity is the weakness and inaction of state institutions. The peace accords laid out an ambitious agenda to rebuild effective justice and security institutions that responded to the needs of the population.[41] In the aftermath of the conflict, important advances were achieved. A new criminal code was approved which established an accusatory or adversarial legal system. New institutions were also established including the Institute of Criminal Public Defense, the Attorney General's Office, and a new civilian police force to replace the old public security bodies that had been complicit in gross human rights violations.[42] These measures, however, proved insufficient. Poor political decisions and the improvisation that accompanied the creation of the new institutions made it impossible to root out old practices and carry out a profound transformation of the security and justice apparatus. The persistent meddling of powerful sectors, both licit and illicit, have perpetuated institutional weaknesses and a lack of judicial independence.

From the onset, the Attorney General's Office suffered from unqualified personnel, poor leadership, corruption, and lack of independence and impartiality. Without direction, the office grew into a costly, ineffective, and burdensome institution lacking a clear strategy and infiltrated by criminal groups.[43] During its first three years, the institution grew from 47 to 1,700 employees (including prosecutors and administrative staff) with little training and adequate controls.[44] Five years later, the situation remained unchanged. Of the 2,217 employees, 67 percent handled administrative tasks and only 33 percent were assigned to handle investigations.[45]

The lack of policies and guidelines for how cases should be investigated and prioritized greatly contributed to the agency's dismal performance. As the United Nations Development Programme (UNDP) described, "the investigations are routine, without a concrete line of investigation or the formulation of hypothesis as the starting point for the work. In many cases, the investigation is limited to performing three or four boilerplate investigative steps and continuing to shelve the case formally or informally."[46] The result of this ineffectiveness has been a staggering low conviction rate and widespread impunity, with an over 95 percent impunity rate for crimes against life.[47] Because many crimes are never reported, the percentage of all resolved crimes is actually even lower.

Powerful sectors, both licit and illicit, also jeopardize the independence of the judicial system through regular attempts to influence the appointment of high-level justice officials, including Supreme and Appellate Court judges, Constitutional Court magistrates, and the Attorney General. The selection processes for these posts are carried out by selection commissions: Supreme Court and Appellate Court magistrates are elected by Congress every five years from a list of candidates selected by the American Bar Association, law school deans, a university rector, and appellate judges; in the case of the attorney general, the president selects from a list of six candidates shortlisted by the head of the American Bar Association, the president of the Ethics Tribunal of the Association, and the head of the Supreme Court.[48]

The commissions were adopted in 2009 to increase transparency of the selection process and allow for civil society oversight. In practice, however, the process has been affected by conflicts of interest and overrun by outside interests seeking to control the membership of the commissions or negotiate quotas of final candidates. Moreover, candidates themselves have competed for political support in order to be elected or maintain their positions. Judges exchange power for access and influence over their decisions.[49]

The PNC suffered a similar fate as the criminal justice system. The desire to respond quickly to rising crime led to measures that further compromised the professionalization of the new force and consequently resulted in serious deficiencies in recruitment, training, leadership, and internal discipline. In a rush to fill the ranks of the new body, the government hastened the vetting and the training of the force, opting to staff the police command and force with officers from the former military police agencies. So extensive was the recycling of the old police into the new force that by 2002, six years after the signing of the accords, 11,000 of 19,000 rank and file officers in the new PNC were members of the old security force.[50] The same situation occurred with the police agencies in charge of investigations.[51] The consequences were foreseeable and long-lasting: corruption, inept police, serious human rights abuses, and a loss in public trust.[52]

Since the creation of the new force, efforts at long-term reform have repeatedly failed due to a lack of resources, poorly trained personnel, and instability at the top. The barrage of allegations of police abuse, corruption, and drug-related offenses have furthered damaged its reputation and fueled citizen mistrust. According to a 2011 poll, a mere 15 percent of the population feels some or much confidence in the police.[53] At the heart of the problem to professionalize the police has been the failure of a coherent strategy and real political commitment to a reform agenda.[54] Contrary to being a model of reform, "the police have become a symbol of instability, corruption, impunity, and ineptitude."[55]

A renewed effort to overhaul the police was undertaken through the creation of the Presidential Police Reform Commission (Comisión Presidencial para la Reforma Policial) in 2010. First led by renowned human rights activist Helen Mack and currently by former interim Interior Minister Adela de Torrebiarte, its efforts center on improving criminal investigations, crime prevention, training and human resources, internal controls, and police planning and management.[56] Among its accomplishments, the Commission set up two regional academies, a training school for high-ranking officers and a continuing education program, launched a new police education model, and strengthened the capacity of the internal affairs unit.

Several police stations have been remodeled and furnished with computers, internet access, and digital registries.[57] The Commission also established a fully equipped and trained pilot police precinct.

While positive, the measures have fallen short at being able to truly address the institutional deficiencies of the institution. Base salaries remain low and working conditions poor and unsanitary, with many precincts throughout the country deteriorating, cramped, and without showers or enough beds.[58] Still pending are reforms to the law on police to guarantee the implementation of a new policing model, including the strengthening of internal controls and establishment of a career track for officers.[59]

Finally, decades of neglect and poor management have fed overcrowding, poor conditions, criminality, and corruption within the penitentiary system. In 2014, Guatemala's prisons were at 280 percent over capacity, placing the country among the 10 most overcrowded in the world. According to authorities, 80 percent of extortions are perpetrated from behind prison walls.[60]

THE IRON FIST RESPONSE

Institutional deficiencies and the lack of political commitment have resulted in a failure to enact a long-term national strategy to combat crime and violence. Pressure to curb high crime rates have often made it harder for authorities to resist calls for tough crime-fighting operations that provide short-term gains without addressing long-term problems.

This heavy-handed approach has characterized the government's responses towards gangs. Although Guatemala did not formalize an anti-gang law, it did follow its neighbors in implementing its own *mano dura*, or iron fist strategy. Known as "Operation Broomsweep" (*Plan Escoba*), the plan involved roundups in marginalized neighborhoods and the mass arrest of suspected gang members. Suspected gang members were commonly arrested on charges of drug possession for consumption. From June 2003 to June 2004, some 10,500 individuals were arrested for possession in the department of Guatemala.[61] Instead of reducing crime and slowing the growth of gangs, the measures exacerbated prison overcrowding and transformed gangs into more sophisticated criminal organizations,[62] while generating a climate of tolerance toward abuses and extrajudicial executions by members of the police.[63]

The lackluster results of the get-tough approach, combined with strong criticisms from various national and international actors, led authorities to distance themselves from the iron fist rhetoric. Nevertheless, governments continued to rely on periodic police operations to round up youth suspected of gang membership. The hardline law enforcement measures have also come at odds with the limited violence prevention and community policing programs authorities have sought to implement.

Another common pattern has been the heavy use of the military to carry out internal security duties. It was under the administration of Otto Pérez Molina (2012–2015), the first career military officer to assume the presidency since the war, that the army experienced its largest expansion in policing matters. Within a week of taking office, Pérez Molina had deployed more than 700 soldiers to man 32 roadblocks across the country.[64] The measure was followed by the establishment of four military brigades to combat drug trafficking and organized crime, and the creation of special task forces made up of soldiers, police and prosecutors dedicated to tackling extortion, femicides, car-theft, kidnapping, and homicides in high crime areas.[65] The government deployed Reserve Army Battalions for Citizen Security (*Escuadrones Reservistas de Seguridad Ciudadana*) to support the police in different regions of the country. The battalions started as three groups of 503 soldiers at a cost of more than Q108 million (U.S.$13.8 million), according to a local newspaper.[66] By 2014, they had extended their presence to 12 of the country's 22 departments.[67]

Deploying the military to assist in public security functions is not unusual in Guatemala. The rise in violent crime and police inefficiency and corruption have been used to justify the use of military to support anti-crime operations by every administration in the post-conflict era beginning with President Alfonso Portillo (2000–2004).[68] Even President Álvaro Colom (2008–2012), of the center-left Nation Unity for Hope (UNE), embraced the involvement of the army in policing matters. In addition to increasing the size of the armed forces to over 20,000 troops, Colom oversaw the reopening of several military bases and outposts, declared two states of siege to confront drug cartels, and abolished the limit on military spending, which had been capped at 0.33 percent of GDP, as set out in the peace accords.[69]

While popular, the involvement of the military in public security has been counterproductive in terms of violence reduction and respect for human rights. According to a United Nations report, in two areas of the capital where joint task forces were deployed the number of attempted murders and homicides rose by five percent and nearly 39 percent, respectively. Prior to their deployment in 2012 murder attempts in those areas were on the decline.[70] Critics also note that the strategy further demoralizes and weakens the police by taking away needed resources and attention. Nor is it the case that the military is less prone to corruption, as evidenced by the number of cases of military involvement in organized crime and other illicit activities.

A TURNING POINT

November 2016 was the least violent month in Guatemala in the past ten years. The same year, Guatemala's national homicide rate hit its lowest point in the past 15 years, at nearly 27 murders per 100,000 people, with a decrease of 258 violent deaths—from 4,778 to 4,520—according to police statistics.[71]

The trend of declining murders began in 2010. The dramatic shift has been due in great part to the arrival of reform-minded leaders committed to building competent, transparent, and accountable institutions and transforming the way criminal investigations are conducted. Under the leadership of Attorney General Claudia Paz y Paz,[72] a new approach to prosecutorial decision making, oversight, and supervision was implemented and priority was given to reducing the dismal conviction rates for homicides and other violent crimes. The model introduced a new methodology for investigating crimes involving group investigations of criminal phenomena and establishing patterns and connections between cases as opposed to looking at cases as isolated incidents. The shift enabled prosecutors to better understand the structure and modus operandi of criminal networks.[73]

These changes were accompanied by measures to increase the use of criminal intelligence and scientific evidence, including DNA, ballistics data and wiretaps; better training and support for those investigating complex cases; the creation of a witness protection program; and the implementation of a results-based evaluation system.[74] To improve inter-institutional coordination, the police created, vetted, and trained specialized units to work jointly with teams of prosecutors, a move that generated greater trust and a sense of comradeship.[75] Twenty-four hour courts for certain crimes were introduced to reduce the number of suspects held for long periods in pretrial detention, as were courts for high risk crime, with headquarters in the capital but with jurisdiction throughout the country.

By the end of her term, the new strategy had achieved unparalleled results. After decades of inaction, many prominent local drug lords had been captured and the Zetas operating in the country were debilitated.[76] In the department of Guatemala, convictions for homicide cases improved from an estimated two percent to ten percent, and impunity dropped from 95 percent in 2009 to 72 percent in 2012.[77]

Paz y Paz's successor, current Attorney General Thelma Aldana, has continued the reform efforts and the relentless pursuit against organized crime and high level political corruption. In 2015, attempting a distinct approach to gang violence, the Attorney General's Office created a specialized division to combat extortions with separate units dedicated to the MS-13 and 18th Street gangs. A 24-hour hotline and free smartphone application were set up to report and help prevent extortions.[78] Working in collaboration with the police, judicial authorities have been able to successfully dismantle large extortion rings. In 2016, after several months of investigations, three major operations against extortion rackets were carried out, producing more than 200 arrests.[79] Aldana's efforts have also resulted in the unprecedented investigation of high level criminal networks, including the prosecution of former President Otto Pérez Molina, his vice president, and many members of his cabinet on corruption charges.[80] Under Aldana's leadership, the Guatemalan Democratic Criminal Policy (*Política Criminal Democrática del Estado de Guatemala*) was created in 2015 to promote a comprehensive model to address criminal phenomena based on four lines of action: prevention, investigation, sanction, and social reintegration.[81]

Positive steps have also taken place within the Ministry of the Interior, the institution in charge of security and the police, particularly since the appointment of former prosecutor Francisco Rivas as Interior Minister. Under Rivas' direction, a smarter preventive and deterrence security strategy has been adopted centered on concentrating a greater police presence during critical days and hours in the 30 most violent municipalities in the country.[82] The increase in the size of the police force, which reached 37,000 in late 2016, has contributed to the implementation of the strategy.[83] The largest decline in homicides in 2016 occurred in the departments in which a significant number of the selected municipalities are concentrated.[84]

Critical to this impressive shift has been the International Commission against Impunity in Guatemala (CICIG). Established in 2007 at the request of the Guatemalan government and with the support of the United Nations, the CICIG is an independent, international body tasked with supporting state institutions in investigating and dismantling criminal networks embedded in the state. The Commission has helped the Public Prosecutor's Office solve several high impact cases of corruption and organized crime and removed thousands of corrupt police officers and officials, while equipping the institutions with many of the modern crime-fighting techniques used today.[85] Its presence has helped promote important legislative and institutional reforms and made it possible for new, more independent and better-trained teams to assume greater direction of the criminal justice system.[86]

AN UPHILL BATTLE

The improvements in investigative capacities and downward trend in violence are undoubtedly encouraging and illustrative of what unequivocal commitment, effective leadership and proper training can achieve. Nonetheless, Guatemala still faces daunting challenges and resistance from certain sectors unwilling to relinquish power and influence.

Despite the overall drop in killings, violent crime remains high and certain regions have experienced increases in violence. Still, in 2016, 4,520 people were murdered in Guatemala, a figure that still places the country at a rate above the Latin America regional average and places it among the ten most violent countries in the world.[87] That same year, only five percent of homicide cases received by the Attorney General's Office resulted in guilty verdicts, and many violent crimes continue to go unreported.[88] The ongoing violence and lack of protection has driven many Guatemalans to abandon their homes or migrate, both within the country and beyond its borders. By some estimates, as of 2016, there were 257,000 persons internally displaced due to conflict and violence in the country.[89] Moreover, as impressive and necessary as the efforts to rein in the country's powerful criminal groups are, these measures alone have been insufficient. Without addressing the structural issues that have allowed criminality to thrive, the vacuum has been quickly filled by other groups or newer generation of criminals. In many regions of the country, large criminal networks continue to operate unimpeded.

To consolidate recent gains, the criminal justice system needs to expand its reach and services, including to rural areas where the state remains virtually non-existent. However, at present, financial constraints have translated into Guatemala having the lowest judges to population ratio in the region.[90] The poorly financed Attorney General's Office has offices in just 53 of the country's 338 municipalities, leaving many border regions and areas with high incidences of crime defenseless.[91] The lack of resources has also contributed to a huge backlog of cases. By some estimates, at current efficiency levels, it would take prosecutors until 2031 to clear the backlog of homicides reported from 2008 to 2015.[92]

Building credible, responsive, and more competent institutions would also require implementing much needed institutional reforms. In 2016, an effort was launched to define a set of legal and constitutional reforms intended to strengthen the independence and impartiality of judges and prosecutors and safeguard the judiciary from political and outside interference. Yet since the proposed package of reforms was submitted to Congress for consideration in October 2016, its approval has stalled due to strong opposition from factions of the private sector, political parties—including the party of President Jimmy Morales—and illicit interests that until now have benefitted from a fragile system.

At the same time, many of the prosecutors, officials and judges leading reform efforts have been the target of threats, lawsuits, and defamation campaigns to discredit their work. Threatened by the work of the Public Prosecutor's Office and CICIG, criminal groups and their allies have responded with death threats against Aldana and a coordinated smear campaign directed against Commissioner Velásquez.

While there is much that needs to be done to build competent institutions and expand impartial access to justice, prevention should not be forgotten. Guatemala is the biggest economy in Central America, yet it is also among the most unequal countries in Latin America. According to World Bank figures, the poverty rate rose from 51 in 2006 to 59.3 in 2014.[93] Poverty is most prevalent in the rural areas, where eight out of ten people are poor.[94] Malnutrition rates in children under five are the sixth highest worldwide.[95] It is estimated that 350,000 young Guatemalans are neither in school nor employed.[96]

Adequate resources are fundamental to addressing these challenges. This will require reforming the tax code, improving tax collection, and reducing tax evasion in order to raise the needed revenue. Yet these measures have repeatedly been opposed by political and economic elites despite the fact that, according to the World Bank, Guatemala continues to have the lowest percentage of social public spending in the world in relation to its economy.[97] Ultimately, Guatemala's ability to fully build on the advances it has achieved and bring about needed reforms will depend on the resolve and political commitment of its leaders. A telling sign of which direction the country might head will be the election of the next Attorney General in early 2018.

Chapter Eight

Violence in Mexico: An Examination of the Major Trends and Challenges

Roberto Zepeda and Jonathan D. Rosen

Mexico's decade-long war on drugs represents and effort to combat organized crime and drug trafficking in the country. The results, however, have been underwhelming when examining official figures on violence, crimes, and perceptions about security. A decade of drug trafficking, organized crime, and drug-related violence has resulted in approximately 200,000 homicides, 60 percent of which can be classified as narco-executions or linked to organized crime. Moreover, there have been almost 30,000 people who have disappeared as well as tens of thousands of bodies discovered in narco-graves around the country. The aforementioned statistics reveal that an estimated 150,000 people have been killed or disappeared as a result of drug trafficking and organized crime in Mexico. Although the majority of people—90 percent—killed have been classified as criminals, 10 percent of the victims have been innocent victims as well as police forces and members of the Army.[1]

This chapter examines the levels of violence in Mexico and contrast them within both the regional and global contexts. This work also identifies and assesses the factors contributing to the upsurge of violence in Mexico during the past decade, classifying them by political, institutional, and economic factors. In addition, this chapter examines the historical legacy that has determined the development of contemporary Mexico that has been characterized by a transition from an authoritarian to a democratic regime—this transition is still an ongoing process. Next, this work focuses on the war on drugs launched by Felipe Calderón and its consequences.[2] Despite the capture of the most wanted criminals and the seizures of illicit drugs, drug trafficking continues and drug cartels have flourished. Subsequently, this chapter analyzes President Enrique Peña Nieto's counternarcotic strategies and the fluctuations in violence during his administration. The initial years of the Peña Nieto administration experienced success as the government implemented a variety of reforms in various sectors (e.g., energy, educational, and fiscal).[3] Nevertheless, violence escalated again in 2015 and 2016, in such a way that the Peña Nieto *sexenio* will be even more violent than the one of its predecessor, Felipe Calderón. This chapter also analyzes the levels of violence in Mexico, considering the number of intentional homicides and narco-executions. The chapter concludes with an evaluation of the counternarcotics strategies of the current and previous administrations.

TRENDS IN GLOBAL VIOLENCE

According to the Global Study on Homicide 2013,[4] produced by the United Nations Office on Drugs and Crime (UNODC), the countries with the highest levels of violence in the world were found in Latin America. Honduras had the highest homicide rate worldwide. Moreover, Latin America became the region with the largest number of violent deaths perpetrated by firearms. Honduras ranked first in the list of the most violent countries, with a homicide rate of 90.4 per 100,000 inhabitants. Other countries in the region with high homicide rates per 100,000 inhabitants include: Venezuela (53.7), Belize (44.7), El Salvador (41.2), Colombia (30.8), Puerto Rico (26.5), Brazil (25.2), Dominican Republic (22.1), Mexico (21.5), and Panama (17.2) (see table 8.1).

As we can see in table 8.1, Mexico is far from being the most violent country in Latin America, as it occupies the ninth position in the region, with a homicide rate of 21.5 per 100,000 people. It is highly likely that the characteristics of the narco-executions in Mexico in recent years (i.e., decapitations, dismembered bodies, among other brutal forms of homicide) make violence more evident and notorious in Mexico than in other countries.

Not only was Latin America the most violent region in the world, but America ranked as the continent with the highest number of intentional homicides in the world. According to the UNODC, 2012 had around 437,000 intentional homicides committed in the world, out of which more than one third (36 percent) occurred in the Americas, followed by Africa and Asia, which registered 31 percent and 28 percent of the intentional homicides, respectively, in that year. Europe had only five percent of intentional homicides.[5]

El Salvador ranked as the most violent country in 2016, replacing Honduras. El Salvador registered a homicide rate of 103 per 100,000 inhabitants in 2015, which declined to 91 in 2016. In this year, according to data from the Igarapé Institute, 43 of the 50 most murderous cities in the world and eight of the top ten countries, were from countries in Latin America and the Caribbean. In the same way the capital city of El Salvador, San Salvador, was the city with the most murders.[6] San Pedro Sula, Honduras, which for years

Table 8.1. Homicide Rate per 100,000 Inhabitants, 2013

Ranking	*Country*	*Homicide Rate per 100,000 Population*
1	Honduras	90.4
2	Venezuela	53.7
3	Belize	44.7
4	El Salvador	41.2
5	Colombia	30.8
6	Puerto Rico	26.5
7	Brazil	25.2
8	Dominican Republic	22.1
9	Mexico	21.5
10	Panama	17.2
11	Ecuador	12.4
12	Bolivia	12.1
13	Nicaragua	11.3
14	Haiti	10.2
15	Paraguay	9.7
16	Peru	9.6
17	Costa Rica	8.5
18	Uruguay	7.9
19	Argentina	5.5
20	Cuba	4.2
21	Chile	3.1

Source: prepared by the authors with data from UNODC, 2013.

remained as the world's most dangerous city, ranked third in 2016. According to the report, "Conflicts between gangs, corruption and weak public institutions all contribute to the high levels of violence across the region."[7]

In the case of Mexico, the levels of violence climbed notably between 2007 and 2011. The homicide rate per 100,000 people spiked from eight in 2007 to a high of 24 in 2011; it declined to 16 in 2014, but then increased to 18 in 2016. Moreover, the total number of intentional homicides more than doubled between 2007 and 2011 from 10,253 to 22,852. Subsequently, the number of homicides decreased in 2012 to 21,736. While the Calderón administration witnessed violence across the country, it is important to note that the majority of violence was concentrated in the following states: Sinaloa, Chihuahua, Tamaulipas, Nuevo León, and Michoacán. Violence declined during the last year of the Calderón government. The downward trend in violence continued during the first half of the Peña Nieto administration. As mentioned above, the levels of violence in Mexico spiked in 2015 and 2016.

An examination of violence in the country also shows emerging trends at the regional level. Mexico is home to the second most violent city in the world, Acapulco, which is a popular tourist resort located in the southeastern state of Guerrero. This city registered a homicide rate of 108 per 100,000 people in 2016, making it the second most violent city in the world after San Salvador.[8] This could also be explained by the fact that Guerrero has become one of the most important centers of heroin production that supplies the United States. At the same time, local criminal groups, such as *Los Rojos* and *Guerreros Unidos*, are fighting for control of the drug trafficking routes and *plazas*. In addition, five drug cartels operate in the state: El Cártel del Pacífico, La Familia Michoacana, el Cártel de los Hermanos Beltrán Leyva, Los Caballeros Templarios, and the Cártel Jalisco Nueva Generación (CJNG), which has emerged on the scene as a powerful organization.[9] In sum, the case of Guerrero is one example of the high levels of violence because of fighting among organized crime groups[10] for control of drug production and trafficking routes.

VIOLENCE IN MEXICO: EXPLANATORY FACTORS

When analyzing the characteristics and factors accounting for the high levels of violence in Mexico over the last decade, it is likely that the Peña Nieto administration will finish with higher levels of violence than the Calderón government. Various factors explain the high levels of drug trafficking, organized crime, and drug-related violence in Mexico. First, one cannot understand the high levels of drug-related violence without understanding the imperfect or "failed" democracy that characterizes the country. In addition to various political and institutional variables (e.g., high levels of corruption and lack of transparency) there are also socioeconomic factors that have contributed to drug trafficking, organized crime, and violence. Economic and labor factors, including poor economic performance and scarce labor opportunities, are also important to examine. Moreover, organized crime groups have taken advantage of the "dark side" of globalization and neoliberal policies, which have created more interconnectedness in the world today.

POLITICAL AND INSTITUTIONAL FACTORS

To understand violence in Mexico, it is important to examine some of the underlying structural issues that have permitted violence, high levels of corruption,[11] and impunity. Mexico had 71 years of single-party authoritarian rule by the Institutional Revolutionary Party (*Partido Revolucionario Institucional*—PRI).[12] While the PRI began to lose political control at the state level in the 1980s, this party controlled the federal government until 2000, when for the first time in history, the National Action Party (*Partido Acción Nacional*—PAN) assumed power with the election of Vicente Fox Quesada to the presidency. Despite the transition to democracy, Mexico remains plagued by high levels of corruption and impunity.[13] According to Transparency International's Corruption Perceptions Index (CPI), Mexico has become more corrupt over time. From 2000 to 2015, Mexico moved from the 57th to the 106th position on the corruption ranking, with one being the least corrupt country and 174 being the most corrupt country. The levels of corruption between 2000 and 2012 increased dramatically, which is paradoxical as this period marked the democratic transition in the country. According to the CPI, Mexico scored a 35 in 2014, with 0 being highly corrupt and 100 being very clean. Furthermore, Mexico ranked 103 out of 175 countries, with the higher the number the more corruption.[14]

One of the institutions that has experienced major challenges in terms of corruption has been the Mexican police.[15] The police, especially the local police, are perceived as one of the most corrupt institutions in the country. At the national level, the municipal preventative police forces accounted for nearly 40 percent of the police force, while the federal ministerial police, accounted for only 1.6 percent of the total police forces. Working as a police officer is very dangerous and many individuals have died while in the line of duty. Moreover, police are not well paid, which also makes them vulnerable to accepting bribes from organized crime groups.

A recent survey conducted by the Center of Social Studies and Public Opinion (*Centro de Estudios Sociales y de Opinion Publica*—CESOP) of the Chamber of Deputies of Mexico,[16] reveals that most people in Mexico think that the police forces are controlled by organized crime groups. For example, two thirds of the respondents believe that police are very or reasonably controlled by organized crime. The military are perceived to be more professional and less corrupt than the police forces. The marines and armed forces are the highest-rated public security institutions, while municipal police forces ranked the lowest.[17]

In addition to police corruption, Mexico has faced major challenges with high levels of impunity. For example, the impunity rate for homicides in Mexico is around 90 percent. In 2016, Mexico had an impunity rate of 99 percent.[18] The high levels of impunity in the country persist despite major reforms to the judicial system that began in 2008. According to a Washington Office on Latin America (WOLA) report, there remains much "to be done for Mexico to enjoy a system that holds perpetrators accountable for crimes while ensuring respect for human rights."[19] There are various challenges that must be addressed, such as the need to change entrenched practices, pass new laws, and train personnel. Reforming a judicial system is a decades-long process.

In sum, Mexico lacks an effective structure of transparency and accountability to prevent corruption in the official institutions. High levels of corruption and impunity can be explained in part by the weak institutions present in the country. Corruption weakens institutions, and, in turn, weak institutions permit corruption. The vicious circle of corruption is so rampant in Mexico that drug trafficking, organized crime groups, and even government officials are not charged for their corrupt acts. The result has been that criminals remain unprosecuted. For instance, Mexico has not been able to determine the whereabouts of 27,000 people who have disappeared in the country.[20] Increasing transparency, implementing the rule of law, and increasing access to information and oversight, especially in terms of security-related institutions, are fundamental as the country seeks to consolidate democracy and combat some of these underlying institutional challenges.

ECONOMIC AND LABOR FACTORS

Since the 1980s, Mexico has been part of the neoliberal global market. This economic model has had both positive and negative effects. The rapid interchange of information and the mobility of persons and resources facilitated by new communication technologies, transportation, and free trade policies has integrated the world economy. These conditions have also facilitated the international trade of goods and legal services. However, criminal organizations have also used such advances to increase their illicit operations. Thus, the openness of markets and borders have multiplied the opportunities to invest money stemming from organized crime in legal markets and businesses around the world.

Poor economic performance, poverty, and the disconnected youth problem have been underlying factors that have contributed to illicit activities as well as violence in Mexico. While neoliberal policies[21] have been implemented in Mexico since 1982, the results have been low economic growth and recurrent crises that have created a labor environment characterized by precarious jobs, informality, unemployment, and high levels of economic and social inequality. This economic and labor context has been used by drug cartels to mobilize the support of marginalized sectors of society, which are not only located in rural areas but also in urban centers. Drug traffickers recruit vulnerable individuals working in the informal economy and living in precarious conditions. Drug traffickers often provide people from marginalized communities with higher salaries than they can receive performing various other menial jobs.

Mexico has millions of youth who neither work nor study (*ni estudian, ni trabajan*), who are referred to as the ninis. The World Bank correlates the nini[22] problem with crime and violence in Latin America. For example, "in Colombia, Mexico, and Central America, where the share of ninis is above the regional average, the problem is compounded by the widespread presence of organized crime. In such environments, new evidence shows that the 'nini' problem is correlated with crime and violence, heightening risks for the youth and for society as a whole."[23] Regarding the case of Mexico, the ninis contributed to violence, particularly in the border states from 2008 to 2013.

FELIPE CALDERÓN'S DRUG WAR

President Felipe Calderón (2006–2012) assumed the presidency after a contested election against Andrés Manuel López Obrador of the Party of the Democratic Revolution (*Partido de la Revolución Democrática*—PRD). Thousands of protestors hit the streets to protest the massive levels of fraud that allegedly occurred during the elections. Given this context, Calderón, who assumed power as a relatively weak president, sought to increase his power and demonstrate his toughness by launching a war on drugs against the major drug cartels and organized crime groups operating in the country. As stated by Rubén Aguilar and Jorge Castañeda,[24] the main reason that Calderón declared the war on drugs was political to gain the legitimation, supposedly lost in the 2006 presidential elections, in the middle of the protests in the streets of Mexico City. Other scholars also observe that the war on drugs[25] was launched immediately after Calderón was sworn in and had the intention of drawing attention away from the highly controversial 2006 election.[26]

President Calderón sought to weaken the increasing power of the cartels in the country and elevated the threat of drug trafficking and organized crime groups to the top national security threat. The Calderón administration, however, did not launch the drug war without support from the United States. The George W. Bush administration (2001–2009) pledged to assist the Calderón administration in combating drug trafficking and organized crime in Mexico through the Mérida Initiative,[27] which began in earnest in 2008. The Mérida Initiative has four pillars: combat organized crime groups, strengthen the rule of law, create a twenty-first century border, and build resilient communities.[28] The Calderón administration, in partnership with Washington, focused on Pillar 1: combating organized crime.

President Calderón focused on capturing the leaders of the major cartels. His government sought to capture the major kingpins of the drug trafficking organizations.[29] The Calderón administration had various successes combating the drug kingpins. However, the killing of one major cartel does not mean that drug trafficking and organized crime will disappear. Instead, what occurred in Mexico—as well as other countries such as Colombia—is that drug trafficking organizations fragmented. In 2006, for example, Mexico had six major drug trafficking organizations. The number of cartels continued to proliferate. For example, eight cartels existed between 2007 and 2009. By 2010, the number of cartels increased to twelve.[30] In 2012, the Attorney General of Mexico, Jesus Murillo Karam, contended: "I would calculate between 60 and 80 [groups], including medium and small ones. They are in various areas of the country, we are identifying their exact geographic location."[31] Thus, the nature of organized crime in Mexico has evolved over time, demonstrating that the kingpin strategy has had some successes, but it has not eliminated drug trafficking and organized crime. Small drug trafficking organizations are often more difficult to combat as they are more agile than the large cartels.

UNDERSTANDING VIOLENCE DURING THE CALDERÓN ADMINISTRATION

Drug trafficking and violence increased during the Calderón administration.[32] First, organized crime groups battled among each other for control of territory and drug routes.[33] In turn, such activities resulted in increases in violence over time. Second, drug trafficking organizations fought with the government, who deployed the military to combat these criminal groups. President Calderón used the military instead of the police because he did not have high levels of confidence in the police forces, which remain laden with high levels of corruption. In addition, the Mexican military is better trained than the police forces. The deployment of the Mexican military to the streets required changes in the constitution as the military is supposed to defend against outside threats while the police maintain law and order.[34]

The militarization of the drug war led to high levels of violence in Mexico. Drug-related killings spiked over time: 2,120 in 2006 to 5,153 in 2008. In 2009, 6,587 drug-related killings occurred.[35] Violence in the drug war was concentrated in certain states. According to data from *Reforma*, Chihuahua accounted for 31 percent of the total drug-related killings in 2009. Other states also had high percentages of drug-related homicides: Sinaloa (12 percent); Guerrero (10 percent); and Durango (10 percent).[36]

According to various official sources, the number of narco-executions increased notably from 2007 to 2011, when the violence reached its peak.[37] In 2012, violence began a declining trend as the number of narco-executions related to organized crime reduced notably compared with the previous year (see table 8.2). Furthermore, between 2006 and 2012 approximately 26,000 people disappeared.[38] At least 10,000 individuals were murdered and buried in "narco-graves" over the same period.[39] Thus, considering the total number of narco-executions, as well as the number of individuals disappeared and those killed and buried in "narco-graves," it is likely that more than 100,000 murders took place during the Calderón government as a result of the war on drugs.

Table 8.2. Number of Homicides and Narco-executions in Mexico 2006–2012

	Narco-executions			*Homicides*	
	Reforma	*Milenio*	*Semanario Zeta*	*SNSP*	*INEGI*
2007	2,275	2,773	2,826	10,253	8,867
2008	5,207	5,661	6,837	13,155	14,006
2009	6,587	8,281	11,753	16,118	19,803
2010	11,583	12,658	19,546	20,680	25,757
2011	12,718	12,284	24,068	22,852	27,213
2012	8,926	11,412	18,161	21,736	26,037
Total	47,296	53,069	83,191	104,794	121,683

Sources: Reforma, Milenio, and Semanario Zeta databases; INEGI, 2013; SNSP, 2013.

INITIAL SUCCESSES OF THE PEÑA NIETO GOVERNMENT

In 2013, Mexico was labeled as an emerging global power. Jim O'Neill, the creator of the term BRICS, which refers to the rise of Brazil, Russia, India, China, and South Africa,[40] has discussed new economic powers on the scene: the MINTs—Mexico, Indonesia, Nigeria, and Turkey.[41] According to O'Neill, the countries of this group are characterized by large populations. Based on this projection, these countries will have a demographic advantage as a result of an expanding labor force. Recent data from CONAPO[42] and INEGI[43] reveal that around 29 percent of the population in Mexico is between 14 years old or younger. Sixty-five percent are between 15 and 64 years old and approximately six percent are aged 65 years or older. If Mexico can implement political reforms to overcome such internal problems as corruption, poor education, lack of transparency, and weak democracy, it could achieve the rates of economic growth experienced by China between 2003 and 2008. Furthermore, O'Neill recognizes the geographic location of Mexico as an advantage in terms of international trade because it is a neighbor of the United States, but also part of Latin America. Moreover, in economic terms, Mexico is a producer of raw materials.

In 2015, Mexico was the second largest economy in Latin America—behind Brazil—with a Gross Domestic Product (GDP) valued at U.S.$1.14 trillion.[44] At the same time, it was the fifteenth largest economy in the world. During the 2000 to 2010 period, Mexico experienced on average less than two percent economic growth. However, economic growth increased to approximately four percent per year between 2010 and 2014. Nevertheless, the levels of economic growth dropped to around two percent between 2014 and 2016.

Daron Acemoglu and James Robinson discuss development in Mexico. They compare two border cities, Nogales, Sonora in Mexico and Nogales, Arizona in the U.S. While these cities are close in proximity, differences between these cities can be explained by the nature and characteristics of their institutions. Such contrasts create different incentives for their citizens. In Mexico, political institutions permeated by corruption have hindered the creation of economic institutions conducive to prosperity.[45] Furthermore, global inequality is explained by how political and economic institutions interact with each other to create poverty or prosperity. The authors observe that economic success requires an organized economy that creates incentives and opportunities for people. In addition, it depends on the performance of the political system and the nature of political institutions. It is a political problem to create economic institutions that generate prosperity.[46]

In addition to underlying structural issues, violence has had a negative impact on the Mexican economy. According to the Institute for Economics and Peace, the economic impact of violence in the country is estimated to be nearly a fifth of Mexico's GDP. For instance, "in 2016, the economic impact of violence increased by 3 percent or 79 billion pesos, reaching a total of 3.07 trillion pesos or U.S.$180 billion. This is equivalent to 18 percent of the country's GDP and represents 25,130 pesos per person, equivalent to more than one month's salary for the average Mexican worker."[47]

THE PEÑA NIETO GOVERNMENT

Enrique Peña Nieto assumed the presidency in 2012. Kate Linthicum contends, "Although Peña Nieto won with just 38 percent of the votes in an election with two other major candidates, many Mexicans had high hopes for the young, charismatic and handsome politician whose telenovela star wife, Angelica Rivera, they had followed in the tabloids."[48] The new president distinguished himself from the previous government by focusing less on the discourse of the drug war and more on various reforms.[49] For example, Peña Nieto successfully passed educational and energy reforms, although they have been quite controversial in nature. In addition, the new president spent less effort marketing the victories of the war on drugs, which is a stark contrast from the Calderón government, who invested tremendous resources marketing to the public the successes of the drug war.[50] For instance, Mexican television stations would routinely show the capture of major kingpins who were paraded in front of the public. In sum, while the discourse regarding drug strategies might be different, the drug policies have remained quite similar.

It is very likely that the Peña Nieto *sexenio* will be marked by a higher number of homicides than the one of his predecessor, Felipe Calderón. According to data provided by INEGI, 120,341 homicides occurred between 2006 and 2012. However, there have been 90,573 homicides from December 2013 to February 2016. Thus, it is possible that there are more than 130,000 by the end of Peña Nieto's government (see table 8.3).[51] It is argued that "[t]he surge in violence around Mexico reflects an increasingly volatile criminal landscape and the limitations of North America's counternarcotics strategy."[52] Moreover, such high levels of violence have contributed to low levels of approval ratings of Peña Nieto. Kirk Semple contends, "the Mexican government's fight against organized crime—backed by hundreds of millions of dollars in American aid—has been to aim at the kingpins, on the theory that cutting off the head will wither the body." However, this has contributed to the fragmentation of "monolithic, hierarchical criminal enterprises into an array of groups that are more violent and uncontrollable."[53]

Violence has increased in Sinaloa due to the capture and extradition of Joaquín "El Chapo" Guzmán, the former leader of the Sinaloa cartel. Between January and February 2017 there have been 235 murders, according to official figures, which is 30 percent higher compared to the same period last year. The extradition of El Chapo Guzmán "has sparked a power struggle in the cartel he founded." For Alejandro Sicairos, a security analyst, the new state governor Quirino Ordaz Coppel, who assumed office in January, has been unable to contain the violence. In addition, local police have failed to impose order, and, therefore, the army and navy have been utilized. However, they have had little impact thus far.[54]

Furthermore, criminal activities linked to drug trafficking organizations, such as kidnapping and extortion, increased during the first year of the Peña Nieto *sexenio* by 33 percent and 10 percent, respectively. Nevertheless, these crimes have declined between 2013 and 2016. The decline is more evident in the case of extortions, while kidnappings have barely decreased. If we com-

Table 8.3. Number of Homicides, Kidnapping and Extortion in Mexico, 1997–2016.

	Homicides	*Kidnappings*	*Extortions*
1997	16,866	1,047	876
1998	14,216	734	1,020
1999	14,619	590	3,391
2000	13,849	591	1,168
2001	13,855	505	1,337
2002	13,148	435	1,636
2003	12,676	413	1,910
2004	11,658	323	2,416
2005	11,246	278	2,979
2006	11,806	733	3,157
2007	10,253	438	3,123
2008	13,155	907	4,869
2009	16,118	1,162	6,332
2010	20,680	1,222	6,113
2011	22,852	1,432	4,594
2012	21,736	1,418	7,284
2013	18,332	1,683	8,196
2014	15,653	1,395	5,773
2015	17,028	1,054	5,046
2016	20,789	1,128	5,239

Prepared by the authors with data from the SNSP, 2017.

pare the levels of such crimes with years, it is evident that they increased notably after 2007, when the war on drugs began, and from then on have remained significantly higher than in the first half of the 2000s (see figure 8.1). In other words, the war on drugs has triggered not only narco-executions but also other criminal activities, which are carried out by drug trafficking organizations such as Los Zetas and La Familia Michoacana.

President Peña Nieto has been hampered by various blunders, one of which was the escape of Joaquín "El Chapo" Guzmán, the notorious leader of the Sinaloa cartel. While the Mexican government captured Guzmán in January 2016,[55] the previous escape constituted an international embarrassment for the Peña Nieto government who refused to extradite Guzmán to the U.S. In addition to the escape of Guzmán, the Peña Nieto administration faced an international scandal with the killing of 43 students from a local teachers college in Ayotzinapa, Guerrero, who were murdered in the city of Iguala. Hannah Stone argues, "A crime of this scale—the abduction and killing of 43 people—could not be carried out in secret. It required a culture of fear and complicity to prevent other authorities in Iguala from intervening, and keep the residents silent."[56] The police allegedly handed over the students to

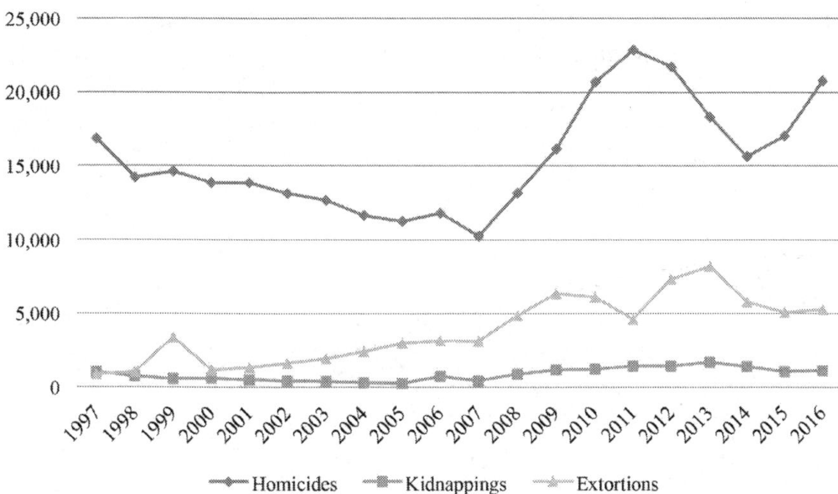

Figure 8.1. Homicides, Kidnappings and extortions en Mexico, 1997–2016
Created by the authors with data from the SNSP, 2017.

a local gang in Guerrero, Guerreros Unidos, who helped dispose the bodies. Investigations demonstrate that the government played an important role in the cover-up of such horrific events. WOLA's Maureen Meyer asserts that "[t]his is one of the worst cases of human rights violations seen in Mexico's recent history. Two years later, the Mexican government has done very little to help these wounds heal. It is shocking that, despite dedicating significant resources, the Mexican government has not found the students, and that its own officials have obstructed the investigation."[57] In sum, the events that occurred in Guerrero have harmed Mexico's international reputation—or soft power[58]—and have called into question the ability of the Peña Nieto government to maintain law and order in the country.

Human rights violations have continued to plague the Peña Nieto government. In September 2016, international human rights officers demanded that the Mexican government examine human rights abuses that occurred in 2006 in San Salvador Atenco, which is a town located in the State of Mexico, where President Peña Nieto served as governor during this period. The case involves 11 women who were sexually assaulted by police during demonstrations.[59] Regarding the event, Maria Patricia Romero Hernández, a victim, contends: "I have not overcome it, not even a little. It is something that haunts me and you don't survive. It stays with you. I could never tell my son and my father of the fact I was raped by not one but several policemen, because they would have gone mad."[60] Another victim, Georgina Edith Rosales Gutiérrez, stated: "The fact we are going to the Inter-American Court is a way of accepting that we were really affected. It was not an accident but rather a state practice towards social movements, and the people in general, and it is a step forward into putting an end to all of this."[61] In sum, the Mexican government has been responsible for systematic human rights abuses that have haunted the lives of many citizens and have harmed the reputation of the current president.

THE SUBNATIONAL PROBLEM

Combating drug trafficking and organized crime in Mexico has resulted in challenges as a result of differences between state governments and the federal government. State governments do not always cooperate with the federal government, particularly when governors are from a different political party than the party in power at the federal level. Thus, there has not been effective collaboration between the different levels of government because of political interests and rivalry. However, it is important that a robust institutional framework of coordination for security-related issues between the different levels of government is created. This political framework must go beyond political interest and should prioritize national and public security.

In addition, another problem that has been present in Mexico is the various legal issues that hinder counternarcotics strategies. For instance, municipal police are not involved directly in the struggle against drug trafficking organizations because it is not under their legal jurisdiction. Drug trafficking and organized crime are federal crimes and therefore are under the jurisdictions of federal institutions such as the Attorney General's Office (*Procuraduría General de la República*) and the federal police. Combating organized crime and the trafficking of illicit drugs in Mexico has been an assignment of the federal police and security related agencies. Nevertheless, the participation of the armed forces (i.e., the army and navy) has been a decision historically promoted by the federal government as a provisional measure since police forces do not have the professional capacity to assume these responsibilities.

Several states have implemented strategies to reduce violence linked to organized crime. For example, the government of Nuevo León—and its capital city Monterrey—promoted a strategy in coordination with businessmen associations and other social organizations to prevent and reduce the levels of violence and other crimes committed by organized crime groups. The number of homicides in this state decreased in recent years due to the participation of non-governmental actors. In contrast, Guerrero, which lacks strong business groups and is one of the poorest states in the country, has not been able to design a strategy to reduce criminal violence in recent years. Thus, subnational governments must be given more legal capacities and attributions as well as more resources to have more professional police bodies. Mexico is a centralized country and financial resources are mostly managed by the federal government. This complicates the flow of resources for security-related issues from federal to subnational governments.

Furthermore, organized crime groups are infiltrating government structures, especially in local governments. For example, high level officials, including governors, from various states like Michoacán,[62] Nayarit, Tamaulipas, and Quintana Roo have been involved in recent years in cases of corruption and protection related to drug cartels. The complex relationship between states and organized crime groups presents major challenges when attempting to implement strategies to combat drug trafficking and organized crime. In the last decade (2007–2017), at least 17 Mexican governors have either been under investigation, captured, or are fugitives of a diverse array of crimes and felonies.[63]

CONCLUSION

Violence and bloodshed have ravaged Mexico during the Calderón and Peña Nieto administrations. While violence initially decreased during the Peña Nieto government, violence has increased over time. Peña Nieto has been plagued by various scandals and is quite unpopular in Mexico.[64] His administration has not been able to combat the massive levels of drug-related violence. In addition, human rights abuses remain rampant. Drug trafficking, organized crime, and violence will continue if the Mexican government does not reform the institutions and combat the high levels of corruption and impunity. Despite the judicial reforms that occurred in 2008[65] and various other reforms, the impunity rate remains at 99 percent. More needs to be done to increase the levels of transparency in the government and combat the high levels of corruption. Mexico also needs fundamental reforms in the penitentiary system, where many of the leading drug traffickers operate with high levels of impunity as demonstrated by the escape of Joaquín “El Chapo” Guzmán. Prisons serve as schools of crime and are in dire need of reform.[66] In sum, reforms to institutions cannot only take place at one level, but instead must occur at all three branches of government: the executive, legislative, and judiciary.

In addition, the government faces many challenges in terms of why individuals participate in drug trafficking and organized crime. The drop in the price of oil has had a significant economic impact on Mexico as the country is a major oil producer and much of the annual budget is from oil profits. These economic challenges will only exacerbate the socioeconomic situation in Mexico. More than half of the country works in the informal sector, and this number could increase if there are not sufficient jobs.[67] In addition to high levels of unemployment and lack of jobs, the government must seek to address the lost generation problem in Mexico.[68] There are 7.5 million youth in Mexico who are known as *ninis* because they neither work nor study (*ni estudian, ni trabajan*).[69] This is extremely problematic because these individuals are vulnerable to being recruited by organized crime groups. People without the proper education and job skills to compete in the formal economy, which is highly competitive, could also be attracted to organized crime and the prospects of earning money quickly.

Violence in Mexico will continue as long as the Mexican government does not address the various structural problems mentioned above. Moreover, *mano dura*[70] strategies will only result in higher levels of violence as has been seen during the previous administration. Strategies seeking to incarcerate delinquents—whether minor level drug traffickers or kingpins—will only increase the number of people in the prisons system. The hardline policies also will lead to continued—if not increases in—violence on the streets. Drug trafficking and organized crime groups will fight between each other for control of territory and markets. In addition, criminal organizations will battle government-led campaigns, which will result in spikes in violence, as clearly seen during the Calderón government.

Mano dura strategies do not address the demand for drugs. Drug traffickers and organized crime groups will continue to kidnap, extort, and participate in other violent acts to protect their businesses and trafficking of illicit goods as long as drug trafficking remains profitable. While the legalization of drugs is not a panacea to organized crime, as criminal groups participate in a plethora of illicit activities, debates have occurred among policymakers and academics about alternative approaches to the drug war.[71] The U.S. remains the leading drug consumer in the world, yet the demand for hard drugs has decreased in recent years. This, however, does not mean that the U.S. government could not do more to combat the demand and focus less on the supply of drugs. In 2016, for example, heroin epidemics have plagued various parts of the country. Kevin Johnson contends, "Overdose deaths attributed to heroin, fentanyl (a powerful synthetic opiate at least 30 times stronger than heroin) and other opiate abuse has spiked from 14 in 2013 to 69 last year, according to city records. The grim numbers do not account for the hundreds of other non-fatal overdose calls that have flooded local public safety agencies, stressing the city's capacity to respond."[72] Thus, the demand issue will remain a major public health problem in the U.S.

Chapter Nine

Violence in Haiti: History, Reforms, and Current Trends

Christa L. Remington

The nation of Haiti lies on the island of Hispaniola in the heart of the Caribbean. Plagued by natural disasters, extreme poverty, political instability, and social unrest, Haiti is an unpredictable and perpetually fragile state. Over the decades, violence in Haiti has taken many forms from politically motivated coups to violent street crimes to government sanctioned torture and mob justice. This chapter will explore the nature of violence in Haiti and the historical, political, and social forces which have shaped it. It will examine general trends in violence, including the resurgence of violent crime after the 2010 earthquake and the current protests and riots following the 2015–2016 elections. Additionally, it will discuss the security measures that have been proposed or enacted by the Haitian government and other international actors, and examine the potential challenges to these security measures.

HAITI IN CONTEXT

Approximately 700 miles from the Florida coast and 600 miles from Venezuela, Haiti's strategic location has long made it a valuable prize. From the days of Christopher Columbus until now, Haiti has served as a point of transit and as a critical location in global trade.[1] Haiti, along with Cuba, is the strategic guardian of the Windward Passage, a direct route to the Panama Canal. Despite its valuable geography, Haiti is a nation seemingly in perpetual turmoil. Home to more than 10 million people, it is a place of rich culture and national pride mixed with a persistent atmosphere of instability resulting from decades of poverty, corruption, national disasters, and political volatility and unrest.

Formally a wealthy French colony, Haiti was known as the "Pearl of the Caribbean," producing half of the world's coffee and over 40 percent of all sugar consumed in Europe.[2] Its natural beauty, climate, and prime geographical location made it a highly desirable territory to European powers and a hotly contended economic prize. Once the Americas' most profitable colony, Haiti was previously called St. Domingue and, during the colonial era, was known for its particularly brutal form of slavery, which culminated in a bloody slave rebellion and the formation of the world's first black republic.[3] Haitians won independence from France and freedom from slavery in 1804, but peace in the island nation was short-lived. From the 1806 assassination of revolutionary leader Jean-Jacques Dessalines, who declared himself emperor-for-life, to the ruthless secret police of dictator Francois Duvalier (1957–1971), division, dictatorships, assassinations, and violence have characterized Haitian history.[4]

Additionally, 21 years after Haitian independence, France demanded the payment of 150 million francs (U.S.$20 billion) to compensate for the loss of valuable plantations, export revenue, and slaves in exchange for recognition of the nation's sovereignty. This debt crippled the economy and left it vulnerable to foreign control, including a U.S. occupation which lasted from 1915–1934.[5] Throughout the twentieth century, Haiti has continued to be subject to a series of military takeovers, coups, and dictators which has strained the practice of democracy and resulted in a weak government with a limited capacity to respond to disasters, corruption, and violence.

Haiti is unique in the Caribbean for many reasons. It is the poorest country in the Western Hemisphere and one of the 20 most impoverished nations on the planet. According to the World Bank, 80 percent of Haiti's population lives below the poverty line.[6] Low rates of literacy and employment, and high rates of malnutrition and disease have combined with other forces to make Haiti a perpetually fragile state. With the Western Hemisphere's lowest life expectancy, highest rates of infant mortality, and with tragic rates of childhood death, stunted growth, and starvation, Haiti has proven particularly susceptible to both external and internal violence. Repeated humanitarian disasters have contributed to a relatively low rate of tourism and a lack of foreign investment when compared with other Caribbean countries.[7] The 2010 earthquake, which claimed over 200,000 lives and 2016's Hurricane Matthew, stalled nascent economic progress and hindered internal security efforts aimed at reducing violence and organized crime.

VIOLENCE

Violence in Haiti primarily stems from three sources—the government (i.e., Haitian National Police), organized crime units such as gangs and armed mili-

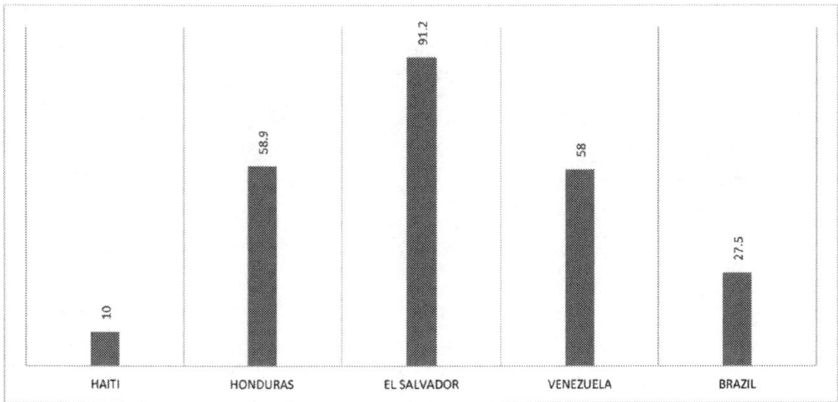

Figure 9.1. Homicide Rate per 100,000 (2016)
Created by the author with data from Homicide Monitor, Igarapé Institute.

tia groups, and individuals. While official rates of violent crime in Haiti have traditionally been lower when compared to other nations in the region, the recent advent of social media and the rise of affordable mobile technologies in Haiti have led to public exposure of incidents of crime, police brutality, and domestic violence that were formally only conjecture or rumor.

Additionally, crime statistics in Haiti are woefully underreported by both the Haitian National Police (HNP) and by victims and observers of violent crime.[8] Therefore, reports indicating that Haiti is statistically safer than other countries in the Caribbean are inaccurate. The U.S. Overseas Security Advisory Council (OSAC) ranks Haiti as a critical threat location for crime. The 2017 Crime & Safety report states that crime statistics, which show Haiti to be safer than surrounding countries, are inaccurate due to underreporting. In addition, Haiti's far lower rates of tourism, when compared to other Caribbean nations, lead to less tourism-related crimes, such as pick-pocketing and muggings (see figure 9.1). Despite this, violent crime, including kidnapping, armed robbery, carjacking, rape, and domestic violence remain an enormous challenge.[9]

Governmental Violence

The current state of violence in Haiti is inextricably tied to its unstable and violent history and the government's complicity, both tacit and explicit, in violent oppression and organized crime. From 1964 to 1986, dictator François "Papa Doc" Duvalier and his son Jean-Claude "Baby Doc" used brutal violence and intimidation to maintain control over the country. During the Duvalier era, the *tontons macoutes*, the Duvalier's personal militia, terrorized dissidents, squashed uprisings, and executed an estimated 30,000 to 60,000 civilians. In Fort Dimanche, a prison known as "the Auschwitz of Haiti," thousands of political prisoners were tortured, electrocuted, maimed, and beaten.[10]

In 1986, with the help of foreign powers, Baby Doc was exiled and a series of internationally led reforms attempted to stabilize the country and reestablish the democratic process.[11] In 1995, the Haitian army was disbanded and the government established the HNP. The HNP became riddled with corruption as Jean Bertrand Aristide, the nation's first democratically elected president, filled top positions with political allies.[12] In 2004, after an American-sanctioned coup which forced the resignation of president Aristide, the United Nations Stabilization Mission in Haiti (MINUSTAH) was tasked with reestablishing stability and training the HNP.[13]

Despite this foreign assistance, the HNP's own role in Haiti's violent and turbulent history has been a thorny one and the police force has been continually plagued by allegations of turning a blind eye to organized crime, facilitating drug trafficking, and carrying out violence on behalf of those willing to pay for it.[14] In 2004, the World Bank's Country Policy and Institutional Assessment Program ranked Haiti in the bottom one percent of all countries for corruption, while Transparency International consistently ranks Haiti among the most corrupt nations in the world (see figure 9.2).[15] Despite occasional seasons of perceived stability, the relationship between the Haitian National Police and the nation at large remains characterized by fear and mistrust which are undergirded by the police force's perpetual lack of capacity, training, and infrastructure.

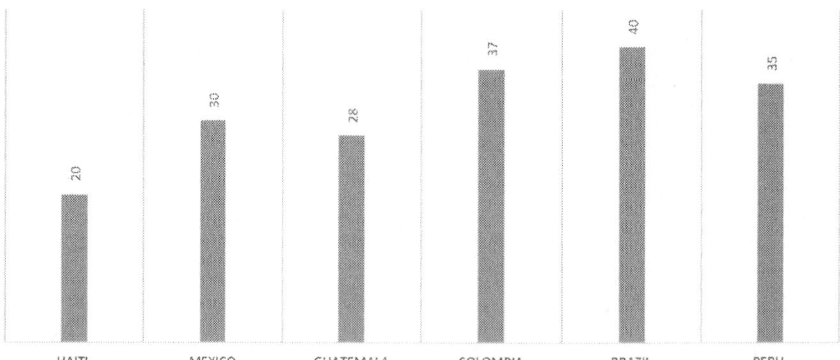

Figure 9.2. Corruption Perceptions Index Score (2016). Note: Zero is highly corrupt and 100 is very clean.

Created by the author with data from Transparency International's Corruption Perceptions Index.

The persistent perception of corruption has led to a volatile relationship between the HNP and the greater Haitian population. According to OSAC, Haitian police are generally perceived as apathetic and incompetent and both unwilling and unable to respond to crime.[16] As a result, violent crimes such as rape, armed burglary and assault, often remain unreported.[17] This lack of reporting, when combined with other social, cultural, and political factors such as the pervasive stigma against rape victims and fear of a corrupt judiciary, make accurate statistics on violence hard to collect. What is certain is that there is a generalized lack of trust between the HNP and the populace, with over 50 percent of Haitians reporting that they would not report a burglary to the police.[18] According to OSAC, this lack of confidence is echoed among criminals, reporting: "Neither violent or passive criminal seems overly concerned with police response, as they know none will be dispatched quickly."[19]

In addition to accusations of complicity in and apathy toward violent crime, the relationship between the HNP and the Haitian population is further complicated by persistent accusations of police brutality that range from allegations of abuse of prisoners to homicide. According to Human Rights Watch, "HNP officers reportedly use excessive and indiscriminate force, commit torture, make arbitrary arrests, and are involved in criminal activity, including kidnappings."[20] While much remains unproven, The National Human Rights Defense Network, Haiti's leading human rights group, released a report detailing an upsurge in police brutality and violence toward civilians.[21] Additionally, the rapid increase in national access to the internet through smart phone proliferation has led, nationwide, to numerous instances of exposure of police brutality.

Organized Crime Units

In the mid-1980s, Haiti became a key player in international drug trafficking because of its strategic position between the United States and South America. The more than 1,100 miles of unmonitored coastline and the government's complicity in the trade presented additional challenges to combatting it.[22] In 2006, eight percent of the total cocaine entering the United States passed through Hispaniola.[23] Organized crime and drug trafficking thrived unchecked under a weak and disjointed administration and an underdeveloped and overstretched national police force. As the drug trade flourished, so did drug-related violence, such as kidnapping, gang wars, and executions. Violent kidnappings reached their peak in the early 2000s when as many as 12 kidnappings took place a day in Port-au-Prince alone.[24]

Although there has been a decline in gang activity since MINUSTAH's presence, this type of organized crime and the resulting violence has long played an important role in Haitian politics and society.[25] During the Aristide era, gangs received firearms and weapons in order to intimidate dissenters and to coerce individuals to vote for a particular candidate.[26] Many neighborhood gangs, although small and disorganized, acted as a source of protection for their neighborhood in place of the failing HNP.[27] Wars between rival gangs were common and casualties frequent and numerous.

By the early 2000s, gang violence had become so prolific that certain neighborhoods, such as Cité Soleil, were off limits to even the HNP and to MINUSTAH.[28] It was not until 2006, under the administration of President René Préval, when HNP anti-gang units in collaboration with MINUSTAH began infiltrating the most turbulent areas in an effort to stem the violence.[29] After the arrests of many prominent organized crime leaders, including those who had fled to the United States, gang activity began to lessen and kidnapping, drug trafficking, and rates of violent crime dropped in Cité Soleil.[30]

Although less visible than in past decades, Haitian gangs remain an influential tool to obtain or protect political power. Often hired by Haitian politicians, these armed gangs intimidate and threaten voters, and blockade, vandalize, or even attack polling stations. Prior to the Presidential election in 2015, 12 individuals were killed in one weekend as rival gangs clashed over who would control voting stations.[31]

General Violence

In addition to organized crime and government related violence, Haiti also struggles with general violence. This includes individual violent crime, domestic violence, violence related to public protests, and issues of lynching and mob justice. As of November 2017, violence in Haiti continues to be persistent and complex. Violent protests, known in Haiti as *manifestations*, remain a primary means by which groups and individuals seek to express displeasure or effect change. Currently, violent protests occur at national, local, and regional levels and against everything from the hiring decisions of small NGOs to the actions of the nation's president. Even as this chapter is being written, violent protests are taking place in Haiti's Ouest department over the tuition costs of public school, an NGO's refusal to hire only local workers, and another NGO's educational program, while anger over President Jovenel Moise's 2017 proposed tax increases has led to nationwide protests, resulting in shootings, the burning of vehicles, destruction of businesses, and the threat of physical harm to any dissenter.[32]

While not every protest in Haiti is violent, violence is more common than not and can be expressed in everything from random gunshots and fiery blockades to looting, window smashing, and mob attacks. Protests are so unpredictable that the U.S. Embassy in Port-au-Prince frequently issues warnings reminding citizens of the volatility and danger surrounding protests in Haiti. One recent warning of a road block and protest in Port-au-Prince explained:

> U.S. citizens are reminded to always use caution when traveling, and to avoid roadblocks and demonstrations. Please keep in mind that demonstrations, even peaceful ones, can escalate quickly and even turn violent. The Embassy urges all U.S. citizens to remain vigilant, be aware of their surroundings, and avoid large crowds as much as possible. Should you find yourself among or near protesters, depart the area immediately.[33]

Likewise, the U.S. State Department has issued and reissued a travel warning for Haiti, encouraging travelers to carefully consider any trip to the island and to remember that "[p]rotests, including tire burning and road blockages, are frequent and often spontaneous." Visitors should "[a]void all demonstrations" and remember that "The Haitian National Police's ability to assist U.S. citizens during disturbances is limited."[34]

During much of 2015 and 2016 and part of 2017, the historic city of Arcahaie endured nearly constant protests. These manifestations were peppered with significant violence, leading to multiple deaths as protestors denounced the government's intention to separate the seaside resort city of Montrouis from its historic commune, severely impacting the commune's tax base and budget.[35] However, violent protests in Haiti are not always what they appear to be and are, even today, part of the complex relationship between Haiti's wealthy elite and impoverished general population and the bureaucratic systems and national history they both share.

Since the days of Baby Doc Duvalier, many of Haiti's wealthy and educated have frequently encouraged violent protests for their particular factions, distributed weapons, provided "stipends" to those willing to "manifest" and fomented rumors among those who are not literate and live in the greatest poverty, such as Cite Soleil, the nation's most famous slum. Violence and mob force are frequently hinted at or even threatened outright by prominent national figures. This has been seen most recently in the 2017 outrage over proposed hikes in fees and taxes. The pushback, led primarily by former senator Jean Charles Moise, whose commanding role in violent protests has been described as "military-style," has been intense and marked by veiled threats of violence on a larger scale.[36] Many of Jean Charles Moise's followers have threatened "a new day of Dessalines," warning the current president, Jovenal Moise, that "the revolution has just started."[37] The political party Jean Charles Moise founded, *Pitit Dessalines*, takes its name from the Haitian founding father Jean-Jacques Dessalines, famous for his "whatever it takes philosophy" during the Haitian revolution, the 1804 massacre of the nation's remaining white population, and his subsequent self-declaration of his own autocratic rule.

Whether or not such threats result in revolutionary-level violence remains to be seen, but protests have already led to the destruction of businesses and cars and violence against the Haitian National Police. Fears over what *may* come have prompted a strong response from both the HNP and the current presidential administration and concerns over violence toward HNP officers is not unfounded. In October 2017 alone, six HNP officers were murdered in Haiti, including a policewoman attacked by a motorcycle gang.[38]

In addition to unpredictable violent protests, Haiti is currently facing a new surge in violent individual crime, such as robbery, kidnapping, and murder. According to OSAC, current trends suggest that violent criminals are "innovating," transitioning from traditional burglary and assault to violent and strategically planned home invasions.[39] During spring and early summer of 2017, concerns over an increase in violent homicide plagued Port-au-Prince, with dozens of violent deaths occurring in the city between April and June.[40]

Moreover, violence in Haiti often takes a more complex form. The nation's lack of capacity and infrastructure, and the inability of the HNP to adequately respond to crime, threat, and accusation has led to a both common and nationally pervasive problem with vigilantism, lynching, and mob justice. From allegations of thievery to claims of child abuse or witchcraft, Haitians frequently take justice "into their own hands," executing perceived criminals through stoning, machete attacks, decapitation, or even mob beating. Though illegal and punishable by life in prison, lynching and mob justice remain a common recourse for Haitians who suspect or observe a wrong, but feel that there is no chance of help from the police or judiciary. According to the United Nations, vigilante justice is the source of 11 percent of the nation's killings.[41] The United Nations Human Rights Office of the High Commissioner explains, "The phenomenon of lynching is often seen as resulting from the failures of the justice system. The lack of access to justice and the population's mistrust in the judiciary leads to a sense of impunity. For the Executive Secretary of the Platform of Haitian Human Rights Organizations (POHDH), Antonal Mortimé, it is that mistrust which in turn fosters 'popular acts of vengeance.'"[42]

Public support for vigilantism remains high, and the Haitian government's failure to condemn and prosecute the practice has kept it entrenched in Haitian culture.[43] Out of more than 400 reported cases of vigilante killing only one has ever reached conviction and the majority have never reached even a semblance of prosecution.[44] Such high levels of impunity amounts to tacit approval of vigilante violence, despite the fact that it is considered a violation of basic human rights and is rife with injustice itself. While most lynching victims are men accused of stealing, at least 25 percent of female victims receive retribution for such suspect reasons as casting spells and practicing witchcraft.[45]

2010 Earthquake

No conversation on violence in Haiti would be complete without a discussion of the potent impact of the 2010 Haitian earthquake on national life and socio-political trajectory. On January 12, 2010, a 7.0 magnitude earthquake crippled Haiti's nascent infrastructure and devastated the national police force, causing enormous nationwide setbacks in terms of security. At least 400 HNP officers were killed or wounded during the quake, and the already fragile state of national security quickly deteriorated.[46] With communications damaged, buildings destroyed, and little coordination of resources, violent crime escalated at an astounding rate.

Adding to the national misery was the reemergence of some of Haiti's most notorious violent criminals. More than 5,000 inmates escaped from the collapsed National Penitentiary, never to be caught again. Some escaped inmates quickly banded together and formed into armed militias, such as the *Armée Federale*, and coordinated organized attacks against political opposition groups or other wealthy targets.[47] A 2010 Brief from the United States Institute of Peace explains how escapees initiated new waves of crime in areas with high poverty and weak police presence. Many gang members returned to their former neighborhoods, leading to "violent turf battles and increased street crime. A new armed group known as the *Armée Federale* has brought together the escaped prisoners from several neighborhoods. They hide out in the hills of the Martissant section of Port-au-Prince and conduct increasingly organized criminal activities throughout the city. Cases of kidnapping and assault increased during the first half of 2010 and crime has been reported in the previously quiet suburbs above Port-au-Prince."[48]

Due to the loss of many top officials and officers and the collapse of ministerial buildings and infrastructure, the HNP was unable to adequately respond to the new waves of crime. During this period, rates of violent crimes and violent sexual assaults skyrocketed, as inmates who had ties to local gangs began reclaiming their neighborhoods. In the immediate aftermath of the earthquake, violence increased nationwide. In the six weeks following the disaster, nearly 11,000 women and girls in the capital city were raped or sexually assaulted. Most of these violent assaults occurred during the daytime in public areas. With the HNP unable to respond to the crime wave, violent assaults increased dramatically and the rate of kidnappings nearly tripled.[49]

Such violent crimes were coupled with the almost unhindered looting of stores and businesses by the hungry and desperate as well as the opportunistic. Gun battles broke out in the streets as businesses owners attempted to protect their property, while churches, aid trucks, and even coffins were looted in broad daylight. The security situation became so intense that UN aid could not be distributed in some areas. Coordination became increasingly difficult and secondary suffering from hunger, thirst, and exposure exacerbated the desperate situation.[50]

In the early aftermath of the earthquake, hundreds of aid groups and nongovernmental organizations (NGOs) flooded into Haiti. While public opinion toward the NGOs was initially favorable, sentiments quickly deteriorated as frustrations over lack of coordination and allegations of corruption spread across the nation. Violent protests broke out in localized areas, but anti-NGO sentiment did not reach its zenith until many months later.

Following the 2010 earthquake, a cholera epidemic which quickly spread across Haiti's central plateau, was traced back to leaking sewage pipes from a Nepalese UN base. According to PAH/WHO, there were 814,551 suspected cases of cholera and 9,693 deaths between 2010 and 2017.[51] As a result, an infuriated public took to the streets in protest, attacking UN bases and barricading streets with burning tires which prevented humanitarian aid from delivering treatment to cholera patients.[52] Violent protesting led to many NGOs restricting locations of travel and service for their personnel, leaving many regions unserved and compounding national resentment.

The cataclysmic impact of the 2010 quake not only led to a complex increase in national violence, but it helped to create the long term and problematic security context in which contemporary Haiti is embedded. While pre-quake Haiti had its share of violence, the nation's progress toward standardization and national sovereignty was upended by the disaster and many Haitians were left, once again, without resource or recourse.

Furthermore, recent political events, both domestic and international, also pose challenges for Haiti's internal security, and its broader relationship with other international actors. The nation's ability to curb violence, strengthen human rights, and protect its citizens is part of a complex system with implications on government legitimacy and the strength of the state and poses grave questions for potential investors and international partners.

Recently, repeated delays in presidential elections raised questions about national capacity and resulted in violent protests and instability throughout Haiti.[53] Throughout 2015 and 2016, thousands of Haitians took to the streets in protest over allegations that the outgoing president, Michel Martelly, used fraud, voter intimidation, and corruption to postpone elections and maintain power. During frequent protests, police arrested demonstrators and fired tear gas into crowds who vandalized buildings and blockaded roads with burning tires. In May 2016, after yet another delayed runoff election, gunmen stormed police headquarters in southern Haiti, beating multiple police officers, stealing weapons, and leaving six dead.[54]

SECURITY REFORMS

Attempted security reforms to combat violence in Haiti have been shaped, funded, and even controlled by international influences such as foreign governments and nongovernmental organizations (NGOs). As of November 2017, most reforms have focused on combating drug trafficking, reforming the justice system, and fighting corruption rather than targeting violence directly.

While many reforms to investigate and combat police corruption had been enacted prior to the earthquake in 2010, the disaster caused major setbacks to their progress. A 2011 report by the UN Office of the High Commissioner for Human Rights (OHCHR) classified the HNP's progress as insufficient in terms of investigation allegations of police violence, human rights abuses, and extrajudicial killings.[55]

In 2011, the OAS Inter-American Drug Abuse Control Commission (CICAD) adopted the "Hemispheric Drug Strategy" and its "Plan of Action 2011–2015," which coordinated international drug trafficking reduction efforts.[56] Through this initiative, bilateral aid from the U.S. and Canada, among other actors, has funded upgrades to police stations and provided surveillance and communications equipment. The United States has provided direct training to the HNP and five coast guard vessels with the intention of guarding the Haitian coast from drug smuggling.

One of the most successful of initiatives was a collaboration between the United Nations and the HNP, where anti-kidnapping expert Robert Arce teamed up to train HNP members on how to both prevent and solve kidnappings. Within a short period of time kidnapping arrests increased five-fold and kidnappings themselves decreased dramatically.[57]

In 2006, the UN Mission in Haiti Community Violence Reduction section (CVR), one of the few initiatives to directly combat violence was implemented in Haiti to "reorient its disarmament, demobilization and reintegration efforts . . . towards a comprehensive community violence reduction programme adapted to local conditions, including assistance for initiatives to strengthen local governance and the rule of law and to provide employment opportunities to former gang members, and at-risk youth."[58] In 2013, a joint program by MINUSTAH, the UNDP, and the Haitian Ministry of Justice and Public Security was developed to maximize the impact of the UN assistance to the Community Violence Reduction program. Since then, the progress of the CVR has been classified as *partially satisfactory*, claiming to have reduced gang violence and increased community stability. Yet despite these and other moderate successes, progress remains mitigated by continued instability, perpetual problems with corruption, and lack of clear priorities, practices, and benchmarks of success.

FUTURE CONCERNS

Despite the eventual election and inauguration of President Jovenal Moise, the results continue to be disputed by former opponents. In October 2017, the United Nations Stabilization Mission in Haiti (MINUSTAH) withdrew from Haiti after 13 years. Although MINUSTAH's presence brought improved security and stability, the nation remains precariously on the verge of chaos.[59] Fears that without MINUSTAH's presence, the political instability and social upheaval of decades past will resume, are not unfounded and only time will tell how Haiti handles the full control of its own internal security. Replacing MINUSTAH will be a smaller number of U.N. police known as the United Nations Mission for Justice Support in Haiti (MINUJUSTH), tasked with strengthening the police force, justice system, and democracy.

Another potential impact on national violence is the recent revival of Haiti's national army. Disbanded in 1994, it opened for recruitment in 2017. With the United Nation's diminished presence, Haiti's military has the opportunity to become the nation's primary security force, but concerns over the army's history of political involvement and role in military coups has some unsettled.[60] Only time will tell whether Haiti's new army will become a source of stability or a token of volatility in the island nation.

Additionally, Haiti's historic and complex relationship with the United States became even more complicated when, in November 2017, President Trump announced the end to the temporary protected status for Haitians who had sought refuge in the U.S. after the 2010 earthquake.[61] Within the next 18 months, nearly 60,000 Haitians will return from the relative stability of the United States to poverty, high unemployment, and political uncertainty in Haiti.[62] While its broader impact on domains of national violence cannot yet be fully known, this influx of Haitians will strain an already weak and burdened system and create the potential for a new array of security challenges.

Furthermore, Haiti's notoriously strained physical infrastructure remains profoundly vulnerable to disasters, despite the influx of money and projects in the years after the earthquake. 2016's deadly Hurricane Matthew demonstrated the weakness of both physical and social institutions and the perilous state of security in the island nation. With 90 percent of south Haiti destroyed,[63] and countless homeless, violence spiked and armed carjacking, lootings, and sexual assault rose again. Without changes to Haiti's fragile infrastructure and an increase in the national government's response capacity, there is little hope that the pattern of disaster, dismay, and violence will not repeat itself again.

Chapter Ten

Transnational Organized Crime and Violence in the Americas

R. Evan Ellis

From the perspective of U.S. national security, Latin America and the Caribbean is often characterized as a region without interstate conflicts, whose principle security issues are limited to natural disasters, drugs and other transnational organized crime. Yet the high rates of murders and other criminal violence in Latin American cities from Caracas to San Pedro Sula and San Salvador, to Kingston to Rio de Janeiro,[1] demonstrates that the region is hardly "at peace," even if there has not been a traditional war between states of the region since the 1995 Cenepa war between Peru and Ecuador.

Although in the post-Cold War era, the U.S. has devoted relatively little attention to Latin American and Caribbean security issues, the insecurity of the region has, ironically, played a central role in U.S. domestic policy and politics. The 2014 crisis of child migrants from Central America,[2] and the central role immigration and the proposed Mexico border wall occupied in the November 2016 U.S. presidential elections highlight the shared understanding among many in the U.S. that conditions in the region to which it is geographically contiguous, affect U.S. security and prosperity to such a degree, as to be a key factor in selecting its president.[3]

THE TRANSNATIONAL ORGANIZED CRIME: VIOLENCE CAUSAL RELATIONSHIP

Transnational organized crime is arguably the single biggest driver expanding violence in Latin America, thus indirectly enabling threats that impact U.S. security and the U.S. economic relationship with the region. Transnational organized crime's contributions to violence in the region are multiple, and both direct and indirect. Criminal groups commit violent acts in the pursuit of profit, including robberies and kidnapping, acts against those who do not pay extortion, or who cooperate with authorities or rivals, battles with police or other state organizations, and fights with rival groups over drug routes, markets to extort, and other revenue streams. Indirectly, criminal activity contributes to a culture in which respect for the state, laws, moral norms, and family values are undercut or perverted, fueling further violence as a mechanism for the resolution of disputes, the expression of anger, or even entertainment as part of a culture of nihilism.

Beyond its direct contributions to violence, a fundamental attribute of transnational criminal groups, deliberately or incidentally, is to undermine the functionality of the state in those areas that would put their activities or organization at risk. This includes corrupting and/or intimidating police, customs authorities, prosecutors, judges, administrators, and elected leaders to permit or protect operations by those groups. In some cases, those personnel are induced to actively participate in the revenue generating operations or other acts of the group. Such activities, however unintentional, erode important portions of the bond between the state and society. Examples include intimidation or bribes by criminal groups to prevent persons from cooperating with the state as witnesses or informants. It also includes enlisting them to participate in the activities of the group, from serving as drug mules and informants, to growing illegal crops such as coca or heroine poppies, or working in the illegal mining sector. Participation in such illicit activities requires a weakening of the moral fabric of the society, in which the lure of money or the fear of retribution by the group is a stronger incentive than the moral imperative to obey the law, or the risk of sanction for not cooperating with legitimate authorities.

By contributing to the deterioration of the state, and its bond with those residing in the national territory, and to the weakening of the moral fabric of society through their activities, transnational organized crime groups create an environment in which violence is increasingly prevalent. Such violence and perceived impunity of those who participate in it, in turn, decreases the population's confidence, and deference to, the state as the mechanism for providing security and justice, while undermining the moral obligation, and fear of sanctions, that prevent residents of the territory from employing violence themselves to achieve security, justice, or other goals.

With incomplete confidence in, and deference to, the state as the holder of the monopoly over the use of violence, individuals, groups, and commercial entities are compelled to hire private security organizations, or to form vigilante groups, to protect themselves. Moreover, absent faith in the state to impose law and order, some feel the need, and liberty, to take justice into their own hands, killing or otherwise punishing those who threaten or harm them.

As seen in the origin of groups such as the self-defense militias of Michoacán, Mexico,[4] the need for resources by those vigilantes to achieve their goals in a sustained fashion, combined with the erosion of moral authority and other incentives, often helps those vigilante groups themselves to become involved in extortion, narcotrafficking, or other illicit activities.

Further complicating matters, the activities of transnational organized groups in the expanding criminal economy, including extortion and other crime, fosters a culture of corruption and inefficiency in the state, and discourages legitimate business activities and investment. Such distortions increase the difficulty of earning a living in the legitimate economy, further driving youth and others to collaborate with criminal groups, whether violent gangs, narcotraffickers, contraband or illegal mining entities. Such collaboration, in turn, swells the membership of such groups and their influence on society. Within such reinforcing cycles of crime, violence, state and social deterioration, drugs play a particularly insidious role. Transnational organized crime groups trafficking narcotics through the region commonly pay for their services through product, rather than money, creating a local drug consumption market, where the gangs and others, which dominate the area and provide services or access to the narcotraffickers become the local distributors of the drugs in which they are paid.[5] Not only does the use of narcotics by some gang members directly contribute to their resort to violence, but the addiction that they foster in the areas they sell drugs to, creates economic needs, and situations where altered consciousness makes violence more probable.

This chapter now turns from the theoretical link between transnational organize crime and violence to particularly worrisome trends in transnational organized crime in Latin America and the Caribbean. This work finds that such transnational organized crime not only contributes to violence in the region, but that its current evolution creates the risk of a significant expansion of that violence, with potentially disastrous consequences for the hemisphere, including the U.S.

TRANSNATIONAL ORGANIZED CRIME OVERVIEW

As suggested in the previous section, transnational organized crime involves a diverse, and evolving set of activities and groups. While the term "narcotrafficking" and "transnational organized crime" is often used interchangeably, TOC groups typically obtain their income from a variety of sources, both legitimate and illegitimate. Such sources of group income may change over time. They may include not only manufacturing, transporting, and distributing drugs, but also illicit mining, human smuggling and trafficking, extortion, kidnapping and contraband goods, among other activities. Different criminal groups may focus on different parts of the same value chain. Within narcotrafficking, for example, the Mexico-based Sinaloa organization manages global supply chains from the sourcing of precursor chemicals to the transformation of coca into base and cocaine, to shipment of the final product and distribution in North America, Europe and Asia.[6] By contrast, the organization Los Zetas tends to focus more on moving drugs and extracting extortion from areas within its control.[7]

In virtually all cases, transnational organized crime groups rely on legitimate businesses, as well as illicit ones, and on the informal economy. In the Northern Triangle, for example, Mara Salvatrucha and Barrio 18 operate nightclubs, taxi and bus companies, among other income sources. Legitimate businesses provide key services required by criminal entities, from electricity, water and other utilities for their operations, to transportation networks to get their goods to market, to commercial establishments and financial systems which allow them to launder their illicit income.

The informal economy is similarly important for organized crime as a supply of human resources for TOC group operations, such as "mules" to transport drugs and launder cash through their bank accounts, those who grow drugs and turn it into base, those who do the illegal mining work, etc. Moreover, the informal economy, because it generally operates on a "cash basis" without electronic records that tie income to specific clients, is particularly useful for the laundering of criminal proceeds.

While some TOC groups are structured in a more hierarchical fashion than others, such entities, and criminal value chains generally demonstrate characteristics of self-organizing, adaptive networks. While some groups such as Mexico's Sinaloa cartel may seek to manage parts of that chain at a global level, others are more specialized in one, or a small number of parts of the criminal value added chain. In Central America, some smuggling groups such as Guatemala's Huistas, specialize in buying product at the country's southern border with Honduras or Salvador, and smuggling it to the Mexican border, where it is sold to a different group at a higher price.[8] Nonetheless, the generation of value from the growing and harvesting of coca to the production of coca base, to transportation and distribution to the final market, generally involves multiple actors responding to a combination of signals from direct clients, purchasers, financiers, and others in the illicit market.

One implication of such self-organizing, adaptive structure, is that, in general, arresting or killing the leadership of a particular group does not disrupt the value chain in an enduring fashion. Rather, in the short term, it generates more violence by inducing subordinates to vie for control of the newly leaderless group, or tempting rivals to encroach on its routes and markets. In Mexico, for example, both the government of Felipe Calderón and that of his successor Enrique Peña Nieto pursued cartel leaders, with considerable success. Notable examples include the November 2010 killing of Gulf cartel leader Antonio Ezequiel Cárdenas Guillén, the arrest of senior Zeta boss Miguel Treviño Morales in June 2013, the arrest of Hector Beltrán-Leyva in October 2014, the 2014 killing of Nazario Moreno González of *La Familia Michoacana*, the February 2015 arrest of Servando Gómez Martínez (*La Tuta*), head of the Knights Templar organization, and the multiple arrests of Sinaloa cartel boss Joaquín Guzmán Loera, ending with his January 2017 deportation to the United States. Yet during the same period, the number of groups in Mexico expanded from seven to over 40, and violence expanded significantly.

In addition to generating fragmentation, increased uncertainty, and violence in the strategic environment, disruption of a group or its leaders also typically spawns a search by its clients, suppliers, and other associates for new business relationships. The arrest of the leadership of the Cachiros[9] and Valle Valle[10] smuggling organization in Honduras in 2013 to 2015, for example, spawned a scramble by Mexican groups such as Sinaloa (which had formerly bought their product) to establish new direct ties with those subgroups that had previously worked for them.[11]

In virtually all the countries of the region, except in Costa Rica and Panama, which formally do not have militaries, the challenge of organized crime has raised the question of the appropriate use of the armed forces in domestic law enforcement operations. In a small number of states such as Chile, where the problem of transnational organized crime has not significantly exceeded police resources (and where previous military rule is a debated historical legacy), the armed forces have not involved themselves in such operations. Yet in the rest, from El Salvador to Argentina, the insufficient capabilities of the police to confront transnational organized crime, combined with the potential contribution of military manpower and assets, have led governments to involve the armed forces in different ways.

The nature of that involvement has varied according to the laws, constitution, needs, and tradition of each nation. In El Salvador, where the military lacks the authority to perform arrests in most circumstances, the armed forces operate in support of the police through entities like Zeus Command, and most recently, through the integrated special units FERES and FIRT, although with police still conducting the actual detention of suspects.[12] In Honduras, by contrast, where the military is constitutionally authorized to perform police functions, the government has formed an elite police force within the military itself, the PMOP.[13] Elsewhere, such as in Argentina, the military role against organized crime is more marginal. There, under Decree 228 of the government of Mauricio Macri, the military has been empowered to support counterdrug operations, including the detection and interdiction of aircraft potentially smuggling drugs,[14] yet the 1988 Defense Law, which forbids military involvement in internal security affairs, has made many in the armed forces uncomfortable regarding the performance of even this limited role.[15] Similarly, in Brazil, whose constitution authorizes military involvement in support of domestic order in extreme circumstances, the armed forces have deployed to augment state security in marginalized neighborhoods during special events such as the World Cup and the 2016 Olympics, as well as in response to police strikes and prison riots such as those at the beginning of 2017.[16] Yet as in Argentina, the Brazilian military remains uncomfortable with such internal security activities.

REINFORCING TRENDS TOWARD EXPANDED VIOLENCE

Throughout Latin America and the Caribbean, the activities of transnational criminal organizations threaten to expand violence and insecurity. Five dynamics are particularly of concern: Destabilizing new alliances among Mexican cartels in a fragmented and unpredictable environment, the evolution of Central American gangs and drug smuggling groups, the interaction of the Colombian peace process with the collapse of Venezuela, the development of the Europe-oriented mid-South America drug corridor, and the maturation of transpacific criminal networks.

In Mexico, the decade-long war against criminal cartels that began with President Felipe Calderón's November 2006 deployment of the Mexican military into Michoacán[17] has transformed that nation's criminal landscape in ways that make it more unpredictable and prone to violence; from three to eight major cartels, Mexico now has 40 or more major criminal groups and affiliated gangs, and infighting between multiple groups in states such as Michoacán, Guerrero, and the State of Mexico.[18] In that context, which has made the interaction between groups less predictable and potentially more violent, the January 2017 extradition to the United States of Joaquín Guzmán Loera (*El Chapo*),[19] has tempted his rivals to contest the power of the Sinaloa organization that he formerly headed. Whereas the latter was arguably Mexico's wealthiest and most internationally connected cartel, its emerging competitor Jalisco Nuevo Generación, under the leadership of Nemesio Oseguera Cervantes (*El Mencho*), has similar international connections, has shown a greater disposition toward violence,[20] and appears to have formed alliances with the remnants of other Mexican cartels, including the Beltran Leyva, Carrillo Fuentes, and Arellano Felix organizations to contest routes and territory once dominated by the Sinaloa cartel,[21] including the February

2017 attack against El Chapo's son, and his former lieutenant Ismael Zambada García (*El Mayo*).[22]

In addition, other powerful Mexico-based groups, such as the Gulf cartel and Los Zetas, who have previously fought Sinaloa, and whose territory has been challenged by CJNG since 2015,[23] and could join an expanded fight. Such attacks raise the prospect of a significant new wave of inter-cartel violence across Mexico, in a criminal environment far more fragmented and less predictable than it was before, at a time that coincides with potential major new stresses on Mexico, including a significant increase in protectionism from its principal market, the United States, and the possible deportation from the U.S. back to Mexico of an expanded number of Mexican citizens.[24]

In Central America, transnational criminal violence is fueled by an interaction between local smuggling groups, which move drugs and people through the region at the behest of Mexican and other cartels, and violent street gangs, which dominate its major urban areas. The most threatening of Central America's gangs, Mara Salvatrucha (MS-13) and Barrio 18, are concentrated in the northern triangle countries of El Salvador, Honduras, and Guatemala. While estimates vary widely, the United Nations Office of Drug Control (UNODC) calculated in 2012 that El Salvador had 20,000 gang members, Honduras had 12,000, and Guatemala had 22,000.[25] The domination of urban neighborhoods by MS-13 and Barrio 18, including their engagement in extortion and other criminal activities and fights with each other, has made the Northern Triangle the most violent sub-region in the hemisphere; in El Salvador, the murder rate reached 103 per 100,000 people in 2015,[26] while in Honduras, it topped out at 86 per 100,000,[27] and in Guatemala, it reached 46 per 100,000 inhabitants.[28]

To the south, in Costa Rica and Panama, although the challenge of gang violence is less severe, the interaction of drug flows and local gangs continues to elevate violence. In Costa Rica, the growth of the murder rate to over 11 per 100,000, while modest by Northern Triangle standards, has become a matter of national concern. Similarly, Panama, which has over 200 gangs[29] loosely grouped into two federations involved in the drug trade and other violent crime, Bagdad and Calor Calor,[30] Rising violence has sparked significant political attention. As in the northern triangle, Panama and Costa Rica's gangs mostly focus on drug sales and minor crimes in areas under their control, but have become involved in drug smuggling to some degree.[31]

With respect to smuggling groups, in general, intermediary organizations move drugs through the region at the behest of, or explicitly selling their product to Mexican organizations such as the Sinaloa cartel, paying extortion to the gangs whose territory they transit, or often using them to conduct operations or sell drugs in the neighborhoods that they control.[32] With time, however, portions of the gangs, particularly Mara Salvatrucha, have leveraged ties of their members to major markets such as the United States to become more directly involved in drug shipments as well.[33] In El Salvador, individual groups with Mara Salvatrucha have begun to smuggle drugs up Salvador's Pacific coast, and along newly constructed highways in the east of the country.[34]

As in Mexico, actions by authorities against the leadership of intermediate groups such as the Cachiros and Valle Valles in Honduras, and the Mendozas, Lorenzanas, Leones, and Lopez Ortiz clans in Guatemala, has fractionalized the criminal networks. Smaller entities that once moved drugs for these groups, such as the Brus and Sizo cartels in Honduras, and the group "Los Pinto,"[35] are now forging new relationships with the Mexican cartels, such as Sinaloa, that once financed or bought their shipments. Other groups, such as the Huistas, in Guatemala, are expanding what were once modest operations in the shadows of larger organizations.[36] The prospect of a shakeup on the Mexican side of those financing drug flows through the region, and the decapitation of the leadership of those smuggling the drugs through Central America, could easily spark a new struggle between groups, complicated by the inflow of deportees from the U.S. into the ranks of the region's criminal street gangs, potentially unleashing a major new wave of violence.

In the northern part of South America, Colombia and Venezuela have developed separate but interacting cultures of criminal violence. In Colombia, a 53-year long civil war, combined with the status of the country as a major source country for drugs and illegal mining, has left a legacy of criminal bands and a culture of violence. While neighboring Venezuela has also long wrestled with corruption, in that country, the attempt to impose a flawed populist authoritarian economic and political model has led to a collapse of the formal economy and associated political violence.[37] By May 2017, for example, escalating protests across Venezuela had claimed almost 40 lives, with over 130 arrests and 1,300 arrests.[38] Even before the latest protests, however, endemic corruption and complicacy of the country's leftist leadership in a range of criminal activities has caused criminal violence to spiral out of control,[39] With the murder rate of 120 per 100,000 in the nation's capital, Caracas, making the city among the most dangerous in the hemisphere.[40]

As of April 2017, the interaction between emerging crises in each country threatened to create an explosive situation. In Colombia, the implementation of a peace accord between the government and The Revolutionary Armed Forces of Colombia (Fuerzas Armadas Revolucionarios de Colombia—FARC) created a risk that a non-trivial portion of the 7,000 members of the FARC being demobilized, uncapable of being absorbed into Colombia's slow-growing economy, would instead continue to rely on their principal skill, the use of instruments of violence, by either joining the rival National

Liberation Army (Ejército de Liberación Nacional—ELN), one of the nation's criminal bands (BACRIM), or form one of their own.[41] As occurred during the similar flawed demobilization of the paramilitary forces of The United Self-Defense Forces of Colombia (Autodefensas Unidas de Colombia—AUC) in 2005, the flow of the former FARC fighters into the ranks of the ELN and BACRIM, possibly with arms and other resources not turned over to authorities,[42] is driving an expansion of those groups and new violent struggles for criminal territory.[43]

Compounding the instability, with the suspension of aerial spraying of the pesticide glyphosate against coca crops in 2015,[44] and the positioning of local coca growers to receive benefits under post-agreement crop substitution programs, the amount of coca being produced in Colombia has skyrocketed, from less than 100,000 hectares in 2014, to an estimated 188,000 hectares in 2016,[45] putting more money in the hands of the narcotraffickers, even while the Colombian military operations and maintenance budget has fallen by an estimated 40 percent in real terms.[46] In addition, two facets of the Colombian government agreement with the FARC increases the likelihood of expanded violence in the countryside. On the one hand, the accord promises to redistribute land in the Colombian countryside, yet increased the protection of existing landholders against having their property confiscated, and left doubts about the adequacy of funding for land redistribution. In addition, by creating a mechanism for the FARC to resurrect itself as a political party, the accord creates the risk that FARC-affiliated candidates could be killed in large numbers by anti-FARC death squads, as happened in the mid-1980s, when almost 5,000 former guerillas who formed the Patriotic Union political party after a previous peace accord, were assassinated.[47]

Complementing Colombia's crisis, as noted previously, the "Bolivarian socialist" regime of neighboring Venezuela has both become thoroughly corrupted by criminal activity. Complicacy of the Venezuelan military and National Guard in narcotrafficking and illicit activities is so extensive that the main criminal group in the country is referred to as the "Cartel of the Suns," referring to the rank insignia of the Venezuelan generals who are believed to be its leaders.[48] Venezuela is also in the process of an economic and political crisis that could lead to a breakdown of order, possible civil war, and a significant outflow of refugees and criminals into some of the most troubled areas of neighboring Colombia. The mismanagement of the Venezuelan economy by the Maduro regime has created broad scarcity for even the most basic goods in Venezuela, prompting hundreds of thousands to cross over the border into Colombia in areas such as Cúcuta,[49] fueling a substantial black market economy in Norte de Santander, one of the greatest zones of BACRIM and guerilla activity in Colombia.

By April 2017, as the desperation of the Venezuelan people, and their rejection of the perceived usurpation of power by the Maduro regime, fueled a cycle of protests and state repression, the government and military felt compelled to hold onto power at any cost. The January 2015 defection to the United States of Leamsy Salazar,[50] security chief to former Chavista parliamentary speaker Diosdado Cabello, and the July 2014 Interpol "Red Notice" against Venezuelan leader Hugo Carvajal when he left the country to accept a diplomatic posting in Aruba,[51] arguably reinforced fears among Venezuela's Chavista government and military leadership that if they ceded power, they would also risk extradition to the United States and possible imprisonment for their involvement in criminal activities. Such fears prevented the Venezuelan military from acting as a guarantor of the constitutional order, and helped push the crisis toward an extreme where the armed forces could potentially fragment amidst an escalation of violence between an intransigent regime and protesters who cannot feed their families and have lost faith in the possibility of peaceful change.

To the south of Colombia and Venezuela, an expanding illegal economy, built around drugs, illegal mining timber, and other illicit flows, is generating its own wave of societal and institutional stresses and violence. In this criminal economy, Peru and Bolivia have become the key source zones for cocaine and illegal mining products, as well as people, while the east of Paraguay has become the principal supplier of marijuana for the Southern Cone. The drugs generally flow east across South America to feed growing markets in the principal cities of Southeastern Brazil, northern Argentina and Uruguay, as well as Europe, although drugs also flow southwest from Peru to Chile, and both drugs and contraband pass from Peru through its own ports, and through those of northern Chile to Asia. In Peru, illegal mining and the production of cocaine has fueled criminal competitions and violence not only within the country itself, but across the mid-continent belt and beyond.[52] The Peruvian cocaine economy is in the hands of a myriad of family-based groups, including multiple separate entities involved in the supply of precursor chemicals, the harvesting of cocaine, its transformation to paste, its transportation, and export.[53] A portion of the cocaine produced in Peru is transported to the Pacific coast, principally for shipment to European and Asian markets, where it is principally exported through the port of Callao, and secondarily, through the northern ports of Paita and Tumbes, and the southern port of Tacna.[54] Violence in the Principal Peruvian port of Callao which forced the deployment of the Peruvian military to the area, was reportedly driven by a struggle between multiple criminal groups for control over illicit exports from the port, and illustrates how the fragmentation of the local criminal economy could drive violence.[55]

Some of the cocaine produced in Peru, as well as Bolivia, is smuggled south into Chile, to supply the internal market of that nation, one of the highest per capita consumer of cocaine in Latin America,[56] and from Chile, to markets in Asia through ports such as Iquique. The smuggling of drugs into Chile has contributed to significant violence in the north of that otherwise relatively peaceful country, including an incident in March 2017 involving Bolivian customs officials crossing the border into Chile,[57] that became a diplomatic dispute between the two nations.

In the interior of Peru, while coca production once helped fund the terrorist group *Sendero Luminoso*, whose war against the Peruvian state cost an estimated 69,000 lives,[58] the principal problem today is the spread of coca production beyond traditional *Sendero Luminoso*-dominated growing regions such as the Upper Huallaga Valley and the Apurimac, Ene and Mantaro river valley (VRAEM), more extensively along the eastern side of the Peruvian Andes, including north of the VRAEM in Pichis Palcazu, and even near Oxapampa.[59]

That Peruvian cocaine which does not flow west to the coast, or to Chile, generally flows East, to European or South American markets. A portion flows from the eastern side of the Andes into the jungle of Brazil, where it is managed by increasingly powerful Brazilian gangs such as the First Capital Command (PCC) and the Red Command (CV). Another portion is smuggled southeast, through provinces such as Madre de Dios, to Bolivia.

Cocaine smuggled from Peru through Bolivia, as well as that produced from Bolivian coca or processed in Bolivian laboratories, is, in part, smuggled south to Argentine ports such as Rosario and Buenos Aires, Uruguayan ports such as Montevideo, or through Paraguay and southern Brazil, to ports such as Santos, for export to Europe.[60] The South American urban centers associated with these flows have accordingly registered an expansion of drug consumption, with associated crime and violence, including cheaper and deadlier substances based on the alkaloids of the coca leaf, known as *paco* in Argentina, [61] and *basuko* in Brazil.[62] With the competition between gangs to control the illegal narcotics market in Argentina, the city of Rosario, a major transport hub for cocaine bound for Europe, has become the most violent urban area in the country.[63]

In Paraguay, the flow of cocaine from Peru and Bolivia for Brazilian and European markets, and the export of marijuana produced in Paraguay itself, has transformed Eastern departments such as Concepción into major drug trafficking areas,[64] With Brazilian groups such as the First Capital Command (PCC) and the Red Command (CV) playing a major role, in conjunction with local groups.[65] The volume of illicit products passing through Paraguay is so extensive that one study estimated that 40 percent of Paraguay's GDP could come from illicit sources.[66] The flow of drugs through the Paraguayan city of

Pedro Juan Caballero, on the border with Brazil, and the struggles between narcotrafficking groups that operate there, has made the city one of the major foci of drug violence in the region.[67]

In Brazil, in a similar fashion, the flow of narcotics through the country has fueled an expansion of drug consumption in major urban areas, including but not limited to the slums (*favelas*) of Rio de Janeiro, São Paulo and other major cities, and with it, the size and power of groups such as the PCC, CV, and other groups such as the "Third Pure Command," and "Amigos do Amigos." Of these groups, the PCC is the largest, operating in all of Brazil's states, with 20,000 or more members.[68] The organization has developed an array of illicit activities and global ties, including working with the radical Shia Islamic organization Hezbollah,[69] and laundering money in Chinese banks.[70] A series of violent incidents in prisons across the northeast of Brazil in January 2017,[71] highlighted how the rise of the PCC and other groups has fueled violence in all facets of Brazilian society.

Finally, with the expansion of commercial and financial flows between Asia and Latin America, and the corresponding growth in supporting infrastructure, trans-Pacific organized crime ties are becoming an increasing problem, and source of violence, in the region.[72] Interactions include the importation of precursor chemicals for drug production from China and India from groups such as the Sinaloa cartel, the laundering of money through Chinese banks, currency exchange houses, and trade based money laundering schemes, and the smuggling of Chinese through the region, generally headed for the United States. While the "Chinese mafia" operating in Latin America generally prefers to keep a low profile, a series of assassinations following the decapitation of the Chinese triad Pi Xue in Argentina illustrates the potential for violence from the activities of Asian groups in Latin America and the fight against them.[73]

SOLUTIONS

Overall, in the fight against transnational organized crime in the region, three centers of gravity can be identified: the resources of the criminal groups, corruption and impunity, and the political will to take on the problem. Criminal groups depend on money and other resources for everything that they do, from the ability to recruit and retain their membership, to the organizations and networks involved in illicit operations such as the production and movement of drugs, to the purchasing of weapons and technology, to the bribing of officials. Across the region, financial intelligence units and similar organizations, bolstered by stricter laws on banking and financial disclosure, are making it increasingly difficult and costly for criminal groups to repatriate and legitimize their ill-gotten gains.[74] With respect to corruption, the compromise of police and other officials—whether through bribes or threats—decimates their effectiveness, no matter what level of resources, training or technology is given to law enforcement.

In addition, the perception of corruption, whether justified or not, makes effective interagency and international coordination virtually impossible. Moreover, when judicial and law enforcement officials are perceived as corrupt and/or ineffective, residents of the area will not take the time, or the risk, to bring cases, or to cooperate as informants and witnesses, reinforcing the cycle of impunity.

The threat of transnational organized crime in Latin America and the Caribbean requires continued attention and resources from the U.S., operating in conjunction with its partners in the region. Efforts against transnational organized crime should incorporate a holistic approach, attacking not only criminal groups themselves, but also their revenue generating activities, resources, and ability to launder money, their recruitment and organizational coherence, and other factors. Moreover, activities against groups should be sequenced in time and space based on an understanding of the dynamics of the criminal organization as a system. This includes anticipating and exploiting the uncertainty and competition that the takedown of a group leader may have on subordinates and rivals. It also involves coordinating security and development activities to take advantage of the clearing of bad actors from an area, in a timely fashion, to re-establish state presence.

Beyond the criminal groups, an effective strategy must also focus on strengthening the institutions that combat and resist them, including combatting corruption in law enforcement, military and judicial institutions, increasing prison controls, strengthening laws governing financial reporting, and growing the formal economy to deny such groups a basis from which to operate. The fight against corruption must leverage technical solutions such as polygraph tests and databases, in a manner that is coordinated with legal and administrative reforms to ensure that the identification of problematic people from an organization results in their permanent removal in a fashion that does not simply put them on the street in the service of an organized crime group, or allow them to move to another organization.

As illustrated by the impact of immigration and NAFTA on the 2016 U.S. Presidential election, no region of the world impacts the security of the United States as directly as Latin America and the Caribbean. By addressing the challenge of transnational organized crime in the region, the U.S. advances is own national interests, as well as those of its neighbors in the hemisphere in which all share.

Chapter Eleven

United States Security Policy in Latin America and the Caribbean[1]

Eric L. Golnick

The United States and Latin America and the Caribbean are intimately linked through common geography, history, and security.[2] The regional policy formulated by the Obama administration prioritized four principal objectives: promoting economic and social opportunity, ensuring citizen security, strengthening effective democratic institutions, and securing a clean energy future.[3] It is still not clear how the Trump administration will interact with other countries in the region. While there are some indicators about wherc the Trump administration's policy will move, it is still opaque. Currently, there are more questions than answers on how the new administration will conduct security policy in the region. This chapter will address a variety of security policy topics relative to the United States and Latin America and the Caribbean. This is by no means an exhaustive list of the varied and complex security relationship the United States government has with partners in the region.

This chapter explores a particular segment of United States foreign policy strategy in Latin America and the Caribbean. The U.S. Department of State directs the execution of U.S. foreign policy in the world. Thus, the objectives of the Department of State determine the appropriate defense and security cooperation activities with partner nations. In the context of engagement with Latin America, U.S. security policy is merely an instrument in the larger U.S. foreign policy toolkit. In many cases, coordination on trade and development in the region are more effective in advancing strategic foreign policy goals. While it is still unknown what the new administration's policy posture in the region is, with the Trump administration's plan to cut the budget of the U.S. Department of State, it could easily be suggested that the United States will rely more on the Department of Defense and other agencies to conduct security policy.[4]

President Obama's security policy in Latin America and the Caribbean was similar to the Bush administration. However, the Obama administration introduced several significant policy distinctions, including a greater emphasis on partnership and a shared responsibility of the security situation.[5] It essentially shifted to a policy of increased engagement.[6] For instance, the reestablishment of diplomatic relations with Cuba in 2015 demonstrates this shift toward a more engagements-based approach to the region.[7] However, the Trump administration has cooled relations with Cuba soon after taking office. It is still unknown what the relationship with Cuba and the United States will be moving forward.

The Obama administration's type of security engagement activities in Latin America closely mirrored that of the Bush administration. Yet the nature and underlying principles of U.S. security policy in conducting these activities is less restrictive, and more open to cooperation. While the Obama administration was more open to dialogue with adversaries, it could be characterized as reactive in implementing that strategy and sometimes disjointed in a unified message to partners.

While the reactive nature of the Obama administration may be interpreted as a lack of focused policy and strategy for the region, the administration considered this approach to be the best fit for the complex and distinct issues that have characterized the U.S. relationship with Latin America and the Caribbean. In 2010, Frank Mora, the former U.S. Deputy Assistant Secretary of Defense (DASD), explained that the lack of a policy catchphrase such as "Good Neighbor Policy" or "Monroe Doctrine" was not indicative of a lack of cohesive strategy.[8] According to Mora, the umbrella approaches of past engagement policies and activities in the region can be counterproductive, and the policy should adjust to the vastly different issues for each partner in the region.[9] This *ad hoc* approach has proven necessary and best suited to productive engagement with partners in a fluid and dynamic geopolitical climate.

Unlike in the Obama era, the Trump administration is relying heavily on the National Security Council and the Department of Defense to make foreign policy decisions instead of the U.S. Department of State, which is normally the lead federal agency for all foreign policy. Alex Daugherty from the *Miami Herald* explains, "Usually, the State Department takes the lead on situations that still require U.S. attention but may not be an immediate threat to national security, but the current upheaval at the agency leaves it unable to effectively do its job."[10] This is further exasperated by the fact that almost a year into his administration, President Trump has yet to appoint dozens of high-level State Department officials, including the Assistant Secretary of State for Western Hemisphere affairs, which is the top diplomat for the region.[11]

Given the proximity to the region, specific security issues that affect both the United States and Latin America and the Caribbean should seemingly be of high priority to U.S. policymakers. However, the U.S. government's overarching policy places Latin America and the Caribbean in a lower national security priority than other regions such as the Middle East or Asia, especially in security policy prioritization. Between the growing economic and homeland security threats posed by ISIS and the rise of China, the United States Government—in particular, the Department of Defense—understandably views Latin America and the Caribbean as a low priority. Security policymakers necessarily must concentrate on what they consider to be the most significant and imminent threat. While Latin America has several security concerns that affect the United States, it receives little attention and funding considerations from Congress and policymakers in Washington when compared to the other aforementioned regions.

BRIEF HISTORICAL CONTEXT OF SECURITY POLICY IN LATIN AMERICA

The United States Department of Defense has been—and continues to be—a crucial force in shaping the modern history of the security and political landscape of Latin America and the Caribbean. However, this history has not been without controversy. Past interventions have served as a source of inspiration for regional adversaries of the United States to author their political rhetoric. These leaders, such as President Nicholás Maduro of Venezuela, often recall the anecdotes of U.S. soldiers overthrowing governments and enabling or supporting brutal dictators in the past. The objective and result of this rhetoric is to paint the Department of Defense as the face of American imperialism and interventionist policy in the Western Hemisphere.

Historically, U.S. policy toward the region has been centered upon the prevention of interference by extra-hemispheric actors in the Western Hemisphere.[12] The Monroe Doctrine of 1823 originally purported that the U.S. and new nations in Latin America and the Caribbean shared democratic values, and that the United States would protect them by force if any outside world power attempted to recolonize.[13] The principles underlying the Monroe Doctrine set the course for U.S. policy and defense of the region.[14]

This strategic approach was exceedingly significant in shaping U.S. security policy in the region during the Cold War. Factions that clashed during civil conflicts in countries such as Guatemala, El Salvador, Nicaragua, Chile, and Argentina effectively served as proxies for the United States and the Soviet Union as each continued to vie for worldwide hegemony. The memories and wounds of those conflicts are still fresh in the minds of many people in the region and affect their perceptions of the United States in terms of defense engagement. In "The Monroe Doctrine: Meanings and Implications," Mark Gilderhus explains:

> Later with the onset of the Cold War, perceived international imperatives led to a series of new interventions in countries such as Guatemala, Cuba, the Dominican Republic, and Chile. Though typically couched in idealistic rhetoric emphasizing Pan-American commitments to solidarity and democracy, the various versions of the Monroe Doctrine consistently served U.S. policy makers as a means for advancing what they understood as national strategic and economic interests.[15]

In 1986, President Ronald Reagan designated drug trafficking as a threat to "the national security of the United States."[16] The United States government and the Department of Defense shifted their focus from countering the Soviet influence in the region to the "war on drugs." The United States' use of the military and law enforcement as a means of combating the flow of drugs from Latin America continues to this day. In fact, the majority of law enforcement and military aid to Latin America and the Caribbean remains focused on counternarcotic operations.[17]

As the world moved into the twenty-first century, various actors across the globe pushed back against U.S. foreign policy as promulgated by the Bush administration including extra-hemispheric actors such as Russia, China, Iran, and Hezbollah. President Hugo Chávez of Venezuela launched the Bolivarian Alliance of the Americas (*Alianza Bolivariana para los Pueblos de Nuestra América*—ALBA) in 2004 with the objective of counteracting U.S. influence in the region.[18] ALBA members include Bolivia, Cuba, Ecuador, and Nicaragua, and the Caribbean island nations of Antigua and Barbuda, Dominica, Grenada, St. Kitts and Nevis, St. Lucia, and St. Vincent and the Grenadines.[19] The relationship between the U.S. Department of Defense and various leaders and actors in the region suffered as a result of ALBA's anti-American rhetoric. The influence of ALBA has diminished significantly after the death of Hugo Chávez in 2013 and the drop of global oil prices in 2015.[20]

The Obama administration's policies underscored the importance of changing the perceptions of U.S. assistance in the region. Secretary of State John Kerry announced in 2010 that "the era of the Monroe Doctrine is over," and that it was vital for the United States to partner with the region on issues regarding security, democracy, and climate change.[21] The Obama administration accordingly attempted to refocus U.S. policy in Latin America and the Caribbean from the "war on terror" and "war on drugs" to social, economic, and citizen security issues.[22]

While it is still too soon to see where the Trump administration will move in the region, early indications show a willingness to reverse course and shift back to a "war on drugs" mentality. Helping this shift is the unfortunate opioid epidemic that is killing thousands of Americans. The Trump administration views this issue as a direct result of illicit drugs coming north from Latin America and the Caribbean.[23]

U.S. NATIONAL SECURITY POLICY

In the U.S. government, the word "policy" is used liberally and at times, carelessly. Many in the highest levels of the United States government mistakenly confound "policy" with law, regulations, and strategy. In the realm of security policy, these interrelated but distinct concepts confuse many commanders regarding the capabilities they possess to conduct operations in their areas of responsibility. A useful definition of policy, in the most simplistic terms, is a "high-level overall plan embracing the general goals and acceptable procedures."[24]

In order to conduct an effective analysis of security policy, it is crucial to understand the manner by which policy filters down to the Department of Defense and to frame how the agency comes to define and create strategies in Latin America and the Caribbean. In contrast to legislation, policy has its origins in the highest levels of the U.S. executive branch. A useful way of understanding this stratified concept of "policy" is to think about an aircraft's perspective while looking at the ground. The President's formulation of policy is at 32,000 feet—meaning the policies are high-level, conceptualized with less detailed, and tend to emphasize the overall picture. As one descends further down the government strata, there is an inversely proportional relationship between level of detail and altitude.

Specifically, the higher stratum of United States foreign policy originates from the President of the United States, the National Security Council, and the Department of State—with the primary conduit being the National Security Council. The National Security Council consists of the President, Vice President, Secretary of State, Secretary of Defense, Secretary of Energy, Secretary of the Treasury, Attorney General, Secretary of Homeland Security, U.S. Representative to the U.N., Chief of Staff to the President, and National Security Advisor.[25] The Council's purpose is to advise and assist the President on security and foreign policy, and to be the President's principal arm for coordinating these policies among various government agencies.[26] Within the National Security Council framework, the NSC Principals Committee is a meeting with solely the secretaries of each agency; likewise, there are lower meetings at the deputy secretary and assistant deputy secretary levels that conduct the day-to-day policy determinations that provide a feedback loop of information and recommendations to the higher-level meetings.[27]

The National Security Council provides a forum in which the senior leadership of the United States government can discuss and come to a practicable consensus on potentially contentious foreign policy issues. For example, if there were an issue or disagreement between the Department of State and the Department of Defense on a particular issue, the National Security Council would convene and act as the arbitrator to determine the path forward.

For issues in defense policy, decisions trickle down from the National Security Council and the Secretary of Defense to the Office of the Secretary of Defense for Policy (OSD Policy). From here more detailed policies are formulated. When OSD (P) formulates its policy, considering guidance from the Secretary of Defense, OSD forwards its policy approach to the Joint Chiefs of Staff and the Combatant Commands. From there, the Combatant Commands devise various policies and strategies with greater specificity, taking into account the higher-level policy abstractions. As the policy descends these strata, each successive level can shape its policy to be more restrictive than the prior level, but it cannot render policy any less restrictive.

Returning to the 32,000-foot view paradigm, the role of the NSC should be to frame the entire perspective in such a way that would enable it to easily anticipate the second and third order effects of its policy determinations. Applying this paradigm to policy formulation in Latin America and the Caribbean, there are a number of difficulties that arise for the National Security Council in thinking long term and strategic. The fluid political and security situation in the region, coupled with domestic political pressures in the U.S., has clouded the NCS's ability to devise policy with the requisite foresight for that level of planning. Unfortunately, reactive policy can create confusion among those responsible for its implementation, and it can indicate a lack of resolve to partner nations.

The individual responsible for defense policy recommendations for Latin America and the Caribbean is the Deputy Assistant Secretary of Defense for Western Hemisphere Affairs (DASD/WHA). The DASD (WHA) reports to both the Undersecretary of Defense for Policy and the Secretary of Defense. The nature of this position can make it frustrating and inefficient when addressing policy issues in the region. For important policy decisions, most ideas must go through five stages of refinement before reaching the Secretary of Defense.[28] The relative civilian-military rank structure presents another difficulty: A DASD is roughly equivalent to a major general (2 star general/ admiral equivalent), while Geographic Combatant commanders (4 star general/admiral) are among the highest-ranking officers in the Defense Department.[29] Although policy decisions should structurally flow from the DASD to the Combatant Commanders, oftentimes the Combatant Commanders will directly recommend policy decisions to the Secretary of Defense. This practice can project a lack of a unified message.

U.S. POLICY IN LATIN AMERICA AND THE CARIBBEAN

As the lead federal agency for U.S. foreign policy, the Department of State sets the policy direction for the other U.S. government agencies and departments dealing with any international issues. Chiefs of Mission, who are considered the President's personal representatives in foreign countries, administrate the embassies and assist (in coordination with the Secretary of State) in implementing the President's constitutional duties of conducting U.S. foreign relations.[30] Structurally, these embassies should report to Assistant Secretaries of State of each designated world region. For the Western Hemisphere, Chiefs of Mission report to the Assistant Secretary of State for Western Hemisphere Affairs. As of early September 2017, the Trump administration has yet to nominate anyone for this role in Latin America and still has an acting assistant secretary for the position.[31]

The Secretary of State, Assistant Secretary of State, and Chiefs of Mission all have input and authority on the direction of U.S. foreign policy in the region. The nature of this structure has the potential to cause friction between the embassies, Assistant Secretary of State for Western Hemisphere Affairs, and the Secretary of State. For instance, the embassy may emphasize certain priorities that are not necessarily at the top of any lists in Washington, D.C. The resulting confusion and infighting within Department of State on policy issues dealing with defense can often stall or cease certain engagements that the Department of Defense had planned on pursuing.

Within each embassy, there is a senior Defense Official or Defense Attaché (SDO/DATT) who is the Chief of Mission's principal military advisor on defense and national security issues. The SDO/DATTs are the single points of contact for all Department of Defense matters affecting each embassy or U.S. defense components assigned to or operating from the embassy.[32] Within each partner nation there are the Security Cooperation Offices (formerly known as the Military Groups or MILGROUPS). These offices ensure that the security assistance, funding, and training from the United States are executed and military-to-military engagement is coordinated at the operational level. Ideally, there is a representative from each service of the U.S. military who works in partnership with the service counterparts of the partner nation.[33]

DEPARTMENT OF DEFENSE ACTIVITIES IN LATIN AMERICA AND THE CARIBBEAN

For historical reasons mentioned earlier, there are sensitivities among Latin American governments toward the Department of Defense having a lead role of operations in the region. The Department of State is averse to a large military footprint in the region, and many embassies will limit the amount of assistance and activities by the Department of Defense—depending on the political situation on the ground. As a result, the Department of Defense is often not the principal federal agency dealing with the majority of the chief policy issues in Latin America. Instead, it functions as a means of support for the other federal agencies. Examples of the types of activities include conducting counter-illicit trafficking and crime, civilian security assistance, and Humanitarian Assistance Disaster Relief (HA/DR) operations.

The United States Southern Command is one of the seven Geographic Combatant Commands responsible for the ground-level implementation of defense policy in Latin America and the Caribbean. The command is led by a 4-star general or admiral. As of 2017, the U.S. Southern Command maintains that its priorities in the region to become the "partner of choice" for the region, have a rapid response to assist in disaster relief and contingency operations, and to counter transregional threat networks.[34] In all of these priorities, it is the goal of the Department of Defense to help partners in the region to build their capacity to address security issues.

"Building Partnership Capacity" consists of training, mentoring, advising, equipping, exercising, educating and planning with foreign security forces.[35] The objective is to enhance the security capabilities of partners in less capable states, so as to ultimately advance U.S. national security interests by having partners with greater operational capabilities.[36] Building Partnership Capacity is broken into Security Cooperation and Security Assistance programs, which are both managed by the Defense Security Cooperation Agency.[37] Security cooperation refers to Department of Defense interactions with foreign defense and security establishments, including all Department of Defense-administered security assistance programs. Security assistance, by contrast, is a group of programs authorized by Title 22 of the U.S. Code, by which the United States provides defense articles, military training, and other defense-related services by grant, loan, credit, cash sales, or lease, in furtherance of U.S. national policies and objectives.[38] Security Assistance includes programs that assist partner nations in combating drug trafficking and reducing violence and crime. Among these programs are the Mérida Initiative for Mexico, the Central America Regional Security Initiative (CARSI), and the Caribbean Basin Security Initiative (CBSI).[39]

While the Department of Defense is not a law enforcement agency as defined by U.S. laws and regulations, it is the main federal agency leading efforts to detect and monitor aerial and maritime transit of illegal drugs toward the United States.[40] The Department of Defense undertakes this role because it has greater aerial, maritime, information, surveillance, and reconnaissance resources than those possessed by any of the federal law enforcement agencies. The primary executor of these capabilities is Joint Interagency Task Force South (JIATF-S), which is structurally located under the Southern Command. While JIATF-S is technically a Department of Defense entity, it is the embodiment of the "whole of government" approach—coordinating with several law enforcement and intelligence communities.[41] The agency collects and shares information with U.S. government agencies and partner nations' military commands and law enforcement organizations.

U.S. GOVERNMENT SECURITY POLICY TOWARD LATIN AMERICA AND THE CARIBBEAN: TOPICS OF CONCERN

U.S. government policies in Latin America vary according to the particular regime and nation engaged. In terms of security policy, the U.S. focuses primarily on defending the southern approaches of the United States, countering organized criminal activity, counter-narcotics, humanitarian assistance/disaster relief operations, and issues of mass migration to the United States. The Obama administration believed that strategically targeted engagement is the most appropriate course of action in the Americas.[42] The former DASD/WHA, Frank Mora, explained that the current policy direction is to engage and partner with *any* nation willing to work with the United States, and that can offer a mutually beneficial relationship from cooperation: "The United States will also work to cultivate deeper partnerships with new 'key centers of influence,' 'emerging nations,' and even 'hostile nations' because of our conviction that 'our own interests are bound to the interests of those beyond our borders.'"[43] While it is still unclear what direction the new Trump administration will take in the region, the topics listed below will likely remain an important aspect of U.S. security policy in the region.

Counter-Drug Operations

While the Obama administration attempted to move away from the "war on drugs" in theory and from a policy perspective, a large portion of U.S. security policy funding and activities in Latin America and the Caribbean are directed toward counterdrug operations. The 2015 Drug Control Strategy specified that interdiction operations remove dangerous drugs from the supply chain and "provides leads on how to dismantle criminal organizations threatening the United States and countries in the region."[44] The U.S. Southern Command states in its mission statement that it aims to work with federal agencies and partner nations to combat illicit trafficking, which poses a transnational threat to the stability of the region and to U.S. national security.[45]

Remarkably, the 2015 National Drug Control Strategy scarcely mentions the Department of Defense. This shift is likely due to a combination of factors—the most prominent being the Obama administration's treatment of the drug problem as a public health issue rather than a military one. This represents a noteworthy change in course on the manner in which the United States has traditionally fought against the flow of drugs.[46] Yet as the Trump administration begins to formulate its security policy in the region, there are indications that the "war on drugs" will be a main staple. Because of domestic political pressures due to the opioid epidemic, the current administration believes attacking the drug problem needs to be addressed by combating the "supply" of illicit trafficking.[47]

Counterterrorism

Since September 11, 2001, counterterrorism has remained a major focus in all areas and at all levels of U.S. security policy, including strategic planning and policymaking in Latin America and the Caribbean.[48] However, the potential threat emanating from terrorism is relatively low in most Latin American countries.[49] Most terrorist activity in the region is located in Colombia and Peru, coming from the Revolutionary Armed Forces of Colombia (*Fuerzas Armadas Revolucionarias de Colombia*—FARC), the National Liberation Army (*Ejército de Liberación Nacional*—ELN), and the Shining Path (*Sendero Luminoso*—SL).[50] All three of these groups have been officially designated as Foreign Terrorist Organizations by the State Department.[51] In terms of policy, the United States combats terrorism by utilizing sanctions, antiterrorism assistance and training, and law enforcement cooperation.[52] For instance, the United States sanctioned Venezuela in 2006 by imposing an arms embargo after determining that the Chávez regime was not fully cooperating with U.S. antiterrorism efforts.[53]

Humanitarian Assistance/Disaster Relief (HA/DR)

The Department of Defense plays a critical role in HA/DR operations in the region. The United States Agency for International Development Office of Foreign Disaster Assistance (USAID/OFDA) is the primary federal agency charged with U.S. disaster relief operations overseas. U.S. military forces assist when the host nation requests disaster relief assistance for their country from the U.S. Ambassador and USAID/OFDA requests Department of Defense capabilities for the relief effort. The final coordination is conducted at the secretarial level, at which point the Secretary of State formally requests military assistance from the Secretary of Defense.[54] Examples of the use of military assistance in HA/DR include the relief operations following earthquakes in Central America and Haiti.

Mass Migration

Unlawful mass migrations of people into the United States are a significant national security policy matter. There is concern among policymakers in the U.S. that in the case of a natural disaster or collapse of a government in the region, these destabilizing events will spur large-scale attempts to enter the United States illegally. Factors that fueled Latin American migration to the United States have included family ties, poverty and unemployment, political and economic instability, natural disasters, proximity, and crime and violence.[55] If the number of migrants attempting to enter the United States illegally reaches a certain saturation point, no single agency will possess the capability or resources to respond effectively to a mass migration.[56] Migration trends from the Caribbean, and more recently the surge of unaccompanied minors from Central America, are priorities of the United States government.[57]

Peacekeeping Operations

A notable policy initiative for the United States government in the region is the training and equipment of regional partners to provide security forces to enhance global peacekeeping operations. The United States government provides the great majority of this training through both the Department of Defense and the Department of State. Global Peace Operations Initiative (GPOI) is a program that works in close coordination with the Department of State regional bureaus, as well as the Office of the Secretary of Defense, the Joint Staff, Regional Combatant Commands, and other Department of Defense organizations to develop regional program plans and execute these training and equipping activities.[58]

Climate Change

The Obama administration's interest in addressing global climate change influenced all departments and agencies of the United States government.

The 2015 National Security Strategy emphasizes the harmful indirect consequences of climate change, as it can lead to increased refugee flows due to natural disasters and conflicts over food and water.[59] While climate change itself does not create emerging security threats, it does act as a threat multiplier by exacerbating existing political weaknesses and social tensions in the region.[60] However, this is likely to change as the current Trump administration is shifting its focus away from addressing climate change.[61]

Whole of Government

In each of these focus areas, multiple agencies in the U.S. government operate in concert with one another to accomplish objectives. The policy direction and implementation is not designed for any one agency to do all of the lifting on any particular issue. The buzzword or phrase used by U.S. policymakers is the "whole of government" approach. Each agency has some unique capabilities that it brings to the table as part of a policy toolbox to solve issues in the region.[62] Combating transnational criminal organizations is a major thrust area in the whole of government approach to Latin America and the Caribbean, as it requires various law enforcement and military agencies to contribute to the efforts to interdict transnational criminal organizations.[63]

POLICY RESTRICTIONS IN LATIN AMERICA AND THE CARIBBEAN

Although the U.S. government has a wide range of interests directing its activities in the region, there are restrictions that prevent certain defense engagement. While the executive branch can alter policies with reversals or determinations relatively quickly, congressional restrictions are difficult to change and present more of an obstacle to certain actions. Many restrictions on security cooperation and defense engagements are codified in congressional law, which requires a legislative process to overturn or amend laws that may be a hurdle to executing policy. The polarizing state of politics in both the House of Representatives and Senate renders this task very difficult, so policy changes can be extremely slow or impossible in these circumstances.

In particular, the Department of Defense is limited by policy and legal restrictions that dictate the degree of engagement and travel in the Western Hemisphere. These restrictions may either be congressionally mandated (law) or a policy from the executive branch. Oftentimes, these restrictions are difficult to lift or circumvent—as is the case with Cuban engagement restrictions, which have been codified in law for decades.

Human Rights

The practice of utilizing the military for domestic security issues can lead to increased human rights issues and violations. In Latin America, the security situation and the weak government institutions almost necessitate the military in some nations to be used for domestic security. Adherence to human rights conventions is a priority for the United States government worldwide. By virtue of the history of U.S. security policy in Latin America, especially during the Cold War, the United States government is particularly concerned with enforcing compliance to international human rights laws by the governments to which it provides assistance. The complex security issues are often addressed by military forces in the region because of institutional weaknesses and corruption within these governments.[64] To further complicate matters, civil-military relationships in the region are tarnished by a history of harsh military rule that is still fresh in the memories of many in the population.[65]

For the Department of Defense, both congressional law and policy serve to restrict assistance and engagement to those partners that do not have a history marred by human rights violations. Of particular importance to the security policy conversation are the Leahy Laws, or Leahy Amendments. First sponsored in the late 1990s by Senator Patrick Leahy (D-VT), the Leahy Laws were passed in the Foreign Assistance Act of 1961, which prohibits assistance to any foreign security force unit that is credibly believed to have committed a gross violation of human rights.[66] As another backstop, there exists a provision in the annual defense appropriations that prohibits use of Department of Defense funds on support and assistance to such forces.[67] The Leahy laws are essential in legitimizing U.S. assistance in the region; however, they also bear the potential of constraining the Department of Defense's ability to respond to national security needs.[68]

Shoot down Laws

The emergence of domestic shoot down laws in the region is another policy consideration for defense restrictions. As the threat of transnational organized crime continues to plague Latin America and the Caribbean, nations in the region have authorized lethal interdiction of civilian aircraft that they believe to be conducting illicit activities. Countries that have enacted shoot down laws include Bolivia, Brazil, Colombia, Honduras, Paraguay, Peru, and Venezuela. In 2001, Peru ceased its shoot down program following an incident in which the military shot down a civilian aircraft carrying a group of innocent missionaries when they were mistaken for criminals. Subsequently, the United States government and Department of Defense ceased the sharing of any radar track information with the Peruvian military.[69] In

2012, the Honduran military shot down two small planes that were suspected of transporting drugs. This incident induced the United States to suspend anti-drug radar support to Honduras.[70]

International law prohibits the practice of shooting down civilian aircraft. The ICAO (International Civil Aviation Organization) and the Chicago Convention state that civilian aircraft are not to be put in danger within the "in service period" (24 hours prior to take off and 24 hours after landing). JIATF-S shares air and maritime tracks with the region's various militaries to bolster counterdrug operations. Historically, this support and assistance exposed U.S. service members and government officials to possible criminal liability, as participation in the neutralization of civilian aircraft is essentially an extrajudicial killing under U.S. law.[71]

AREAS OF CONCERN IN U.S. SECURITY POLICY

Latin America and the Caribbean have a complex and diverse security environment that necessitates constant and intricate attention from U.S. policymakers. The topics below present a brief synopsis of some of the primary areas of concern.

Emergence of China and Russia in the Region on Defense Issues

The emergence of extra-hemispheric actors is garnering the attention of many in the U.S. policy world, despite the region being considered a low priority to some. The "partner of choice" concept refers to the United States' status as the preferred provider of defense training, equipment, and sales of defense articles. In terms of security partnerships in the hemisphere, the United States is no longer the only actor in the region. American policymakers must now work to remain relevant and engaged with nations in the region that have historically partnered with the United States on security issues.[72] The rise of Russian and Chinese involvement in the region has brought the United States into competition with these eastern powers for dominance as the partner of choice.

China

While China provides defense-related assistance in the region, it does not appear that China's objective is to challenge the United States as a security provider.[73] China does provide some training and defense sales; however, Chinese interest in Latin America and the Caribbean seems to be heavily motivated by economic considerations. The Chinese tend to use the soft power of their military force. For example, the Chinese military has brought over its hospital ship, known as the *Peace Ark*, to provide medical screening and care to the region.[74] The United States provides the same type of assistance when it deploys its own hospital ship, the USS COMFORT.[75] There is, however, a growing concern about the Chinese plans to build a canal in Nicaragua that will have a larger capacity than the Panama Canal. As a result, some in the security policy world surmise that these canal plans could be a justification for increased Chinese military presence and a "counter-pivot" by China to the United States' "Asian Pivot."[76]

Russia

Russia's defense engagement in Latin America is not a new phenomenon. During the Cold War, the United States and Russia fought proxy wars in Central America and the Caribbean. While this engagement waned after the collapse of the Soviet Union, the Russian Federation is engaging in the region more heavily in recent years. Moscow's activities in Latin America and the Caribbean may be an attempt to acquire military facilities in the region and to undermine U.S. influence, while strengthening counter blocs such as ALBA.[77]

Emphasis on Central America

In recent years, violence and insecurity in Central America have shifted the focus of U.S. policymakers. The area of El Salvador, Guatemala, and Honduras, known as the "northern triangle," is of particular worry because of the high levels of violence and crime that beleaguer and exude from these nations.[78] The crime problem has been further exacerbated by the increase of illicit traffickers and gang members.[79] The United States Southern Command based its prioritization of working with Central America upon the 2011 White House Strategy to combat transnational organized crime and the Central American Regional Security Initiative (CARSI), which has received $1.2 billion in U.S. assistance from FY2008–FY2015.[80]

The decision by the Department of Defense to concentrate resources on Central America became further justified when the United States experienced a sharp increase in the number of unaccompanied children from the region arriving at the southern border in 2014.[81] According to the 2015 National Security Strategy, "migration surges involving unaccompanied children across our southern border is one major consequence of weak institutions and violence."[82] Former Assistant Secretary of State Roberta Jacobson explained during her testimony that the number of unaccompanied children flowing into the United States is an indication of the deteriorating security situation in Central America.[83]

Colombia

From a policy perspective, Colombia is touted as a success for Department of Defense engagement and assistance in the region. Colombia resurged from the brink of collapse in the late 1990s and now maintains one of the most objectively powerful security forces in the region. Over the past 50 years, Colombia has endured an internal armed conflict among drug cartels and extremist, armed political groups.[84] In the late 1990s, some analysts feared Colombia would disintegrate into a failed state.[85] As a result of U.S. assistance in what was known as "Plan Colombia," the country has not only thrived[86] but is now a model of security to the surrounding region. The United States government's end objective is for the Colombian military to undertake many of the traditional roles assisting and leading in security engagements throughout the region. In turn, the U.S. wants the Colombian military to eventually be able to export its expertise and capabilities to other countries in the region.

The United States government remains committed to assisting the Colombian government by facilitating peace talks with the FARC and the subsequent demobilization and reintegration of FARC rebels.[87] While the United States Department of Defense has experience in demobilizing and reintegrating enemy forces in other regions, decades of violence and a bitter relationship between the FARC and the Colombian government and citizens will complicate an already daunting task.[88] Although Colombia is often touted as a success story, the degree and volume of U.S. assistance to Colombia is slowly diminishing. While peace talks have finished and the FARC members are demobilizing[89]—as well as the movement of drug cartels and violence into Central America and the Caribbean—U.S. funding and attention is being directed elsewhere.

Brazil

The United States and Brazil enjoy an active and productive political and economic relationship. The two governments maintain at least twenty active bilateral dialogues, many of which are directly related to defense issues.[90] Although U.S.-Brazilian cooperation on security issues has traditionally been limited, law enforcement and military engagement has increased over the past decade with coordination on counter-narcotics, counterterrorism, and defense.[91]

Brazil is a regional power that keeps a large and well-equipped defense force. Brazil's government and military do not often request or desire U.S. defense assistance or training. Nonetheless, they are a powerful partner in defense cooperation in the region. As mentioned earlier in the chapter, an underlying principle of U.S. security policy is the encouragement of partner nations to participate and undertake more comprehensive security roles. Brazil's contribution as the lead country for the United Nations' mission in Haiti is a prime example of this active participation. In 2010, the U.S. and Brazilian governments signed a Defense Cooperation Agreement, promoting defense cooperation in security and defense technology, as well as information sharing.[92]

Caribbean

CBSI

The United States has various security concerns in the Caribbean. Among these antagonists are an increase in illicit trafficking and terrorist threats from individuals that fought for ISIS and have since returned to the Caribbean.[93] As such, the Department of Defense and the Caribbean nations cooperate on topics of mutual security concerns. The geographic location of these Caribbean nations makes them attractive transit countries for illicit drugs destined for the United States.[94] In September 2015, the Obama administration identified the Bahamas, the Dominican Republic, Haiti, and Jamaica as major drug-producing or drug-transit countries in the Caribbean.[95] The President considered factors such as increased homicide rates and political and social instability when making these determinations, as those factors are indicative of illicit trafficking and transnational organized crime.[96]

In 2009, the Obama administration developed the Caribbean Basin Security Initiative (CBSI) with the goals of reducing illicit trafficking, and increased cooperation on issues of security, law enforcement, justice reform, and border security.[97] For FY2016, the Obama administration requested $53.5 million for the CBSI.[98]

Cuba

President Obama was the first American Head of State to visit Cuba since 1928. Like many of the multifaceted issues in American foreign policy, the thaw in relations between the United States and Cuba is contentious. No drastic changes in the defense relationship with the Cubans occurred, and the low-level engagement with Cuban military counterparts continued. Any greater degree of assistance and coordination with the Cuban military is proscribed in congressional law. The Cuban Democracy Act of 1992, the Cuban Liberty and Democratic Solidarity (LIBERTAD) Act of 1996, and the Trade Sanctions Reform and Export Enhancement Act of 2000 preclude the Department of Defense from providing material and security assistance to the government of Cuba.[99]

The Trump administration has indicated that the thaw in relations with Cuba will be under review. Matthew Taylor explains:

> While some lawmakers are pushing for more pressure on Cuba for human rights, it seems unlikely that the administration would be able to completely unwind U.S. investment on the island, given growing U.S. business interests. Even as he has promised to review Cuba regulations, Secretary of State Rex Tillerson seems to have put some space between himself and the most dramatic Trump campaign oratory. But a harder rhetorical line and the possibility of renewed sanctions from Washington may strengthen hardliners within the Cuban regime and diminish the impetus toward reform; already it has led to nationwide military exercises that belie the Cuban regime's concern about a return to a more confrontational relation.[100]

While it is too early in the Trump administration to know how this will play out, it is likely that Trump will reverse some of the policies of the Obama administration.

Haiti

In the Western Hemisphere, Haiti is arguably the most impoverished and troubled state. The 2010 earthquake exacerbated the situation, rendering the government incapacitated and creating much worse conditions for the citizens. The U.S. reaction to the earthquake in Haiti was predominately a military operation. The United States' ability to deliver relief supplies and unique lifesaving capabilities was a direct result of the mobilization of Department of Defense strategy and resources.[101] The United States government continues to provide support and relief to Haiti. However, questions regarding leadership responsibility for the MINUSTAH security mission after the Brazilians depart will dominate security policy considerations in the months to follow.

CONCLUSION: THE FUTURE OF SECURITY POLICY IN LATIN AMERICA

Generally speaking, the United States security policy is convoluted, and nested within a confusing and complex National Security Council system. These policy intricacies are compounded in Latin America and the Caribbean due to the historical and political sensitivities of U.S. military operations in the region.

What was the previous Obama administration's security policy in Latin America? Judging from various policy documents from the National Security

Council and press releases from the White House, the consensus was to foster relationships with partner nations on topics of mutual concern and to engage with all partners in the region. Many policies were left intentionally ambiguous to allow flexibility in engagement with partners in the region. While there are benefits to a flexible and less restrictive policy, oftentimes it produces a lack of clear guidance to the individuals implementing the policy and transmits unclear messages to partner nations.

What will the Trump administration bring in terms of security policy in the region? Early indications show a move to the use of his National Security Council—and in particular the Department of Defense—as the largest instruments in its foreign policy. An increase in the Defense Department's budget will mean that the State Department will experience significant budget cuts. Such changes could impact the United States' soft power in the region. This will likely make Latin American leaders weary of U.S. assistance and may hurt relations in the long term. The Department of State should remain the lead federal agency in promulgating security policy in Latin America and the Caribbean as many of the issues in the region are more likely to be alleviated through diplomacy and development.

Notes

INTRODUCTION

1. Laura Chioda, *Stop the Violence in Latin America: A Look at Prevention from Cradle to Adulthood* (Washington, DC: World Bank Group, 2016); for more on poverty, economics, and inequality in Latin America, see: Tim H. Gindling, "Poverty in Latin America," *Latin American Research Review* 40, no. 1 (2005): pp. 207–222; Alain De Janvry and Elisabeth Sadoulet, "Rural poverty in Latin America: Determinants and exit paths," *Food Policy* 25, no. 4 (2000): pp. 389–409; Carol Graham and Andrew Felton, "Inequality and happiness: insights from Latin America," *Journal of Economic Inequality* 4, no. 1 (2006): pp. 107–122; Nora Claudia Lustig, ed. Declining inequality in Latin America: A decade of progress? (Washington, DC: Brookings Institution Press, 2010); Edwin Goñi, J. Humberto López, and Luis Servén, "Fiscal redistribution and income inequality in Latin America," *World Development* 39, no. 9 (2011): pp. 1558–1569.

2. Laura Chioda, *Stop the Violence in Latin America: A Look at Prevention From Cradle to Adulthood.*

3. UNDP, *Regional Human Development Report 2013–2014. Citizen Security with a Human Face: Evidence and Proposals for Latin America* (New York, NY: UNDP, 2013); Steven Dudley, "Criminal Evolution and Violence in Latin America and the Caribbean," *InSight Crime*, June 26, 2014, www.insightcrime.org/news-analysis/evolution-crime-violence-latin-america-caribbean, accessed April 2017.

4. Charles Parkinson, "Latin America is World's Most Violent Region: UN," *InSight Crime*, April 21, 2014, www.insightcrime.org/news-analysis/latin-america-worlds-most-violent-region-un, accessed April 2017.

5. UNODC, *Global Study on Homicide 2013* (New York, NY: UNDOC, 2014), chapter 1.

6. UNODC, *Global Study on Homicide 2013*, Ch. 1. The number are based on 2012 data or latest year.

7. Ibid.

8. Robert Muggah and Ilona Szabó de Carvalho, "There's a cure for Latin America's murder epidemic—and it doesn't involve more police or prisons," *World Economic Forum*, April 4, 2017, www.weforum.org/agenda/2017/04/there-s-a-cure-for-latin-america-s-murder-epidemic-and-it-doesn-t-involve-more-police-or prisons/?utm_content=buffer369bb&utm_medium=social&utm_source=plus.google.com&utm_campaign=buffer, accessed May 2017.

9. Laura Chioda, *Stop the Violence in Latin America: A Look at Prevention from Cradle to Adulthood*, p. 1.

10. Elyssa Pachico, "Latin America Dominates List of World's Most Violent Cities," *InSight Crime*, January 22, 2015, www.insightcrime.org/news-analysis/latin-america-dominates-list-of-worlds-most-violent-cities, accessed April 2017.

11. For more, see Alicia R. Schmidt Camacho, "Ciudadana X: Gender violence and the denationalization of women's rights in Ciudad Juarez, Mexico," *CR: The New Centennial Review* 5, no. 1 (2005): pp. 255–292; Charles Bowden, *Murder City: Ciudad Juarez and the global economy's new killing fields* (New York, NY: Nation Books, 2011); Jessica Livingston, "Murder in Juárez: gender, sexual violence, and the global assembly line," *Frontiers: A Journal of Women Studies* 25, no. 1 (2004): pp. 59–76.

12. Ibid.

13. Ibid.

14. Ibid.

15. Ibid; see also Seguridad, Justicia y Paz, www.seguridadjusticiaypaz.org.mx/, accessed April 2017.

16. Robert Muggah and Ilona Szabó de Carvalho, "There's a cure for Latin America's murder epidemic—and it doesn't involve more police or prisons."

17. Ibid.

18. For more, see: Adam Isacson, "Colombia peace in tatters," *NACLA Report on the Americas* 35, no. 5 (2002): pp. 10–13; Thania Paffenholz, "Civil Society and Peace Negotiations: Beyond the Inclusion-Exclusion Dichotomy," *Negotiation Journal* 30, no. 1 (2014): pp. 69–91.

19. Nicholas Casey, "Colombia's Congress Approves Peace Accord With FARC," *The New York Times*, November 30, 2016.

20. 15th Anniversary of Plan Colombia: Learning from Its Successes and Failures," *Washington Office on Latin America*, February 1, 2016, www.wola.org/files/1602_plancol/, accessed April 2017.

21. David Wing, "Number of victims of Colombia's conflict surpasses 7 million," *Colombia Reports,* November 18, 2014.

22. Peter A. Lupsha, "Drug trafficking: Mexico and Colombia in comparative perspective," *Journal of International Affairs* (1981): pp. 95–115; Ted Galen Carpenter, *The Fire Next Door: Mexico's Drug Violence and the Danger to America* (Washington, DC: Cato Institute, 2012); Enrique Desmond Arias and Mark Ungar, "Community policing and Latin America's citizen security crisis," *Comparative Politics* 41, no. 4 (2009): pp. 409–429; Enrique Desmond Arias, "The dynamics of criminal governance: networks and social order in Rio de Janeiro," *Journal of Latin American Studies* 38, no. 02 (2006): pp. 293–325; Coletta Youngers and Eileen Rosin, eds.

Drugs and democracy in Latin America: The impact of US policy (Boulder, CO: Lynne Rienner Publishers, 2005).

23. Clare Ribando Seelke, *Gangs in Central America* (Washington, DC: Congressional Research Service 2016); for more on gangs, see: José Miguel Cruz, "Criminal violence and democratization in central America: the survival of the violent state," *Latin American Politics and Society* 53, no. 4 (2011): pp. 1–33; Sonja Wolf, "Mara Salvatrucha: The Most Dangerous Street Gang in the Americas?" *Latin American Politics and Society* 54, no. 1 (2012): pp. 65–99; Sonja Wolf, "Maras transnacionales: Origins and transformations of Central American street gangs," *Latin American Research Review* 45, no. 1 (2010): pp. 256–265.

24. Tristan Clavel, "540 Children were Murdered Last Year in El Salvador: Report," *InSight Crime*, January 31, 2017, www.insightcrime.org/news-briefs/540-children-murdered-last-year-el-salvador-report, accessed April 2017, p. 1.

25. Adriana Beltrán, "Children and Families Fleeing Violence in Central America," *WOLA*, February 21, 2017, www.wola.org/analysis/people-leaving-central-americas-northern-triangle/, accessed May 2017, pp. 3–4.

26. Ibid.

27. Steven Dudley, "Criminal Evolution and Violence in Latin America and the Caribbean."

28. Bruce Bagley, *Drug Trafficking and Organized Crime in the Americas: Major Trends in the Twenty-First Century* (Washington, DC: Woodrow Wilson International Center for Scholars, 2012).

29. Ibid. For more on corruption, see: Joseph S. Tulchin and Ralph H. Espach, *Combating Corruption in Latin America* (Washington, DC: Woodrow Wilson Center Press, 2000); Kurt Gerhard Weyland, "The politics of corruption in Latin America," *Journal of Democracy* 9, no. 2 (1998): pp. 108–121.

30. Robert Muggah and Ilona Szabó de Carvalho, "There's a cure for Latin America's murder epidemic—and it doesn't involve more police or prisons," p. 3.

31. For more on this topic, see: Cynthia L. Arnson and Eric L. Olson with Christine Zaino, eds. *One Goal Two Struggles: Confronting Crime and Violence in Mexico and Colombia* (Washington, DC: Wilson Center, 2014); Bruce Bagley, *Drug Trafficking and Organized Crime in the Americas: Major Trends in the Twenty-First Century.*

32. Bruce Bagley, *Drug Trafficking and Organized Crime in the Americas: Major Trends in the Twenty-First Century.*

33. Patrick Corcoran, "Mexico Has 80 Drug Cartels: Attorney General," *InSight Crime*, December 20, 2012, www.insightcrime.org/news-analysis/mexico-has-80-drug-cartels-attorney-general, accessed April 2017.

34. Paula Miraglia, "Drugs and Drug Trafficking in Brazil: Trends and Policies," *Brookings Institution*, 2016, www.brookings.edu/wp-content/uploads/2016/07/Miraglia-Brazil-final.pdf, accessed April 2017, p. 2.

35. Nick Miroff and William Booth, "Mexico's drug war is at a stalemate as Calderon's presidency ends," *The Washington Post*, November 27, 2012; David A. Shirk, "Drug violence in Mexico: data and analysis from 2001–2009," *Trends in Organized Crime* 13, no. 2–3 (2010): pp. 167–174.

36. Kimberly Heinle, Cory Molzahn, and David A. Shirk, *Drug Violence in Mexico: Data and Analysis Through 2014* (San Diego, CA: University of San Diego, 2015).

37. Ibid.

38. Kirk Semple, "Mexico Grapples With a Surge in Violence," *The New York Times*, December 13, 2016.

39. "Interactive Maps and Charts of Armed Violence Indicators," *Small Arms Survey*, www.smallarmssurvey.org/tools/interactive-map-charts-on-armed-violence.html, accessed April 2017.

40. "Thousands of Girls and Women are Fleeing Rape, Sexual Violence and Torture in Honduras, El Salvador and Guatemala," *Center for Gender & Refugee Studies*, cgrs.uchastings.edu/talking_points_and_stories, accessed April 2017.

41. Julio Jacobo Waiselfisz, Mapa da Violência 2015: Homicídio de Mulheres no Brasil (Brasília, BR, 2015).

42. Mimi Yagoub, "Why Does Latin America Have the World's Highest Female Murder Rates?" *InSight Crime*, February 11, 2016, www.insightcrime.org/news-analysis/why-does-latin-america-have-the-world-s-highest-female-murder-rates, accessed April 2017.

43. Kyra Gurney, "Perceptions of Insecurity Increasing in LatAm," *InSight Crime*, December 9, 2014, www.insightcrime.org/news-analysis/perceptions-of-insecurity-increasing-in-latin-america, accessed June 2017.

CHAPTER 1. VIOLENCE AND SECURITY IN ARGENTINA: MAJOR TRENDS AND POLICY RESPONSES

1. United Nations Development Programme, *Regional Human Development Report 2013–2014. Citizen Security with a Human Face: Evidence and Proposals for Latin America* (New York, NY: United Nations Development Programme, 2014).

2. United Nations Office on Drugs and Crime, *Global Study on Homicides, 2013* (Vienna: United Nations Office on Drugs and Crime, 2013).

3. Robert Muggah, "Latin America's Poverty Is Down, But Violence Is Up. Why?" *Americas Quarterly*, October 20, 2015.

4. United Nations Development Programme, Regional Human Development Report 2013–2014. Citizen Security with a Human Face: Evidence and Proposals for Latin America (New York, NY: United Nations Development Programme, 2014).

5. Latin American Public Opinion Project (LAPOP), *The Political Culture of Democracy in the Americas, 2014*: *Democratic Governance Across 10 Years of the Americas Barometer* (Nashville, TN: Vanderbilt University, 2014).

6. Ministerio de Justicia y Derechos Humanos, *Informe Anual de Estadísticas Policiales 2008* (Buenos Aires: Dirección Nacional de Política Criminal, 2008).

7. Ministerio de Seguridad de la Nación, *Estadísticas Criminales en la República Argentina, 2015* (Buenos Aires: Secretaría de Seguridad Interior, 2016a).

8. United Nations Development Programme, *Regional Human Development Report 2013–2014. Citizen Security with a Human Face: Evidence and Proposals for Latin America* (New York, NY: United Nations Development Programme, 2014).

9. Daniel Pardo, "Qué hay de Real y qué de Exagerado en la 'Epidemia de Inseguridad' por la que Protesta Argentina," *BBC Mundo*, October 11, 2016. Original in Spanish, non-official translation by the author; the same procedure applies for any original quotes that are not in English throughout this text.

10. Latin American Public Opinion Project (LAPOP), *The Political Culture of Democracy in the Americas, 2014: Democratic Governance Across 10 Years of the Americas Barometer* (Nashville, TN: Vanderbilt University, 2014).

11. Latin American Public Opinion Project (LAPOP), *The Political Culture of Democracy in the Americas, 2014: Democratic Governance Across 10 Years of the Americas Barometer* (Nashville, TN: Vanderbilt University, 2014).

12. Ministerio de Justicia y Derechos Humanos, *Informe Anual de Estadísticas Policiales 2008* (Buenos Aires: Dirección Nacional de Política Criminal, 2008).

13. Daniel Pardo, "Qué hay de Real y qué de Exagerado en la 'Epidemia de Inseguridad' por la que Protesta Argentina," *BBC Mundo*, October 11, 2016.

14. Ministerio de Seguridad de la Nación, *Informe del Sistema Nacional de Información Criminal, 2015*, (Buenos Aires: Dirección Nacional de Gestión de la Información Criminal, 2016b).

15. United Nations Office on Drugs and Crime, *Global Study on Homicides, 2013* (Vienna: United Nations Office on Drugs and Crime, 2013).

16. Ministerio de Justicia y Derechos Humanos, *Informe sobre Homicidios, 2014* (Buenos Aires: Instituto de Investigaciones, Consejo de la Magistratura, 2015).

17. Murray Lee, *Inventing Fear of Crime Criminology and the Politics of Anxiety* (Cullompton: Willan, 2007).

18. Gabriel Kessler, *El Sentimiento de Inseguridad. Sociología del Temor al Delito* (Buenos Aires: Siglo XXI Editores, 2009).

19. The first surveys were developed by President's Commissions on Law Enforcement and Administration of Justice in 1967 and its main objective was to provide a measurement closer to the "real crime." Major improvements began in 1972, when the Department of Justice began funding the development of the National Crime Victimization Survey, which is currently the most important as it includes interviews of 80,000 individuals older than 12 (Sozzo, 2008, "Pintando con Números: Fuentes Estadísticas de Conocimiento y Gobierno de la Cuestión Criminal," in *Inseguridad, Prevención y Policía*, ed. Máximo Sozzo (Quito: FLACSO, 2008), pp. 21–66.

20. Máximo Sozzo, "Pintando con Números: Fuentes Estadísticas de Conocimiento y Gobierno de la Cuestión Criminal," in *Inseguridad, Prevención y Policía*, ed. Máximo Sozzo (Quito: FLACSO, 2008), pp. 21–66.

21. Ibid.

22. Gabriel Kessler, "Rising Levels of Insecurity in Latin America," *Global Dialogue*, July 13, 2012, http://isa-global-dialogue.net/rising-levels-of-insecurity-in-latin-america/, accessed January 4, 2017.

23. Latin American Public Opinion Project (LAPOP), *The Political Culture of Democracy in the Americas, 2014: Democratic Governance Across 10 Years of the Americas Barometer* (Nashville: Vanderbilt University, 2014).

24. Gabriel Kessler, *El Sentimiento de Inseguridad. Sociología del Temor al Delito* (Buenos Aires: Siglo XXI Editores, 2009).

25. Nicolás Rodríguez Games, Santiago Fernández, & Marcelo Sain. *Seguridad y Gobiernos Locales en Argentina* (Buenos Aires: Universidad Metropolitana para la Educación y el Trabajo, 2016).

26. Guillermina Seri, *Seguridad: Crime, Police Power, and Democracy in Argentina* (New York, NY: Bloomsbury Academic, 2012).

27. Gabriel Kessler, *El Sentimiento de Inseguridad. Sociología del Temor al Delito* (Buenos Aires: Siglo XXI Editores, 2009).

28. Ibid.

29. Before the administration of Cristina Fernández (2007–2015), internal security was historically in charge of the Ministry of Interior.

30. In April 1988, the National Congress passed Law 23, 553 (National Defense Law), annulling previous defense legislation. Unlike the prior legal instrument, which expressly allowed the military force to confront domestic threats such as drug trafficking, the new legislation formally divided the spheres of internal security and external defense.

31. Marcelo Sain, "La Reforma Policial en América Latina: Una Mirada Crítica desde el Progresismo," *Nueva Sociedad*, Documentos, pp. 1–69.

32. Organization of American States (OAS), *Seguridad Pública: Argentina* (Washington DC: Departamento de Seguridad Pública).

33. Gabriel Kessler, "Delito, Sentimiento de Inseguridad y Políticas Públicas en la Argentina del Siglo XX, in *La Inseguridad y la Seguridad Ciudadana en América Latina*, ed. José Alfredo Zavaleta Betancourt (Buenos Aires: CLACSO, 2012).

34. Infobae, "Sólo 3 de Cada Mil Personas que Delinquen van a la Cárcel, se Quejó Macri," March 7, 2014.

35. La Nación, "Oficializan la Declaración de Emergencia en Seguridad," January 22, 2016, http://www.lanacion.com.ar/1864382-oficializan-la-declaracion-de-emergencia-en-seguridad, accessed April 6, 2017.

36. Operation Northern Shield was launched during Kirchner administration (2003 to 2007). The initiative intended to control drug smuggling along the South American country's northern border by the installation of different radars operated by the Air Force.

37. The 1988 National Defense Law prohibits the participation of the armed forces in internal security operations, limiting their role to external defense.

38. "Macri Coincide con la Idea de Revisar el Rol de las FF.AA. Contra las Drogas," *Clarín*, January 18, 2014.

39. "Encuesta Nacional sobre Política Migratoria," *Poliarquía Consultores*, January 30, 2017, http://poliarquia.com/encuesta-nacional-sobre-politica-migratoria/, accessed April 17, 2017.

40. Decree 70/2017 modifies Law 25,871. Most importantly, the new legal instrument reduces the deportation process to no more than two months while increasing the prohibition time for expelled foreigners returning to Argentina from five to eight years or more.

41. Santiago Del Carril, "Regional Leaders Alarmed over Macri's Immigration Decree," *Buenos Aires Herald*, February 3, 2017.

42. Currently Argentina's age for legal prosecution of a criminal minor is 16 years-old, although the law does not permit younger criminals to be punished or to be taken to trial.

43. "Age of Criminal Responsibility Should be Lowered, Macri," *Buenos Aires Herald*, January 20, 2011.

44. "Baja de Imputabilidad: el Gobierno Descarta sumar a Zaffaroni al Debate," *Clarín*, January 5, 2017, https://www.clarin.com/politica/baja-imputabilidad-gobierno-descarta-sumar-zaffaroni-debate_0_ryjhNJnBl.html, accessed April 18, 2017.

45. Additional initiatives include the hire of American and Israeli advisers, the imprisonment of drug traffickers, the increasing presence of federal troops in the most insecure areas, the designation of law-enforcement officers as attaches along different diplomatic representations abroad, among others.

46. Adam Isacson, "Latin America's Dangerous Shift to Aerial Shootdown Policies in War on Drugs," *Washington Office on Latin America* (WOLA), February 4, 2014, https://www.wola.org/analysis/latin-americas-dangerous-shift-to-aerial-shootdown-policies-in-war-on-drugs/, accessed April 6, 2017.

47. The Ruta 34 highway is a major transit route for the cocaine smuggled primarily from Bolivia but also from Peru and Colombia. Beginning on the border with Bolivia, the so-called "*ruta blanca*" (white route) connects the provinces of Salta and Santa Fe, respectively the main entry point and hub for drug trafficking in Argentina. Similarly, Ruta 11 plays an analogous role with regard to marijuana trafficking from neighboring Paraguay.

48. Ministerio de Justicia y Derechos Humanos, *Informe Anual del Sistema Nacional de Estadísticas Sobre Ejecución de la Pena 2011* (Buenos Aires: Dirección Nacional de Política Criminal, 2011).

49. UNICEF, *Adolescentes en Conflicto con la Ley Penal* (Buenos Aires: Ministerio de Desarrollo Social de la Nación, 2015).

50. Corte Suprema de Justicia de la Nación, *Homicidios Dolosos 2013* (Buenos Aires: Instituto de Investigaciones y de Referencia Extranjera, 2014).

CHAPTER 2. BRAZIL: VIOLENCE AND PUBLIC (UN)SAFETY

1. Michel Foucault, *The History of Sexuality. Vol. I: An Introduction* (New York: Picador, 2008); Michel Foucault. *Discipline and Punishment: The Birth of Prison* (New York: Picador, 1997).

2. Ibid.

3. Ibid., p. 138.

4. Ibid., p. 140.

5. Ibid., p. 141.

6. Daniel Cerqueira e Danilo Santa Cruz Coelho, *Democracia Racial e Homicídios de Jovens Negros na Cidade Partida* (Brasília: IPEA, 2017), p.5.

7. Daniel Cerqueira, Renato Sergio de Lima Samira Bueno, Luis Iván Valencia, Olaya Hanashiro, Pedro Henrique G. Machado e Adriana dos Santos Lima, *Atlas da Violência 2017* (Brasília: IPEA/Fórum Brasileiro de Segurança Pública, 2017).

8. Daniel Cerqueira e Danilo Santa Cruz Coelho, *Democracia Racial e Homicídios de Jovens Negros na Cidade Partida* (Brasília: IPEA, 2017), p. 7.

9. Ibid.

10. Ibid., p. 20.

11. Ibid., p. 19.

12. Ibid., p. 22.

13. Ibid., p. 10.

14. Thiago Rodrigues and Carol Viviana Porto, *The South American View for a Better Collaboration between South America and Europe Against Drug Trafficking* (Rio de Janeiro: CEBRI/Konrad Adenauer Foundation/European Union, 2017).

15. Thiago Rodrigues, *Política e Drogas nas Américas: uma genealogia do narcotráfico* (São Paulo: Desatino, 2017).

16. Luis Fernando Sarmiento, Ciro Krauthausen, *Cocaína & CO.: un mercado ilegal por dentro* (Bogotá: Tercer Mundo Editores, 1991).

17. Thiago Rodrigues and Carol Viviana Porto, *The South American View for a Better Collaboration between South America and Europe Against Drug Trafficking*

18. Daniel Cerqueira, Renato Sergio de Lima Samira Bueno, Luis Iván Valencia, Olaya Hanashiro, Pedro Henrique G. Machado e Adriana dos Santos Lima, *Atlas da Violência 2017*, p. 43.

19. Ibid.

20. Ibid., p. 43.

21. Ibid., p. 44.

22. Daniel Cerqueira e Danilo Santa Cruz Coelho, *Democracia Racial e Homicídios de Jovens Negros na Cidade Partida.*

23. Wendy Hunter, *Eroding Military Influence in Brazil: Politicians Against Soldiers* (North Carolina: Chaper Hill, 1997).

24. Kai Michael Kenkel, "New Missions and emerging powers: Brazil, peace operations and MINUSTAH," in *Mission Critical: Smaller Democracies' Role in Global Stability Operations* eds, Christian Leuprecht, Jodok Troy, and David Last (Montreal/Kingston: McGill/Queen's University Press), p. 125–147, especially p. 133.

25. Carlos Aguiar Serra and Orlando Zaccone. Guerra é Paz: os paradoxos da política de segurança pública de confronto humanitário In Vera M. Batista, ed., *Paz Armada* (Rio de Janeiro: Editora Revan/Instituto Carioca de Criminologia, 2012), pp. 23–46.

26. Maíra Siman Gomes, "pacificação" como prática de "política externa" de (re) produção do self estatal: reescrevendo o engajamento do Brasil na MINUSTAH. Rio de Janeiro: IRI/PUC-Rio, 2014.

27. Todd Diacom, *Rondon: o marechal da floresta* (São Paulo: Companhia das Letras, 2006).

28. Thiago Rodrigues, *Política e Drogas nas Américas: uma genealogia do narcotráfico.*

29. Depirou A. Labrousse A., *Coca Coke* (São Paulo: Brasiliense, 1988).

30. Misha Glenny, *McMafia: A Journey Through the Global Criminal Underworld* (New York, Vintage Books, 2008).

31. United Nations Office on Drugs and Crime (UNODC), *World Drug Report 2016* (Vienna: UNODC, 2016).

32. Luis Fernando Sarmiento, Ciro Krauthausen, *Cocaína & CO.: un mercado ilegal por dentro*.

33. Cecília Coimbra, *Operação Rio: o mito das classes perigosas. um estudo sobre a violência urbana, a mídia impressa e os discursos de segurança pública* (Niterói: Oficina do Autor/Intertexto, 2001).

34. Marcos Barreira e Maurilio Lima Botelho, Exército nas Ruas: da Operação Rio à Ocupação do Complexo do Alemão. Notas para uma reconstituição da exceção urbana in *Até o último homem*, eds. Felipe Britom e Pedro Rocha de Oliveira (São Paulo: Boitempo), p. 115–128, especially p. 118.

35. Michel Foucault, *The Birth of Bipolitics—Lectures at Collège de France 1978–1979* (New York: Picador, 2004).

36. Frédéric Gros, *States of Violence: An Essay on the End of War* (London: Seagull Books, 2010).

37. Data from Fórum Brasileiro de Segurança Pública, Anuário *Brasileiro de Segurança* Pública: 2015 (São Paulo: Brasileiro de Segurança Pública, 2015)

38. Brazil. "Map of the Imprisonment. Young people in Brazil," available at juventude.gov.br/articles/participatorio/0010/1092/Mapa_do_Encarceramento_-_Os_jovens_do_brasil.pdf, accessed November 2017.

39. See: Estadão. "Detentes filming decapitation and distributing images in Manaus," Noticias UOL, January 4, 2017.

40. See: hypomnemata-extra, May 2006, em www.nu-sol.org/hypomnemata/boletim.php?idhypom=85 hypomnemata 74, June 2006, in www.nu-sol.org/hypomnemata/boletim.php?idhypom=87; hypomnemata 102, October 2008, in www.nu-sol.org/hypomnemata/boletim.php?idhypom=119; hypomnemata 150, November 2012, in www.nu-sol.org/hypomnemata/boletim.php?idhypom=180.

41. Portal of the Planalto, "Government will invest about R$ 2.2 billion in the penitentiary system in 2017," 01/1/2017, In www2.planalto.gov.br/acompanhe-planalto/noticias/2017/01/governo-investira-cerca-de-r-2-2-bilhoes-no-sistema-penitenciario-em-2017, accessed November 2017.

42. See: Fabiana Uchinaka. "Violation of human rights in ES prisons will be discussed at the UN" In UOL Noticias. São Paulo, March 15, 2010, in noticias.uol.com.br/cotidiano/ultimas-noticias/2010/03/15/violacao-de-direitos-humanos-em-presidios-do-es-sera-discutida-na-onu.htm Acesso em 17.3.2017.

43. Camilla Costa. "How Espírito Santo managed to eliminate deaths in prisons–and what still does not work in its system," *BCC*, January 17, 2017.

44. For more, see: Jill Langlois, "126 inmates still at large in Brazil after a prison riot that left 56 dead," *Los Angeles Times,* January 4, 2017.

45. For more, see: Acácio Augusto, "qual democracia?—sobre como a busca por segurança está solapando a Liberdade." This article can be found at www.academia.edu/27800102/qual_democracia_sobre_como_a_busca_por_seguran%C3%A7a_est%C3%A1_solapando_a_liberdade, accessed November 2017.

46. See: "Paulo Hartung guarantees that he closes the year with government budget in good order," *Temp Novo*, December 12, 2016.

47. Michel Foucault, *The Birth of Bipolitics—Lectures at Collège de France 1978–1979* (New York: Picador, 2004).

48. Loïc Wacquant, *Prisons of Poverty* (Minneapolis: University of Minnesota Press, 2009).

49. "Adolescente é morto pelo Exército em bairro da Grande Vitória," *Espírito Santo*, January 11, 2017.

50. See: Vera Carpes' Via Legal TV series, winner of the XXVIII Wladimir Herzog National Award 2006, Human Rights Award for Journalism: Justice and Human Rights Movement/OAB/RS, www.youtube.com/watch?v=T3IPFUfodzg&feature=youtu.be, accessed 03/15/2017.

51. Cleuci de Oliveira in Fortaleza, "Brazil grapples with lynch mob epidemic: 'A good criminal is a dead criminal,'" *The Guardian*, December 6, 2016.

52. See: Didier Bigo, 'Guerres, conflits, transnational et territoire (Partie 1). *Culture & Conflits*, 21 (21): 2002, pp. 1–10; Mark Neocleous, *Power, Police Power* (Oxford: Oxford University Press, 2014); Thiago Rodrigues, Mariana Kalil, Roberto Zepeda, Jonathan Rosen. Warzone Acapulco: urban drug trafficking in the Americas, *Contexto Internacional*, vol. 39 3 (2017): pp. 609–631; Marcelo Souza, *Fobópole: o medo generalizado e a militarização da questão urbana* (Rio de Janeiro: Bertrand Brasil, 2008).

53. Coletta A. Youngers and Eileen Rosin, eds., *Drugs and Democracy in Latin America: The Impact Of U.S. Policy* (Boulder, CO: Lynne Rienner, 2005).

54. Stephen Graham, *Cities Under Siege: the new urban militarism* (London/New York, Verso, 2010).

CHAPTER 3. SPECTACULAR (IN)JUSTICE: IMPUNITY AND COMMUNAL VIOLENCE IN BOLIVIA

1. "Cochabamba: Policía acusa a Fejuve de Entre Ríos por linchamiento," *Correo del Sur*, November 15, 2016.

2. "El representante del Defensor del Pueblo, Marcelo Cox, condenó la 'irresponsabilidad' de los padres y dirigentes de permitir que los niños miren el asesinato. El exasambleísta [sic] Henry Paredes afirmó: 'Es vergonzoso que esté ocurriendo esto.'" All translations are my own. Anonymous, "Linchamiento se convirtió en espectáculo del horror," *Los tiempos*, November 17, 2016. Retrieved on August 3, 2017 from: http://www.lostiempos.com/actualidad/local/20161117/linchamiento-se-convirtio-espectaculo-del-horror.

3. Of course, given that these videos violate YouTube's terms of service, they are generally removed rather quickly.

4. This notion is, as I will discuss, debatable. "Bolivia es uno de los países con más linchamientos en América Latina," *Los Tiempos*, April 1, 2016.

5. There is, of course, much to be said about the permissibility of extreme graphic non-fictional violence and suffering in the face of the impermissibility of mere nudity. This, however, is beyond the scope of this chapter. Goldstein and Castro, "Creative Violence," p. 395.

6. A significant difference being that the former, if interrupted by police, need not lead to loss of life, whereas the latter indicates a 'completed' *linchamiento.*

7. While Goldstein and Castro indicate that the incidence of *linchamiento* is likely heavily underreported, Yates makes note specifically of the underreporting of such incidents in rural communities. See: Daniel Goldstein and Fatima Williams Castro, "Creative Violence: How Marginal People Make News in Bolivia," *Journal of Latin American Anthropology* 11/2 (2006), XX and Donna Yates, "'Community Justice,' Ancestral Rights, and Lynching in Rural Bolivia." *Race and Justice* XX (June 2017): pp. 12–13.

8. Defensoría del Pueblo, *El ejercicio de los derechos humanos en el estado plurinacional de Bolivia: Informe 2015*, La Paz: 2015: pp. 102–103; Daniel M. Goldstein and Fatimah Williams Castro, "Creative Violence: How Marginal People Make News in Bolivia." *Journal of Latin American Anthropology* 11/2 (2006): p. 394.

9. Juan Yhonny Mollericona, "Radiografía de los linchamientos en la ciudad de El Alto." Retrieved from: http://www.pieb.com.bo/UserFiles/File/PDFs/Linchamien tos_Mollericona.pdf; Héctor Luna Acevedo, "Los actos de linchamiento y la inseguri dad ciudadana en Bolivia." *Temas Sociales* 38 (2016): p. 168.

10. Daniel Goldstein and Fatima Williams Castro, "Creative Violence: How Marginal People Make News in Bolivia," *Journal of Latin American Anthropology* 11/2 (2006): p. 394.

11. Jorge-Carlos Derpic-Burgos, "Seguridad ciudadana, estado y sociedad civil en el context boliviano (2001–2013)," *Boletín científico "Sapiens Research"* 4/2 (2014): p. 14.

12. "8 de 10 intentos de linchamiento en El Alto afectaron a inocentes," *Pagina Siete*, September 2014, p. 11.

13. Miguel Rives, "Desde 2014, El Alto tuvo 16 intentos de linchamiento y 3 ajusticiamientos." *La Razón*, April 11, 2016.

14. Guatemala's tracking of lynching was part of the conditions imposed by the United Nations Verification Mission to Guatemala (MINUGUA).

15. "Potosí: Hechos criminales consternan a pobladores." *Correo del Sur*, October 21, 2017.

16. "Bolivia es uno de los países con más linchamientos en América Latina." *Los tiempos*, 01 April 2016. Retrieved August 4, 2017 from: http://www.lostiempos.com/actualidad/nacional/20160401/bolivia-es-uno-paises-mas-linchamientos-america-latina.

17. This is the claim put forward by Brazilian sociologist Joseé de Souza Martins: María Martín, "Brasil tem um linchamento por dia, não é nada excepcional," *El País*, July 8, 2015.

18. Helene Risør, "Twenty Hanging Dolls and a Lynching: defacing Dangerousness and Enacting Citizenship in El Alto, Bolivia," *Public Culture* 22/3 (2010), p. 465.

19. Carlos Vilas claims 1,993 lynchings in Peru between 2002 and 2003. Carlos Vilas, "Linchamientos y conflicto politico en los Andes," *Desarrollo económico* XLIV/187 (2007), p. 429.

20. Angelina Snodgrass Godoy, "When Justice is Criminal: Lynchings in Ciontemporary Latin America." *Theory and Society* 33 (2004): p. 621.

21. UNODC, *Global Study on Homicide 2013* (New York, NY: UNODC, 2016): p. 126.

22. Daniel M. Goldstein, "'In Our Own Hands': Lynching, Justice, and the Law in Bolivia," *American Ethnologist* 30/1 (2003), p. 36.

23. Luna, "Los actos de linchamiento," pp. 170–172.

24. Daniel M. Goldstein, *The Spectacular City: Violence and Performance in Urban Bolivia* (Durham, NC: Duke University Press, 2004), p. 184.

25. Snodgrass, "When Justice is Criminal," pp. 626–627.

26. Goldstein, "In Our Own Hands," p. 38.

27. "orgías de un canibalismo sin límite," while citizens of La Paz and Oruro trembled before "una invasión devastadora a [estas] populosas ciudades . . . cuyos vecindarios sufren la dolorosa inquietud de un asalto posible." As quoted in Martinez, "La peur blanche," p. 269.

28. José de Souza Martins, "As condições do estudo sociológico dos linchamentos no Brasil." *Studos Avançados* 9/25 (1996), pp. 303–305.

29. Snodgrass, "When Justice is Criminal," p. 621, 632. Goldstein, *The Spectacular City*, p. 180.

30. Hinnerk Onken, "Lynching in Peru in the Nineteenth and Early Twentieth Centuries," in *Globalizing Lynching History* (New York, NY: Palgrave Macmillan, 2011): pp. 173–186.

31. Orin Starn, *Nightwatch: The Politics of Protest in the Andes* (Durham, NC: Duke University Press, 1999.

32. Goldstein seems to favor this argument.

33. This is Michael Painter's "melodrama in which the villains are the harsh environment and insensitive agents of change, and the hero the peasantry with its traditional practices and lifeways." Painter, "Re-creating the Peasant Economy," p. 97.

34. Martinez, "La peur blanche."

35. Erick D. Langer, "Andean Rituals of Revolt: The Chayanta Rebellion of 1927." *Ethnohistory* 37/3 (1990): p. 230. This, of course, is just one example. The twentieth century is littered with regional rebellions against landowners. See, for example: Jorge Dandler and Juan Torrico, "From the National Indigenous Congress to the Ayopaya Rebellion: Bolivia, 1945–1947," in: Steve Stern, *Resistance, Rebellion, and Consciousness in the Andean Peasant World. 18th to 20th Centuries* (Madison: The University of Wisconsin Press, 1987): pp. 334–378 and Esteban Ticona Alejo and Xavier Albó Corrons, *Jesús Machaca: la marka rebelde* vol. 3 "La lucha por el poder communal," La Paz: CEDOIN, 1997: pp. 340–341.

36. Herbert S. Klein, *Bolivia: The Evolution of a Multi-Ethnic Society* (New York, NY: Oxford University Press, 1992): p. 234; Maria Lagos, *Autonomy and Power: The Dynamics of Class and Culture in Rural Bolivia* (Philadelphia: University of Pennsylvania Press, 1994): pp. 49–51.

37. Herbert S. Klein, *Bolivia: The Evolution of a Multi-Ethnic Society*. (New York: Oxford University Press, 1992), pp. 219–222.

38. Olivia Harris's work is one of relatively few works that touch on it explicitly. Harris, *To Make the Earth Bear Fruit*, pp. 141–167.

39. Michael Painter, "Re-creating the Andean Peasant Economy in Southern Peru." In: Jay O'Brien and William Roseberry (eds), *Golden Ages, Dark Ages: Imagining the Past in Anthropology and History* (Berkeley, CA: University of California Press, 1991): pp. 81–106.

40. Indeed, the UNDP notes that Bolivia sees the highest rates of violence against women in Latin America. UNDP, *Informe Regional de Desarrollo Humano, 2013–2014* (New York, NY: UNDP, 2013): p. 84.

41. Harris, *To Make the Earth Bear Fruit*, pp. 150–151.

42. Ibid., pp. 147–149.

43. Ibid., pp. 146–147.

44. Canessa, "Memory and Violence," pp. 184–185.

45. Olivia Harris, *To Make the Earth Bear Fruit: Ethnographic Essays on Fertility, Work, and Gender in Highland Bolivia* (London: Institute of Latin American Studies, 2000): pp. 146–147.

46. Ticona and Albó, *Jesús de Machaqa*, pp. 344–351.

47. Canessa, "Memory and Violence," p. 189.

48. Harris, *To Make the Earth Bear Fruit*, p. 141. Also see: Xavier Albó Corrons, "Retornando a la solidaridad y faccionalismo Aymara," Ii Gonzalo Sánchez and Eric Lair (eds), *Violencias y estrategias colectivas en la región andina: Bolivia, Colombia, Perú, y Venezuela* (Lima: Editorial Norma, 2004): p. 460

49. Ibid., p. 157.

50. The exception being the one noted by Canessa. Canessa, "Memory and Violence," p. 189.

51. This ritualistic aspect in many ways mirrors the descriptions of ritualized violence offered by Harris. Harris, *To Make the Earth Bear Fruit*, 141–163.

52. Donna Yates, "'Community Justice,' Ancestral Rights, and Lynching in Rural Bolivia." *Race and Justice* XX (June 2017), pp. 6–7; Risør, "Twenty Hanging Dolls," 481; Goldstein and Castro, "Creative Violence," p. 395.

53. Yates, "Community Justice," p. 7.

54. Risør, "Twenty Hanging Dolls," p. 482; Goldstein and Castro, "Creative Violence," p. 395; Yates, "Community Justice," p. 7.

55. Alex Ayala Ugarte and Jorge Derpic, "Bolivia: los linchados de El Alto," *Revista Anfibia*.

56. Indeed, Goldstein quotes the police report as indicating that "threats have been received to the effect that if any authority were to go to the area, he would receive the same punishment [burning alive] as the thieves." Goldstein, *The Spectacular City*, p. 189.

57. Josué Hinojosa, "Vinculan con narcotráfico linchamiento en San Julián," *Los Tiempos*, May 17, 2017.

58. Carlos Corz, "La Policía decide volver a San Julián tras 16 días de dejar la población por linchamiento." *La Razón*, June 2, 2017.

59. "Bolivia: devuelven cuerpos de policías linchados." *BBC World*, June 4, 2010. From http://www.bbc.com/mundo/america_latina/2010/06/100604_2054_bolivia_linchamiento_devuelven_cuerpos_lav. August 25, 2017.

60. These were two separate incidents. Yates, "Community Justice," p. 7.

61. Risør, "Twenty Hanging Dolls," p. 482.

62. Such as Baldwin Montero, "Difunden imágenes del viceministro Rodolfo Illanes en manos de sus secuestradores," *La Razón*, August 29, 2016.

63. Anonymous, "Murió la mujer que fue atada, junto a sus hijos, a un 'palo santo.'" *El Deber*, 01 April 2017. From: http://www.eldeber.com.bo/bolivia/Murio-la-mujer-que-fue-atada-junto-a-sus-hijos-a-un-palo-santo-20170104-0091.html. August 7, 2017.

64. This is based in large part on my own observation, but is confirmed by Goldstein: Goldstein, *The Spectacular City*, 235. Also see: Risør, "Twenty Hanging Dolls," p. 475.

65. Risør, "Twenty Hanging Dolls," p. 482.

66. Goldstein's notion of *desconfianza*: Goldstein, *The Spectacular City*, pp. 37–45, 187.

67. Risør, "Twenty Hanging Dolls," p. 481.

68. This is rather in line with the argument made by Snodgrass, who states that "[l]ynchings are not about crime." Snodgrass, "When Justice is Criminal," p. 628.

69. Luna Acevedo, "Los actos de linchamiento," p. 167.

70. Miguel Rivas, "Desde 2014, El Alto tuvo 16 intentos de linchamiento y 3 ajusticiamientos." *La Razón*, 11 April 2016; Anonymous, "Los linchamientos convierten a Bolivia en un país con pena de muerte de facto," Última Hora, November 8, 2013.

71. Such as Anonymous, "Queman vivo en Bolivia a un hombre al que confundieron con un ladrón." *El Espectador*, September 8, 2014.

72. Yates, "Community Justice," pp. 3–4.

73. Luna Acevedo, "Los actos de linchamiento," pp. 172–173.

74. "En El Alto, se confunde justicia comunitaria con linchamiento." *El Diario*, March 30, 2016.; Anonymous, "8 de 10 intentos de linchamiento."

75. Such as Goldstein, *The Spectacular City*, pp. 194–196.

76. Ciudadanía/LAPOP, *Cultura política de la democracia en Bolivia, 2014: Hacia una democracia de ciudadanos*. Cochabamba: Ciudadanía/LAPOP, 2014: p. 14.

77. Elizabeth Zechmeister (ed.), *The Political Culture of Democracy in the Americas, 2014: Democratic Governance across 10 Years of the AmericasBarometer*. Nashville: USAID, 2016: p. 150.

78. Zechmeister, *Political Culture*, p. 147.

79. Canessa, "Memory and Violence," p. 189; see also: Goldstein and Castro, "Creative Violence," 394–396.

80. Yates, "Community Justice," p. 7.

81. Human Rights Watch, *World Report 2017*, p. 126.

82. Zechmeister, *Cultura política*, p. 33.

83. Goldstein, *The Spectacular City*, pp. 97–133.

84. Yates, "Community Justice," p. 4.

85. Elyssa Pachico, "Corrupt fighting the corrupt in Bolivia? Majority of prosecutors linked to crimes." *Christian Science Monitor*, November 3, 2014; Anonymous, "Senado exhorta al Fiscal General suspender al menos a 300 fiscales con procesos judiales." *La Razón*, October 30, 2014.

86. United Nations Human Rights Council, *Annual Report of the United Nations High Commissioner for Human Rights and Reports to the Office of the High Commissioner and the Secretary-General. Addendum*. March 5, 2014: pp. 11–14. Organization of American States, *Access to Justice and Social Inclusion: The Road towards Strengthening Democracy in Bolivia*, Washington, DC: 2007.

87. Marten Brienen, "A Special Kind of Hell: The Bolivian Penal System." In Jonathan D. Rosen and Marten Brienen, *Prisons in the Americas: A Human Dumping Ground* (Lanham, MD: Lexington Book, 2015): pp. 150–152.

88. Zechmeister, *Political Culture*, p. 102.

89. E.g. Goldstein, *The Spectacular City*, pp. 186–188.

90. Zechmeister, *Cultura política*, p. 63.

91. Zechmeister, *Cultura política*, p. 8; UNODC, *Global Study on Homicide 2013* (New York, NY: UNODC, 2016): p. 126.

92. Data from the Bolivian *Instituto Nacional de Estadísticas*: http://www.datos.ine.gob.bo

93. Neil Whitehead, *Dark Shamans: Kanaimà and the Poetics of Violent Death*, Chapel Hill: Duke University Press, 2002: p. 5.

94. Snodgrass, "When Justice is Criminal," p. 628.

95. Yates, "Community Justice," 11–12; Franz Chávez, "Lynch Mobs Hide Behind 'Community Justice' in Bolivia." *Inter Press Service* December 9, 2013.

96. Snodgrass, "When Justice is Criminal," p. 630.

97. Yates, "Community Justice," p. 12.

98. Canessa, "Memory and Violence," p. 189.

99. Such as noted also in the case of Peru: Onken, "Lynching in Peru."

100. Marta Irurozqui, "Ebrios, vagos y analfabetos. El sufragio restringido en Bolivia, 1826–1952." In *Revista de Indias*, LVIII/208 (1996), pp. 696–742; Marta Irurozqui Victoriano, *'A bala, piedra y palo.' La construcción de la ciudadanía política en Bolivia, 1826–1952*. Sevilla: Diputación de Sevilla, 2000; Marta Irurozqui Victoriano y Víctor Peralta Ruiz, *Por la Concordia, la fusion y el unitarismo: estado y caudillismo en Bolivia, 1825–1880*. Madrid: CSIC, 2000, pp. 176–177; Marta Irurozqui Victoriano, *La armonía de las desigualdades: elites y conflictos de poder en Bolivia 1880–1920*. Madrid: CSIC, 1992; Marta Irurozqui Victoriano, "The Sound of the Patutos: Politicisation and Indigenous Rebellions in Bolivia, 1826–1921," *Journal of Latin American Studies* 32:1 (2000): pp. 85–114; and Marta Irurozqui Victoriano, "Las paradojas de la tributación. Ciudadanía y política estatal indígena en Bolivia, 1825–1900." In *Revista de Indias* 59:217 (1999): pp. 705–740.

101. Herbert S. Klein, *Bolivia: The Evolution of a Multi-Ethnic Society* (New York: Oxford University Press, 1992), p. 234; Maria Lagos, *Autonomy and Power: The Dynamics of Class and Culture in Rural Bolivia* (Philadelphia: University of Pennsylvania Press, 1994), p. 49–51.

102. Canessa, "Memory and Violence," p. 189.

103. Harris, *To Make the Earth Bear Fruit*, p. 162.

104. Webber, *From Rebellion to Reform*, pp. 57–59. Rüdiger Horst, "Zielkonflikte zwischen Demokratie und ökonomischer Stabilität in Bolivien" in Thomas Jäger, *Bolivien: Staatszerfall als Kollateralschaden*, pp. 127–173: 134.

105. Something community members appear entirely aware of: Goldstein, *The Spectacular City*, 196.

106. Harris, *To Make the Earth Bear Fruit*, pp. 147–149.

107. Snodgrass, "When Justice is Criminal," p. 639. For a critique of the tendency to regard any violence indigenous communities engage in as 'resistance,' see: Brienen, "The Andean Melodrama."

108. This is the main argument in Goldstein and Castro, "Creative Violence."

109. Goldstein, *The Spectacular City*, pp. 191–198.

CHAPTER 4. VIOLENCE IN PERU

1. Portions of this text are reproduced and/or adapted from Barnett S. Koven and Cynthia McClintock, "Cooperation and Drug Policies: Trends in Peru in the Twenty-First Century," in *Cooperation and Drug Policies in the Americas: Trends in the Twenty-First Century*, eds. Roberto Zepeda and Jonathan Rosen (Lanham, MD: Lexington Books, 2014), Barnett S. Koven and Cynthia McClintock, "The Evolution of Peru's Shining Path and the New Security Priorities in the Hemisphere," in *Reconceptualizing Security in the Americas in the Twenty-First Century*, eds. Bruce M. Bagley, Hanna Kassab, and Jonathan Rosen (Lanham, MD: Lexington Books, 2015), and Barnett S. Koven and Cynthia McClintock, "The Obama Administration and Peru," in *The Obama Doctrine in the Americas: Major Security Challenges*, eds. Hanna Kassab and Jonathan Rosen (Lanham, MD: Lexington Books, 2016).

2. Kyra Gurney, "Perceptions of Insecurity Increasing in LatAm," *InSight Crime*, December 9, 2014, www.insightcrime.org/news-analysis/perceptions-of-insecurity-increasing-in-latin-america, accessed June 2017.

3. Gurney, "Perceptions of Insecurity Increasing in LatAm."

4. David Gagne, "InSight Crime's 2016 Homicide Round-Up," *InSight Crime*, January 16, 2017, www.insightcrime.org/news-analysis/insight-crime-2016-homicide-round-up, accessed June 2017.

5. Ibid.

6. Gagne, "InSight Crime's 2015 Latin America Homicide Round-Up"; David Gagne, "InSight Crime's 2014 Homicide Round-Up," *InSight Crime*, January 12, 2015, www.insightcrime.org/news-analysis/insight-crime-2014-homicide-round-up, accessed June 2017.

7. Gurney, "Perceptions of Insecurity in LatAm."

8. Ibid.

9. Peru Reports, *Crime Statistics,* perureports.com/crime/, accessed June 2017.

10. Peru Reports, *Crime Statistics*; Richard Webb and Graciela Fernández Baca, *Perú en Números 2016* (Lima: Cuánto, 2016), 1011.

11. ConsultAndes, *Peru Key Indicators*, May 21–28, 2017, Lima, Peru, p. 11.

12. Enrique Chávez, "El VRAEM es una bomba de tiempo," [interview with Rubén Vargas], *Caretas,* June 23, 2016, 35.

13. Peter Klarén, *Peru: Society and Nationhood in the Andes* (New York, NY: Oxford University Press, Inc., 1999), 376; Cynthia McClintock, *Revolutionary Move-*

ments in Latin America: El Salvador's FMLN and Peru's Shining Path (Washington, DC: United States Institute for Peace Press, 1998), pp. 182–184.

14. Korena Marie Zucha, "Incomplete Developmental Counterinsurgency: The Case of the Shining Path of Peru," (Master's thesis, Texas State University-San Marcos, Dept. of Political Science, 2007), pp. 56–59.

15. James Brooke, "Fugitive Leader of Maoist Rebels Is Captured by the Police in Peru," *New York Times,* September 14, 1992; Daniel W. Fitz-Simons, "Sendero Luminoso: Case Study in Insurgency," *Parameters* (Summer 1993): pp. 72–73; Robert L. Scheina, *Latin America's Wars Volume II: The Age of the Professional Soldier, 1990–2001* (Dulles, VA: Potomac Books Inc., 2003), p. 1993.

16. Barnett S. Koven, "El resurgimiento de Sendero Luminoso (SL)," *Air & Space Power Journal en Español* (Segundo Trimestre 2010): p. 26.

17. ConsultAndes, *Monthly Security Indicators*, December 2010, Lima, Peru, p. 1; ConsultAndes, *Monthly Security Indicators,* October 2011, Lima, Peru, 2; McClintock, *Revolutionary Movements in Latin America: El Salvador's FMLN and Peru's Shining Path*, p. 73.

18. McClintock, *Revolutionary Movements in Latin America: El Salvador's FMLN and Peru's Shining Path*, p. 73.

19. *El Comercio,* "El comando especial VRAE entra en acción," April 12, 2008; Maiah Jaskoski, *Military Politics and Democracy in the Andes* (Baltimore, MD: The Johns Hopkins University Press, 2013), p. 63; Koven, "El resurgimiento de Sendero Luminoso (SL)," 27; Ore and Terry Wade, "Interview-Peru: Shining Path Expands Role in Cocaine Trade," *Reuters: AlertNet,* December 12, 2008.

20. Frank Bajak and Carla Salazar, "Peru Rebel Brothers Lead Retooled Shining Path," *Associated Press,* May 29, 2012.

21. *El Comercio,* "Dircote detecta a 18 senderistas que hacen labor legal, política y de masas en Lima," November 24 2007; Koven, "El resurgimiento de Sendero Luminoso (SL)," p. 27; Américo Zambrano, "VRAEM: La emboscada," *Caretas,* August 15, 2013, p. 16.

22. Evan Ellis, "The Evolution of Transnational Organized Crime in Peru," *Latin America Goes Global*, May 4, 2017, p. 7.

23. Richard Webb and Graciela Fernández Baca, *Perú en Números 2016* (Lima, Peru: Instituto Cuánto, 2016), p. 1011; Richard Webb and Graciela Fernández Baca, *Perú en Números 2007* (Lima, Peru: Instituto Cuánto, 2007), p. 548.

24. Webb and Fernández Baca, *Perú en Números 2016*, p. 1011.

25. Collin Post, "Shining Path ambush kills 10 on eve of Peru's election," *Peru Reports*, April 12, 2016.

26. Bajak and Salazar, "Peru Rebel Brothers Lead Retooled Shining Path."

27. "Latin American Newsletters: Shining Path Today," *Latin News*, November 2013, London, U.K.

28. David Gagne, "Peru's Shining Path Allied With Colombian Drug Traffickers," *InSight Crime*, May 19, 2015, www.insightcrime.org/news-briefs/peru-shining-path-guerrillas-allied-with-colombian-drug-traffickers, accessed June 2017.

29. Óscar Chumpitaz, "Dirandro identifica a 30 mafias del narcoctráfico en la zona del VRAEM," *La República*, July 10, 2016, p. 16.

30. ConsultAndes, *Peru Key Indicators,* April 30–May 2017, Lima, Peru, p. 10.

31. Cynthia McClintock and Fabián Vallas, *The United States and Peru: Cooperation at a Cost* (New York: Routledge, 2003), pp. 122–129.

32. Data is derived from the U.S. Department of State, Bureau of International Narcotics and Law Enforcement Affairs, *International Narcotics Control Strategy Report (INCSR)*, from 2000–2013, Washington, DC.

33. Marco Aquino, "Peru forces set to enter coca-growing areas controlled by cartels," *Reuters,* May 25, 2017.

34. United Nations Office on Drugs and Crime, *Perú: Monitoreo de cultivos de coca 2013,* June 2014, Lima, Peru; U.S. Department of State, Bureau of International Narcotics and Law Enforcement Affairs, *International Narcotics Control Strategy Report (INCSR)*, from 2000–2013.

35. ConsultAndes, *Peru Key Indicators,* June 8–15, 2014, Lima, Peru, p. 9.

36. ConsultAndes, *Peru Key Indicators*, May 21–28, 2017, Lima, Peru, p. 11.

37. ConsultAndes, *Peru Key Indicators* 17–844, May 2017, Lima, Peru, p. 11.

38. Mirella Van Dun, "Cocaine Flows and the State in Peru's Amazonian Borderlands," *Journal of Latin American Studies* 48 (June 2016): pp. 509–535; Ellis, "The Evolution of Transnational Organized Crime in Peru," pp. 2–3.

39. Chávez, "El VRAEM es una bomba de tiempo," p. 35.

40. Elyssa Pachico, "*The Evolution of the Drug Trade in Peru's Cocaine Heartland*," *Insight Crime,* August 31, 2012, www.insightcrime.org/news-analysis/the-evolution-of-the-drug-trade-in-perus-cocaine-heartland, accessed June 2017; Van Dunn, "Cocaine Flows," pp. 516–517; Ellis, "The Evolution of Transnational Organized Crime in Peru," pp. 6–7.

41. Pachico, *The Evolution of the Drug Trade in Peru's Cocaine Heartland.*

42. U.S. Department of State, Bureau of International Narcotics and Law Enforcement Affairs, *International Narcotics Control Strategy Report (INCSR),* Volume I, March 2010, Washington, DC, p. 502.

43. Based on author's calculations using data from *IDL Reporteros,* "Las narcopistas vuelan," December 20, 2013, Gorriti likewise estimates 80 flights per month. See Gustavo Gorriti, "*Hunting Drug Planes in Peru's Jungles*," *InSight Crime,* April 25, 2014, www.insightcrime.org/news-analysis/hunting-drug-planes-in-perus-jungles, accessed June 2017.

44. *IDL Reporteros,* "Las narcopistas vuelan;" Romina Mella, "*Peru's Cocaine Air Bridge,*" *InSight Crime*, November 8, 2013, www.insightcrime.org/news-analysis/perus-cocaine-air-bridge, accessed June 2017.

45. *La República,* "Descubren siete nuevas rutas de la droga que van del Vraem hacia Brasil," May 2, 2017; *The Guardian,* "Peru authorizes military to shoot down cocaine-smuggling planes," August 20, 2015.

46. *La República,* "Descubren siete nuevas rutas de la droga que van del Vraem hacia Brasil"; *The Guardian,* "Peru authorizes military to shoot down cocaine-smuggling planes"; *First Post,* "Peru Eyes Backing Bill to Resume Shooting Down Drug Planes," March 11, 2015; *Mpelembe,* "Peru Considers Lifting Ban on Shooting Down Aircrafts Suspected of Carrying Drugs," March 10, 2015.

47. *La República,* "Descubren siete nuevas rutas de la droga que van del Vraem hacia Brasil"; *The Guardian,* "Peru authorizes military to shoot down cocaine-smuggling planes."

48. Ellis, "The Evolution of Transnational Organized Crime in Peru."

49. *The Conversation,* "How Peru's drug trade is threatening its economic growth," July 28, 2015.

50. Mimi Yagoub, *"Peru's New Homicide Index Shows Spiking Violence in Drug Port," InSight Crime,* July 22, 2016, www.insightcrime.org/news-briefs/peru-first-official-murder-stats-show-spiking-violence-in-drug-port, accessed June 2017.

51. Tristan Clavel, "Retired Military Investigated for Cocaine Trafficking in Peru," *InSight Crime,* February 17, 2017, www.insightcrime.org/news-briefs/retired-peru-military-investigated-cocaine-trafficking, accessed June 2017.

52. ConsultAndes, *Peru's Drug Fight* (Sector Report), July 2016, p. 7.

53. A security expert and retired- Peruvian Army Intelligence Colonel in discussion with Barnett Koven, April 28, 2017, Lima, Peru.

54. Kyra Gurney, "Over 90% of Peru's Mayors Face Corruption Investigations, Highlighting Endemic Problem," *InSight Crime,* July 17, 2014, www.insightcrime.org/news-briefs/90-peru-mayors-facing-corruption-investigation-endemic, accessed June 2017.

55. *DW*, "Perú: por caso de corrupción Odebrecht pueden ir a prisión expresidentes," June 2, 2017.

56. Felipe Puerta, "*Breaking Down LatAm's Lucrative Trade in Stolen Cell Phones*," *InSight Crime,* August 13, 2014, www.insightcrime.org/news-analysis/latam-lucrative-stolen-cell-phone-trade, accessed June 2017; Gerry Smith, "How Stolen Smartphones End Up In the Hands of Colombian Cartels," *Huffington Post,* December 10, 2013.

57. Dylan Waller, "Opportunity in Peru's Construction Industry," *Seeking Alpha*, June 26, 2015; *Spy Ghana,* "Peru's construction industry rebound in 2015," February 12, 2015; *eMarketer,* "Mobile Peru 2016: Updated Forecasts and Key Growth Trends," August 15, 2016.

58. World Bank, Global Poverty Working Group, *Poverty headcount ratio at national poverty lines (percent of population),* 2004–2015, Washington, DC.

59. This paragraph is based on Elohim Monard, "Qué pasó en Tumbes? Una pequeña ciudad de la costa norte alcanzó la tasa más alta de homicidios en el Perú," available at https//blogs.iadb.org/sinmiedos/2016/08/18/qué-pasó-en-Tumbes-una-pequeña-ciudad-de-la costa-norte-alcanzó-la-tasa-más-alta-de-homicidios-en-el-Perú.

60. Ibid.

61. Ibid.

62. Michael Lohmuller, "Peru Extortion Shows Strengthening of Homegrown Criminal Groups," *InSight Crime,* March 25, 2014, www.insightcrime.org/news-briefs/peru-extortion-shows-strengthing-of-homegrown-criminal-groups, accessed June 2017.

63. *El Comercio,* "Extorsionadores en construcción mueven S/.100 mlls. al año," March 22, 2015.

64. Mimi Yagoub, "Construction Site Extortion in Peru Shows Evolution of Local Org Crime," *InSight Crime,* July 21, 2014, www.insightcrime.org/news-briefs/

construction-site-extortion-in-peru-shows-evolution-of-local-org-crime, accessed June 2017.

65. *Spy Ghana,* "Peru's construction industry rebound in 2015"; Waller, "Opportunity in Peru's Construction Industry,"; The World Bank, *GDP growth (annual percent),* 2000–2015, Washington, DC.

66. Yagoub, *Construction Site Extortion in Peru Shows Evolution of Local Org Crime.*

67. M. R., "Stop-start sleuthing: A bizarre system of policing in Peru," *The Economist,* July 10, 2014.

68. *El Comercio,* "Extorsionadores en construcción mueven S/.100 mlls. al año," March 22, 2015.

69. Ibid.

70. Ibid.

71. *El Comercio,* "Extorsionadores en construcción mueven S/.100 mlls. al año"; Yagoub, *Construction Site Extortion in Peru Shows Evolution of Local Org Crime.*

72. Yagoub, *Construction Site Extortion in Peru Shows Evolution of Local Org Crime.*

73. Collin Post, "13 injured in extortion gang's grenade attack at Lima circus," *Peru Reports*, July 23, 2015.

74. Marguerite Cawley, "Peru Confronts Extortion of Construction Companies," *InSight Crime,* November 18, 2014, www.insightcrime.org/news-briefs/peru-confronts-extortion-of-construction-companies, accessed June 2017.

75. M. R., "Stop-start sleuthing: A bizarre system of policing in Peru."

76. Yagoub, *Construction Site Extortion in Peru Shows Evolution of Local Org Crime.*

77. Lohmuller, *Peru Extortion Shows Strengthening of Homegrown Criminal Groups.*

78. Marguerite Cawley, "Growth of Extortion a Major Concern for Peru: Official," *InSight Crime*, October 31, 2013, www.insightcrime.org/news-briefs/growth-of-extortion-a-major-concern-for-peru-official, accessed June 2017.

79. Lohmuller, *Peru Extortion Shows Strengthening of Homegrown Criminal Groups.*

80. Marguerite Cawley, "Peru Extortion Gang Goes Multinational," *InSight Crime,* September 9, 2014, www.insightcrime.org/news-briefs/peru-extortion-gang-now-operating-in-various-andean-states, accessed June 2017.

81. *Xinhuanet*, "Peru to fight cellphone theft by disabling stolen gagets," January 11, 2011.

82. *Perú 21,* "Osiptel: Más de 1.2 millones de celulares se robaron en el primer trimestre"; Puerta, *Breaking Down LatAm's Lucrative Trade in Stolen Cell Phones.*

83. Ibid.

84. *Tiempo de San Juan,* "Por el celular y la mochila, matan a cuchilladas a un trabajador," April 23, 2017.

85. *Canal N*, "Ejecuciones extrajudiciales: video muestra a policías matando a delincuentes," March 10, 2016.

86. *Peru This Week,* "60% of Peruvian citizens are now considered middle class," June 11, 2014. The estimate is by the Association of Peruvian Banks (Asociación de Bancos del Perú; ASBANC).

87. Jacob Poushter, *Smartphone Ownership and Internet Usage Continues to Climb in Emerging Economies* (report for Pew Research Center—Global Attitudes and Trends), February 22, 2016, Washington, DC.

88. *eMarketer,* "Mobile Peru 2016: Updated Forecasts and Key Growth Trends"; *Statista*, "Mobile Phone Penetration In Peru," www.statista.com/statistics/622681/mobile-phone-penetration-in-peru/, accessed June 2017.

89. "Peru GDP per capita," Trading Economics, www.tradingeconomics.com/peru/gdp-per-capita.

90. "Celulares," Saga Falabella, www.falabella.com.pe/falabella-pe/category/cat40591/Celulares?sorter=2, accessed June 2017.

91. "Smartphones," Entel, www.entel.pe/personas/catalogo-equipos/smart phones/apple/.

92. Puerta, *Breaking Down LatAm's Lucrative Trade in Stolen Cell Phones*; Smith, "How Stolen Smartphones End Up In the Hands of Colombian Cartels"; Gerry Smith, "Inside the Massive Global Black Market for Smartphones," *Huffington Post,* December 10, 2013.

93. Puerta, *Breaking Down LatAm's Lucrative Trade in Stolen Cell Phones.*

94. Ibid.

95. Smith, "How Stolen Smartphones End Up In the Hands of Colombian Cartels."

96. Vic Lee, "San Francisco cellphone theft leads to blackmail in Peru," *ABC News,* February 26, 2013.

97. *Diario Uno,* "Seguridad será la prioridad de PPK," June 11, 2016.

98. ConsultAndes, *Monthly Security Indicators*, May 2017, p. 9.

99. Collin Post, "Peru's new government outlines plan to fight rising crime," *Peru Reports*, August 12, 2016.

100. Gustavo Gorriti, "La Acción y sus Actores," *Caretas,* August 15 2013; Zambrano, "VRAEM: La emboscada," 15; Enrique Obando in discussion with Cynthia McClintock, Lima, Peru; Ricardo Soberón in discussion with Cynthia McClintock, May 5, 2014, Lima, Peru.

101. Damien Cave, "How a Kingpin Above the Law Fell, Incredibly, Without a Shot," *The New York Times,* February 24, 2014.

102. "Peru Shining Path Leader Comrade Artemio Captured," *BBC News Latin America & Caribbean,* February 13, 2012; *The Economist,* "One down; Peru's Shining Path," March 3, 2012, 49; Jeremy McDermott, *Peru's Shining Path Leaders Expected Party not Ambush*, *InSightCrime*, August 16, 2013, www.insightcrime.org/news-briefs/shining-path-leaders-expecting-party-not-ambush, accessed June 2017.

103. Dana Priest, "Covert Action in Colombia: U.S. Intelligence, GPS Bomb Kits Help Latin American Nation Cripple Rebel Forces," *The Washington Post,* December 21, 2013.

104. Gustavo Gorriti in discussion with Cynthia McClintock, Lima, Peru.

105. *Canal N*, "Piura: presunto terrorista fue capturado tras 23 años de búsqueda," August 12, 2016.

106. *Canal N*, “Vraem: capturan a presunto líder terrorista,” August 20, 2016.

107. Julieta Pelcastre, “Peru and the United States Learn Together in 2017,” *Diálogo,* February 8, 2017.

108. Ariel Noyola Rodríguez, “The United States Shall Set Up a New Military Base in Peru,” *Voltairenet.org*, January 25, 2017.

109. *Canal N*, “Vraem: ministro González visitó a bases antisubversivas,” August 9, 2016.

110. Tristan Clavel, “Perú reinicia operaciones militares en zona cocalera del VRAEM,” *Insight Crime,* October 13, 2016, es.insightcrime.org/noticias-del-dia/peru-reinicia-operaciones-militares-zona-cocalera-vraem, accessed June 2017.

111. ConsultAndes, *Monthly Security Indicators,* October 2016, p. 1.

112. ConsultAndes, *Monthly Security Indicators*, June 2017, pp. 2–4.

113. Cynthia McClintock, “Like Bush, Has Obama Only Good Intentions? The Case of U.S. Peruvian Relations, 2001–2012,” Paper presented at 2012 Congress of the Latin American Studies Association, San Francisco, CA, May 23–26, 2012; Cynthia McClintock, at off-the-record discussion with a Peruvian minister, May 2017.

114. ConsultAndes, *Peru's Drug Fight*, p. 3; The U.S. Department of State, Bureau of International Narcotics and Law Enforcement Affairs, *International Narcotics Control Strategy Report (INCSR)*, from 2000–2015, Washington, DC.

115. Chemonics International Inc., *Transforming Communities, Transforming Lives* (report for U.S. Agency for International Development, Washington, DC: Chemonics International Inc.), August 2012.

116. U.S. Agency for International Development, *Peru: Country Development Cooperation Strategy 2012–2016*, (Washington, DC: U.S. Agency for International Development), 15.

117. Chemonics International Inc., *Transforming Communities, Transforming Lives*; UNODC Alternative Development Projects in Peru, accessed June 6 2014; U.S. Agency for International Development: Peru, last modified May 27 2014, www.usaid.gov/peru.

118. ConsultAndes, *Peru Key Indicators,* May 21–28, 2017, 11.

119. Eduardo Garcia, “Estado invirtió S/. 5,900 mllns. en el desarrollo del Vraem,” *El Puruano,* March 2, 2016.

120. Enrique Chávez, “El VRAEM es una bomba de tiempo,” 34; Ellis, “The Evolution of Transnational Organized Crime,” p. 7.

121. Ibid.

122. Barnett S., Koven, “Emulating U.S. Counterinsurgency Doctrine: Barriers for Developing Country Forces, Evidence from Peru,” *Journal of Strategic Studies* 39, nos. 5–6 (October): pp. 878–898.

123. Chávez, “El VRAEM es una bomba de tiempo,” 33–35.

124. Luis Fernando Alonso, “Nearly 1,000 Complaints against Peru Police This Year,” *InSight Crime*, October 14, 2016, www.insightcrime.org/news-briefs/nearly-1-000-complaints-against-peru-police-this-year, accessed June 2017.

125. Frank Bajak, “The Peruvian military is letting planes filled with cocaine fly right under their noses,” *Business Insider*, October 14, 2015.

126. *Diario Correo,* "Pedro Pablo Kuczynski condenó asesinato de dos policías en el Vraem," May 31, 2017.

127. Caitlin Fitzgerald, ¿Puede Perú Llevar el Desarrollo a la Principal Región Cocalera del País? (report for Talking Drugs), September 30, 2016.

128. ConsultAndes, *Peru Key Indicators* 17–844, 11.

129. Ellis, "The Evolution of Transnational Organized Crime in Peru."

130. ConsultAndes, *Peru Key Indicators* 17–844.

131. "List of countries and dependencies by number of police officers," *Wikipedia,* en.wikipedia.org/wiki/List_of_countries_and_dependencies_by_number_of_police_officers. The dates for the listed countries vary. The primary indicated source is a 2010 United Nations Commission Report on criminal justice around the world.

132. This paragraph is based on a report by Peru's statistic institute described in ConsultAndes, *Monthly Security Indicators*, February 2017, 6–7.

133. *La República,* "Estos son los salarios de los policías en Perú: ¿Se justifica una protesta?" February 5, 2016.

134. *The Washington Post*, "In Peru, 'an iron hand in a silken glove,'" December 11, 2016, p. B3.

135. Alonso, *Nearly 1,000 Complaints against Peru Police This Year.*

136. Ibid.

137. ConsultAndes, *Monthly Security Indicators*, September 2016, Lima, Peru, p. 9; *The Washington Post,* "In Peru, 'an iron hand in a silken glove,'" December 11, 2016, p. B3.

138. ConsultAndes, *Monthly Security Indicators*, April 2017, 7.

139. ConsultAndes, *Peru Key Indicators,* May 21–28, 2017, 8.

140. *Peru 21,* "Ministro Basombrío tras entrega de patrulleros a la Policía: "¡Por fin! . . . Ya están equipados,"" November 3, 2016.

141. Felix Moreno, "Patrulleros serán controlados en el Callao con sistema GPS," *El Comercio*, October 20, 2011.

142. W. Alejandro Sanchez, *Drones in Latin America* (Washington, DC: Council on Hemispheric Affairs, January 12 2014).; Innocon, accessed April 23 2014, www.innoconltd.com/?CategoryID=156&ArticleID=109; *Interactive Intelligence,* "Brazil's Embraer to Begin Building Drones," September 8, 2011; Christopher Woody, "The world's 2nd-largest cocaine producer is adding drones to its police force," *Business Insider,* March 9, 2017.

143. Woody, "The world's 2nd-largest cocaine producer is adding drones to its police force," The announcement was by General Orlando Velasco Mujica, the director of PNP aviation.

144. Alberto Linares Tejada "Division de investigacion de delitos de alta tecnologia-policia nacional del Peru," post on on *Hypnosis y Psicotraining, Xing* (blog), October 26, 2011 (9:15 a.m.), www.xing.com/communities/posts/division-de-investigacion-de-delitos-de-alta-tecnologia-policia-nacional-del-peru-1006892331.

145. "III Conferencia de Tecnologías de la Información y Comunicaciones 2016." Policía Nacional del Perú. www.pnp.gob.pe/tic_2016_final/index.html.

146. Puerta, *Breaking Down LatAm's Lucrative Trade in Stolen Cell Phones.*

147. See for example the telling story of "El Adusto" in Van Dun, "Cocaine Flows," especially pp. 530–531.

148. ConsultAndes, *Peru Key Indicators*, February 26–March 5, 2017, 10.

149. Cawley, *Peru Extortion Gang Goes Multinational.*

150. *La República,* "Ministerio de Justicia evalúa declarar en emergencia sistema penitenciario," August 30, 2016.

151. Minister of Justice Marisol Pérez Tello, in discussion with Cynthia McClintock, June 12, 2017, Washington, DC.

152. Charles D. Brockett, "The Evolution and Impact of Domestic and Transnational Drug Trafficking Organizations in Guatemala," Paper presented at the Latin American Studies Association meeting, New York, May 27–30 2016, p. 29.

153. Yagoub, *Construction Site Extortion in Peru Shows Evolution of Local Org Crime.*

154. ConsultAndes, *Peru Key Indicators,* April 16–23, 2017, p. 10.

155. Vice Minister of Public Security, Ricardo Valdés Cavassa, in discussion with Cynthia McClintock, May 2, 2017, Lima, Peru; ConsultAndes, *Monthly Security Indicators*, May 2017, p. 9.

156. Cynthia McClintock's report from hundreds of conversations on this topic with everyday Peruvians, in particular taxi drivers, over many years.

157. See for example "Kuczynski gets tough on security and corruption," *Latin America Weekly Report*, May 5, 2016, p. 7.

158. *La República,* "Encuesta nacional urbano rural GfK," December 20, 2015, p. 2.

159. James Bargent, "Vigilante Justice Popular Across Latin America," *InSight Crime*, March 30, 2015, www.insightcrime.org/news-analysis/vigilante-justice-popular-across-latin-america, accessed June 2017.

160. Michael Fraiman, "Peru's Pitchfork Politics: The Rise of Vigilantism and the Right Wing," *Foreign Affairs,* November 2, 2015.

161. Fraiman, "Peru's Pitchfork Politics."

162. Ibid.

163. Ibid.

164. "Chapa tu Choro, Susy Diaz feat. Rony Yeico," YouTube video, posted by "RadioChata," October 17, 2015, www.youtube.com/watch?v=JaWrogkBNQI.

165. "¡Chapa tu choro en Cajamarca!," Youtube video, posted by "Cajamarca Viral," September 8, 2015, www.youtube.com/watch?v=iO365NzG4jU.

166. "Servicio de Serenazgo," *Seguridad Cuidadana,* www.seguridadidl.org.pe/actores/municipalidades/servicio-de-serenazgo.

167. "Platforma de vídeo vigilancia," *Mira Flores,* vwww.miraflores.gob.pe/_contenTempl2.php?idpadre=5300&idhijo=5301&idcontenido=5303.

168. *La República* "Serenos deben recibir al menos 3 meses de entrenamiento antes de usar armas no letales," January 31, 2016; *El Comercio,* "Debate: ¿Debería el serenazgo portar armas no letales?" February 26, 2016.

169. "Serenazgo," *Mira Flores,* www.miraflores.gob.pe/_contenTempl2.php?idpadre=5300&idcontenido=5441.

170. *Peru21* "Las propuestas de PPK y de Fujimori en seguridad," May 1, 2016, p. 18.

171. *Seguridad Cuidadana,* "Servicio de Serenazgo."

CHAPTER 5. NEGOTIATING PEACE AND STRENGTHENING THE STATE: REDUCING VIOLENCE IN COLOMBIA

1. María Victoria Llorente and Jeremy McDermott, "Colombia's Lessons for Mexico" *in One Goal, Two Struggles: Confronting Crime and Violence in Mexico and Colombia,* edited by Cynthia J. Arnson and Eric L. Olson with Christine Zaino, Woodrow Wilson Center Reports on the Americas #32 (2014).

2. Andreas E. Feldmann and Victor J. Hinojosa, "Terrorism in Colombia: Logic and Sources of a Multidimensional and Ubiquitous Phenomenon," *Terrorism and Political Violence* 21 (2009): pp. 42–61. In additional to these groups, a host of other significant guerilla groups have existed in Colombia including the EPL (Popular Liberation Army), M–19 (Movement of April 19), PRT Worker's Revolutionary Party), MAQL (Quintín Lame Armed Movement), JBC (Jaime Bateman Cayón Group), EPLA (Latin American Patriotic Army), ERP (People's Revolutionary Army), and the ERG (Guevarist Revolutionary Army).

3. These groups received financing from other sources as well, including extortion and (for the FARC) kidnapping. The ELN historically avoided a significant role in the narcotics trade, which helps account for its smaller size.

4. Sarah Zukerman Daly, *Organized Violence after Civil War: the Geography of Recruitment in Latin America* (Cambridge, U.K.: Cambridge University Press 2016), p. 57.

5. Ibid., p. 75.

6. The average is 1,068.67 deaths per year. UN Office on Drugs and Crime's International Homicide Statistics database retrieved from the World Bank, data.worldbank.org, accessed August 2017.

7. Guatemala last recorded a battlefield death in 1995, El Salvador in 1991, and Nicaragua in 1990. Ibid.

8. Andreas E. Feldmann and Victor J. Hinojosa, "Terrorism in Colombia."

9. Ibid., p. 42.

10. UNHCR, *Global Trends: Forced Displacement in 2016* (Geneva, SZ: UNHCR, 2017), p. 36.

11. It is important to note, however, that this total is cumulative and dates to 1985. While discussions are underway to establish a de-registration process, none currently exists. Once someone registers as an IDP, they are permanently counted, and Colombia's IDP population continues to grow; for more, see: UNHCR, Global Trends: Forced Displacement in 2016, p. 36, especially fn. 50.

12. Internal Displacement Monitoring Center, "Colombia" available online at www.internal-displacement.org/countries/colombia, accessed June 23, 2017.

13. UNHCR, *Global Trends*, p. 19.

14. Álvaro Camacho Guizado and Andrés López Restrepo, "From Smugglers to Drug Lords to Traquetos: Chances in the Colombian Illicit Drug Organizations," in *Peace, Democracy and Human Rights in Colombia*, ed. Christopher Welna and Gustavo Gallón (Notre Dame, IN: Notre Dame University Press, 2007).

15. Ibid.

16. As this is the most dangerous part of the production chain, it is also the most profitable. This shift has resulted in a significant increase in the power of Mexican crime syndicates and a corresponding increase in violence in Mexico as Zepeda and Rosen note (this volume).

17. A 2007 study by the United Nations found that in 2005 only 20 percent of the country's homicides were politically motivated or related to the armed conflict and that prior to 2001, an average of 10 percent of the country's homicides were related to the conflict. U.N. Office on Drugs and Crime (UNODC), *Violence, Crime, and Illegal Arms Trafficking in Colombia* (Bogotá, CO: UNODC, 2006).

18. Ibid.

19. The FARC has also used kidnapping for expressly political reasons by kidnapping high-value targets including soldiers and political leaders to use as leverage in peace negotiations and prisoner exchanges.

20. Interview with author, Bogotá, Colombia February 2009. Note that there are no paramilitaries not engaged in narcotics trafficking.

21. Jonathan D. Rosen, *The Losing War: Plan Colombia and Beyond* (Albany, NY: State University of New York Press, 2014).

22. Victor J. Hinojosa, *Domestic Politics and International Narcotics Control: U.S. Relations with Mexico and Colombia, 1989–2000* (New York, NY: Routledge 2007), p. 60.

23. European funds for Plan Colombia never materialized.

24. Jonathan D. Rosen, *The Losing War*, p. 27.

25. "Why Colombia is Not the 'Next Vietnam,'" United States Support for Colombia: Fact Sheet, Bureau of Western Hemisphere Affairs, U.S. Department of State, March 28, 2000.

26. Hinojosa, *Domestic Politics and International Narcotics Control*, 60–61.

27. Peter J. Meyer, "U.S. Foreign Assistance to Latin America and the Caribbean: Recent Trends and FY2015. Appropriations." (Washington, D.C: Congressional Research Service, 2014).

28. Jonathan D. Rosen, *The Losing War*, p. 34.

29. Ibid., pp. 24–27

30. June S. Beittel, *Colombia: Background, U.S. Relations, and Congressional Interest* (Washington, DC: Congressional Research Service, 2012).

31. Among others, see "Colombia: President Uribe's Democratic Security Policy," International Crisis Group 2003, www.crisisgroup.org/latin-america-caribbean/andes/colombia/colombia-president-uribes-democratic-security-policy, accessed June 30, 2017.

32. Jonathan D. Rosen, *The Losing War*, p. 65, 68.

33. Sarah Zukerman Dal, *Organized Violence after Civil War*, provides a compelling description of the motivations of the paramilitaries in entering this dialogue. See especially pages 60–64.
34. Sarah Zukerman Daly, *Organized Violence after Civil War*, p. 62.
35. Ibid.
36. Ibid., p. 1.
37. Ibid., p. 52.
38. Ibid., p. 117
39. "Some of the Many Reasons Why the United States Should Keep Supporting Colombia's Peace Accord," *WOLA*, February 1, 2017, colombiapeace.org/2017/02/01/some-of-the-many-reasons-why-the-united-states-should-keep-supporting-colombias-peace-accord/, accessed August 11, 2017.
40. Nicholas Casey and Joe Parkin Daniels, "'Goodbye, Weapons!' FARC Disarmament in Colombia Signals New Era," *New York Times*, June 27, 2017.
41. Ibid.
42. Luis Jaime Acosta, "Colombia's FARC Rebels Hand Over Weapons, Ending Armed War with Government" *The Wire*, June 28, 2017.
43. Nicholas Casey and Joe Parkin Daniels, "'Goodbye Weapons!' FARC Disarmament in Colombia Signals New Era."
44. Luis Jaime Acosta, "Colombia's FARC Rebels Hand Over Weapons, Ending Armed War with Government."
45. "Tasa de homicidios en Colombia de 2016 es la más baja desde 1974," *El Colombiano* December 29, 2016, at www.elcolombiano.com/colombia/baja-tasa-de-homicidios-en-colombia-YD5674203 accessed June 30, 2017.
46. Gimena Sánchez-Garzoli and Sonia Londoño, "The Activists Key to Consolidating Colombia's Peace are Facing Increased Attacks" *Washington Office on Latin America*, February 15, 2017, www.wola.org/analysis/activists-key-consolidating-colombias-peace-facing-increased-attack/, accessed August 11, 2017.
47. "CIDH condena el aumento de asesinatos contra defensoras y defensores de derechos humanos en Colombia," Organization of American States, November 2, 2016, www.oas.org/es/cidh/prensa/comunicados/2016/160.asp, accessed August 11, 2017.
48. Adam Isacson, "Confronting Colombia's Coca Boom Requires Patience and a Commitment to the Peace Accords," *Washington Office on Latin America*, March 13, 2017, available online at www.wola.org/analysis/confronting-colombias-coca-boom-requires-patience-commitment-peace-accords/, accessed June 30, 2017
49. Allen Cone, "U.N.: Colombia's coca cultivation area increased 52 percent from 2015 to 2016," UPI, July 15, 2017, available online at www.upi.com/Top_News/World-News/2017/07/15/UN-Colombias-coca-cultivation-area-increased-52-from-2015-to-2016/7571500128514/, accessed August 16, 2017.
50. Isacson, "Confronting Colombia's Coca Boom Requires Patience and a Commitment to the Peace Accords"
51. Adam Isacson, "The FARC Really Appears to be Abandoning Coca—Which May Mean Violence," May 17, 2017, adamisacson.com/the-farc-really-appears-to-be-abandoning-coca-which-may-mean-violence/, accessed August 12, 2017.

52. Internal Displacement Monitoring Center, "Colombia: Figures Analysis," www.internal-displacement.org/assets/country-profiles/COL-Colombia-Figures-Analysis.pdf, accessed June 23, 2017.

53. William Spindler, "Forced displacement growing in Colombia despite peace agreement" UNHCR 10 March 2017, www.unhcr.org/en-us/news/briefing/2017/3/58c26e114/forced-displacement-growing-colombia-despite-peace-agreement.html, accessed June 23, 2017.

54. Ibid.

55. "New Wave of Violence Threatens Colombia's Peace Prospects" Norwegian Refugee Council, August 8, 2017, www.nrc.no/news/2017/august/new-wave-of-violence-threatens-colombias-peace-prospects/, accessed August 11, 2017.

56. Ibid.

57. "New Wave of Violence Threatens Colombia's Peace Prospects."

58. "Some of the Many Reasons Why the United States Should Keep Supporting Colombia's Peace Accord."

59. Jonathan D. Rosen, *The Losing War*, p. 57.

CHAPTER 6. VIOLENCE: EL SALVADOR'S 'ILL-STRUCTURED' PROBLEM

1. "A rare murder-free day recorded in El Salvador," *Aljazeera*, January 13, 2017.

2. Matt Rocheleau, "El Salvador's Murder Rate Skyrockets," *The Boston Globe*, July 9, 2015.

3. "A rare murder-free day," January 13, 2017.

4. "A day without murder: no one is killed in El Salvador for the first time in two years," *The Guardian*, January 12, 2017.

5. "A day without murder," *The Guardian*, January 12, 2017.

6. See, for example, Randal C. Archibold, "In El Salvador, Violence Falls Amid a Gang Truce," *New York Times*, August 27, 2012.

7. Leonardo Goi, "Tensions Rise over Dissident MS13 Faction in El Salvador," *Insight Crime*, April 20, 2017.

8. Carabel Alegria, "El Salvador," *World Literature Today*, V. 81, N. 3 (May–June 2007): p. 42.

9. See Horst W. J. Rittel and Melvin M. Webber, "Dilemmas in a General Theory of Planning," *Policy Sciences*, V. 4, N. 2 (June 1973): pp. 155–169.

10. Zvi Lanir and Gad Sneh, *The New Agenda of Praxis* (Tel Aviv: Praxis Lanir-Decision and Learning Systems, 2000): 10.

11. Rittel and Webber, "Dilemmas in a General Theory," p. 161.

12. Ibid., p. 160.

13. Daniel Alarcón, "The Executioners of El Salvador," *The New Yorker*, August 4, 2015.

14. *Salvador*—Bulletin No. 58 (Bureau of the American Republics: Washington, 1892): 28.

15. Percy F. Martin, *Salvador of the Twentieth Century* (London: Edward Arnold, 1911): 13.

16. William M. LeoGrande and Carla Anne Robbins, "Oligarchs and Officers: The Crisis in El Salvador," *Foreign Affairs*, V. 58, N. 5 (Summer 1980): p. 1084.

17. Dinorah Azpuru, "The Salience of Ideology: Fifteen Years of Presidential Elections in El Salvador," *Latin American Politics and Society*, V. 52, N. 2 (Summer 2010): p. 107.

18. LeoGrande and Robbins, "Oligarchs and Officers," p. 1085

19. Joaquín M. Chávez, "An Anatomy of Violence in El Salvador," *Nacla*, nd.

20. Martin, *Salvador of the Twentieth Century*, p. 23.

21. See, for example, Eric Ching, "In Search of the Party: The Communist Party, the Comintern, and the Peasant Rebellion of 1932 in El Salvador," *The Americas*, V. 55, N. 2 (October 1998): 205–206.

22. Nathan Gilbert Quimpo, "The Philippines: Predatory Rimes, Growing Authoritarian Features," *The Pacific Review*, V. 22, N. 3 (July 2009): pp. 335–353.

23. David Browning, "Agrarian Reform in El Salvador," *Journal of Latin American Studies*, V. 15, N. 2 (November 1983): p. 407.

24. Browning, "Agrarian Reform in El Salvador," p. 407.

25. See the discussion in Walter C. Ladwig III, "Influencing Clients in Counterinsurgency: U.S. Involvement in El Salvador's Civil War, 1979–1992," *International Security*, V. 41, N. 1 (Summer 2016): p. 111.

26. David Bell, "El Salvador: State Building in El Salvador," *Harvard International Review*, V. 6, N. 7 (May/June 1984): p. 39.

27. Lynn Stephen, "Women's Rights Are Human Rights: The Merging of Feminine and Feminist Interests Among El Salvador's Mothers of the Disappeared," *American Ethnologist*, V. 22, N. 4 (November 1995): p. 808.

28. Stephen, "Women's Rights," p. 808.

29. Nina Lakhani, "El Salvador's dirty warriors to face justice for 1989 massacre of six Jesuits priests, their housekeeper and her daughter," *The Independent*, April 22, 2015.

30. Steven Dudley and Juan José Martínez d'Aubuisson, "El Salvador Prisons and the Battle for the MS13's Soul," *Insight Crime*, February 16, 2017.

31. Sheila Flynn, "The history of MS–13, according to a former member: How one of the most notorious gangs in the world grew from a group of displaced immigrant teens who banded together to smoke weed and listen to music," *The Daily Mail*, March 14, 2017.

32. Elana Zilberg, "Fools Banished from the Kingdom: Remapping Geographies of Gang Violence between the Americas (Los Angeles and San Salvador)," *America Quarterly*, V. 56, N. 3 (September 2004): p. 762.

33. Flynn, "The history of MS–13," March 14, 2017.

34. Carlos A. Rosales and Ana Leonor Morales, "The Re-Emergence of Social Cleansing in El Salvador," *Boomlive*, January 22, 2016.

35. R. Evan Ellis, "The Gang Challenge in El Salvador: Worse Than You Thought," *War on the Rocks*, December 16, 2015.

36. Miguel Galvis, "El Salvador is losing the war it declared on criminals," *Latin Correspondent*, March 9, 2016.

37. Danny Gold, "Are El Salvador's Murderous Gangs the Voice of the Oppressed? They Think So," *Vice News*, November 25, 2015.

38. Gold, "Are El Salvador's Murderous Gangs the Voice of the Oppressed?," November 25, 2015.

39. Christian Krohn-Hansen, "The Anthropology of Violent Interaction," *Journal of Anthropological Research,* V. 50, N. 4 (Winter 1994): p. 376.

40. Viridiana Rios, "Why did Mexico Become So Violent? A Self-Reinforcing Violent Equilibrium Caused by Competition and Enforcement," *Trends in Organized Crime*, V. 16 (2013): p. 139.

41. P. Jeffery Brantingham, et al., "The Ecology of Gang Territorial Boundaries" *Criminology*, V. 50, N. 3 (2012): p. 852.

42. Arron Daugherty, "El Salvador is Most Violent Nation in Western Hemisphere," *Insight Crime*, January 4, 2016.

43. Daugherty, "El Salvador is Most Violent Nation," January 4, 2016. See the discussion here regarding the emergence of MS503, the "*Revolucionarios*," who were said to have broken from MS–13 in 2016.

44. The phase belongs to Kenneth Waltz, depicting the influence of structures upon agents. See his "A Response to my Critics," in Keohane, *Neorealism and its Critics* (New York: Columbia University Press, 1986): p. 343.

45. See Kenneth Waltz in Keohane, *Neorealism and its Critics*, p. 129.

46. Thomas Schelling, "What is the Business of Organized Crime?" *Journal of Public Law*, V. 20 (1971): p. 73.

47. Schelling, "What is the Business of Organized Crime?" p. 73.

48. On ontological security, see Jennifer Mitzen, "Ontological Security in World Politics: State Identity and the Security Dilemma," *European Journal of International Relations*, V. 12, N. 3 (2006): pp. 341–370.

49. Roberto Valencia, "Official Data Suggests El Salvador Police Kill with Impunity," *Insight Crime*, October 7, 2016.

50. Mike LaSusa, "Report Describes Shifting Patterns of Violence in El Salvador," *Insight Crime*, September 22, 2016.

51. Valencia, "Official Data," October 7, 2016.

52. Ibid.

53. Ibid.

54. Ibid.

55. Rosales and Morales, "The Re-Emergence of Social Cleansing, January 22, 2016.

56. Loren Riesenfeld, "El Salvador to Deploy Special Forces to Combat Gangs," *Insight Crime*, May 8, 2015.

57. "El Salvador Transfers 27 Gang Members to Maximum Security Prison for Killing Cops," *Latin American Herald Tribune*, February 6, 2017.

58. Valencia, "Official Data," October 7 2016.

59. Ibid.

60. P. Jeffery Brantingham, et al., "The Ecology of Gang Territorial Boundaries" *Criminology*, V. 50, N. 3 (2012): p. 854.

61. Elijah Anderson, "The Code of the Streets," *The Atlantic*, May 1994.

62. Alfonso Valenzuela Aguilera, "Urban Surges: Power, Territory, and the Social Control of Space in Latin America," *Latin American Perspectives*, I. 189, V. 40, N. 2 (March 2013): p. 21.

63. Sarah Kinosian, Angelika Albaladejo, and Lisa Haugaard, "El Salvador's Violence: No Easy Way Out," *Latin America Working Group*, February 10, 2016.

64. R. Evan Ellis, "The Gang Challenge in El Salvador: Worse Than You Thought," *War on the Rocks*, December 16, 2015.

65. Óscar Martínez, et al., "Killers on a Shoestring: Inside the Gangs of El Salvador," *New York Times*, November 20, 2016.

66. Martínez, et al., "Killers on a Shoestring," November 20, 2016.

67. Ibid.

68. Flynn, "The history of MS–13," March 14, 2017.

69. Ibid.

70. Kate Linthicum, "Why tens of thousands of kids from El Salvador continue to flee to the United States," *The Los Angeles Times*, February 16, 2017.

71. Linthicum, "Why tens of thousands," February 16, 2017.

72. Kinosian, Albaladejo, and Haugaard, "El Salvador's Violence," February 10, 2016.

73. Harris, Desiderio, Millman and Effron, "In El Salvador," May 17, 2016.

74. Madeleine Schwartz, "El Salvador: A Town Without Violence?" *The New York Review of Books*, January 27, 2017.

75. Anastasia Moloney, "Rape, abortion ban drives pregnant teens to suicide in El Salvador," *Reuters*, November 12, 2014.

76. Jason Motlagh, "El Salvador: The Man Who Digs up Dead Bodies for Living," *The Huffington Post*, March 3, 2017.

77. Tristan Claval, "El Salvador's 'Black Widows' and the Growing Sophistication of the MS13," *Insight Crime*, March 1, 2017.

78. Wilson Dizard, "UN: A child dies violently every 5 minutes; Central America hard-hit," *Al Jazeera America*, October 21, 2014.

79. Roberto Lovato, "El Salvador's archives of death," *The Boston Globe*, March 6, 2016.

80. Rosales and Morales, "The Re-Emergence of Social Cleansing," January 22, 2016.

81. Ibid.

82. Angelika Albaladejo, "No Life Here: Internal Displacement in El Salvador," *Latin American Working Group*, February 18, 2016.

83. Daugherty, "El Salvador is Most Violent Nation," *Insight Crime*, January 4, 2016.

84. Carlos Garciá, "How the MS13 Got Its Foothold in Transnational Drug Trafficking," *Insight Crime*, November 30, 2016.

85. "El Salvador commemorates 25 years of peace," *The Economist*, January 21, 2017.

86. "Remittances to El Salvador Surge to Record High in 2016," *Voice of America*, January 23, 2017.

87. "Remittances," *Voice of America*, January 23, 2017.

88. Dan Morse, "Behind the rise in seemingly chaotic MS–13 violence: A structured hierarchy," *The Washington Post*, March 19, 2017.

89. Morse, "Behind the rise," March 19, 2017.

90. Ibid.

91. Jessica Yakeley and J. Reid Meloy, "Understanding Violence: Does Psychoanalytic Thinking Matter?" *Aggression and Violent Behavior,* V. 17 (2012): p. 237.

92. Stephen Gill, "Globalisation, Market Civilization, and Disciplinary Neoliberalism," *Millennium—Journal of International Studies*, V. 24, N. 3 (1995): pp. 399–423.

93. Suzanne Kent, "Symbols of Love: Consumption, Transnational Migration, and the Family in San Salvador, El Salvador," *Urban Anthropology and Studies of Cultural Systems and World Economic Development*, V. 39, N. 1/2 (Spring, Summer 2010): p. 86.

94. Kent, "Symbols of Love," p. 87.

95. Loic Wacquant, "The Militarization of Urban Marginality: Lessons from the Brazilian Metropolis," *International Political Sociology*, 2 (2008): pp. 56–74.

96. Kent, "Symbols of Love," p. 88.

97. Sarah Kinosian, "El Salvador's Security Policy is Increasing Extrajudicial Killings and Abuse," *Latin American Working Group*, February 12, 2016.

98. Bryan Avelar, "The El Salvador Gang That Kills Its Gay Members," *Insight Crime*, January 18, 2017.

99. Javier Auyero, Agustín Burbano De Lara and Mariá Fernanda Berti, "Uses and Forms of Violence among the Urban Poor," *Journal of Latin American Studies*, V. 46, I. 3 (August 2014): p. 452.

100. Polly Wilding, "'New Violence': Silencing Women's Experiences in the Favelas of Brazil," *Journal of Latin American Studies*, V. 42, I. 4 (November 2010): p. 721.

101. Parveen Azam Ali and Paul B. Naylor, "Intimate Partner Violence: A Narrative Review of the Feminist, Social and Ecological Explanations for its Causation," *Aggression and Violent Behavior*, 18 (2013): p. 614.

102. The paradigmatic statement on this matter is Robert K. Merton, "Social Structure and Anomie," *American Sociological Review*, V. 3, N. 5 (October 1938): p. 676.

103. Jose Soltero and Romeo Saravia, "Dimensions of Social Stratification and Anomie as Factors of Religious Affiliation in El Salvador," *Sociology of Religion*, V. 64, N. 1 (Spring 2003): p. 3.

104. Robert Agnew, "Foundations for a General Strain Theory of Crime and Delinquency," *Criminology*, V. 30, N. 1 (1992): p. 48.

105. Agnew, "Foundations for a General Strain Theory," p. 51.

106. Craig A. Anderson and Brad J. Bushman, "Human Aggression," *Annual Review of Psychology,* 53 (2002): p. 31.

107. Anderson and Bushman, "Human Aggression," pp. 31–32.

108. Robert J. Bursik, "Social Disorganization and Theories of Crime and Delinquency: Problems and Prospects," *Criminology*, V. 26, N. 4 (1988): p. 521.

109. Bursik, "Social Disorganization and Theories of Crime and Delinquency," p. 521.

110. Marvin Wolfgang and Franco Farracuti, *The Subculture of Violence: Towards an Integrated Theory in Criminology: Towards an Integrated Theory in Criminology* (Tavistock Publications Limited, 1967): pp. 155–156.

111. Lonnie Athens, *The Creation of Dangerous Violent Criminals* (1989): p. 11.

112. Wolfgang and Farracuti, "*The Subculture of Violence,*" pp. 155–156.

113. Lonnie Athens, "The Self as a Soliloquy," *The Sociological Quarterly* 35, no. 3 (August 1994): p. 524.

114. Lonnie Athens, *Violent Criminal Acts and Actors Revisited* (Urbana: University of Illinois, 1997), p. 138.

115. Lonnie Athens, "Park's Theory of Conflict and His Fall from Grace in Sociology," *Cultural Studies-Critical Methodologies* V. 13, N. 2 (2013): p. 84.

116. Lonnie Athens, "Violent Encounters: Violent Engagements, Skirmishes, and Tiffs," *Journal of Contemporary Ethnography* V. 34, N. 6 (December 2005): p. 649.

117. Andrew V. Papachristos, "Murder by Structure: Dominance Relations and the Social Structure of Gang Homicide," *American Journal of Sociology*, V. 115, N. 1 (July 2009): p. 76.

118. Anne Burnett, "Medea and the Tragedy of Revenge," *Classical Philology*, V. LXVIII, N. 1 (January 1973): p. 1.

119. Richard A. Bogg, "Dostoevsky's Enigmas: An Analysis of Violent Men," *Aggression and Violent Behavior,* V. 4, N. 4 (1999): p. 382.

120. Bogg, "Dostoevsky's Enigmas," p. 384.

121. Manni Crone, "Religion and Violence" Governing Muslim Militancy through Aesthetic Assemblages," *Millennium: Journal of International Studies*, V. 43, N. 1 (2014): p. 294.

122. J. P. Carroll, "Why the Deadliest Gang in the World Might be Rethinking Face Tattoos," *The Daily Caller*, May 15, 2016.

123. Roque Planas, "How El Salvador Became the World's Most Violent Peacetime Country," *The Huffington Post*, March 4, 2016.

124. Ignacio Martín-Baró, "Political Violence and War as Causes of Psychological Trauma in El Salvador," *International Journal of Mental Health*, V. 18, N. 1 (Spring 1989): p. 16.

125. Reinhold Niebuhr, "The Illusion of World Government," *Foreign Affairs*, V. 27, N. 3 (April 1949): 386.

126. Jeff Elison, Carlo Garofalo and Patrizia Velotti, "Shame and Aggression: Theoretical Considerations," *Aggression and Violent Behavior*, 19 (2014): p. 449.

127. Elison, Garofalo and Velotti, "Shame and Aggression," p. 448.

128. Recep Dogan, "The Dynamics of Honor Killings and the Perpetrator's Experiences," *Homicide Studies*, (2014): p. 3.

129. Thomas J. Scheff, "Social-emotional origins of violence: A theory of multiple killing," *Aggression and Violent Behavior*, 16 (2011): p. 454.

130. For the views of James Gilligan on this matter, see Scheff, "Social-emotional origins of violence," p. 454.

131. Elison, Garofalo and Velotti, "Shame and Aggression," p. 447.

132. Elison, Garofalo and Velotti, "Shame and Aggression," p. 448.

133. Ibid.

134. José Cruz, et al., *The New Face of Street Gangs: The Gang Phenomenon in El Salvador* (Miami: The Kimberly Green Latin America and Caribbean Center and the Jack D. Gordon Institute for Public Policy, Florida International University, 2017), p. 6.

135. Jeffrey Jensen Arnett, "Sensation Seeking, Aggressiveness, and Adolescent Reckless Behavior," *Personality and Individual Difference*, V. 20, N. 6 (1996): p. 693.

136. Callie H. Burt and Ronald L. Simons, "Self-Control, Thrill Seeking and Crime: Motivation Matters," *Criminal Justice and Behavior*, V. 40, N. 11 (November 2013): p. 1332.

137. Anderson and Bushman, "Human Aggression," p. 32.

138. Randall Collins, "The Micro-Sociology of Violence," *The British Journal of Sociology*, V. 60, I. 3 (2009): p. 571.

139. Collins, "The Micro-Sociology of Violence," p. 571.

140. Don Weenink, "Frenzied Attacks. A Micro-Sociological Analysis of the Emotional Dynamics of Extreme Youth Violence," *The British Journal of Sociology*, V. 65, I. 3 (2014): p. 413.

141. "El Salvador commemorates 25 years of peace," *The Economist*, January 21, 2017.

142. Joaquín M. Chávez, "An Anatomy of Violence in El Salvador," *Nacla*, nd.

143. Chávez, "An Anatomy of Violence in El Salvador," *Nacla*, nd.

144. Héctor Silva Ávalos, "Negotiations Between El Salvador Government, MS13 Prove Elusive," *Insight Crime*, February 1, 2017.

145. "Murders in notoriously violent El Salvador drop 20 percent in 2016: police," *Reuters*, January 2, 2017.

146. Loren Riesenfeld, "El Salvador to Deploy Special Forces to Combat Gangs," *Insight Crime*, May 8, 2015.

147. Nini Lakhani, "'We fear soldiers more than gangsters': El Salvador's 'iron fist' policy turns deadly," *The Guardian*, February 6, 2017.

148. Lakhani, "'We fear soldiers more than gangsters,'" February 6, 2017.

149. Ibid.

150. "El Salvador mulls suspending some rights as crime spikes," *Reuters*, March 8, 2016.

151. Rosales and Morales, "The Re-Emergence of Social Cleansing," January 22, 2016.

152. Madeleine Schwartz, "El Salvador: A Town Without Violence?" *The New York Review of Books*, January 27, 2017.

153. Kinosian, "El Salvador's Security Policy," February 12, 2016.

154. Steven Dudley and Juan José Martínez d'Aubuisson, "El Salvador Prisons and the Battle for MS13's Soul," *Insight Crime*, February 6, 2017.

155. Roberto Valencia, "Ho El Salvador Handed its Prisons to the Mara Street Gangs, *Insight Crime*, September 3, 2014.

156. Dudley and Martínez d'Aubuisson, "El Salvador Prisons," February 6, 2017.

157. Ibid.

158. Kinosian, "El Salvador's Security Policy," February 12, 2016.

159. Dudley and Martínez d'Aubuisson, "El Salvador Prisons," February 6, 2017.

160. Joshua Partlow, "Trump wants to deport MS–13 gang members. El Salvador is dreading their return," *The Washington Post*, May 24, 2017.

161. "El Salvador: At least 30 slain in bloody 24-hour span," *The Washington Post*, March 16, 2017.

162. Dudley and Martínez d'Aubuisson, "El Salvador Prisons," February 16, 2017.

163. Roque Planas, "How El Salvador Became the World's Most Violent Peacetime Country," *The Huffington Post*, March 4, 2016.

164. "El Salvador struggles with options on returning gang members," *The Washington Post*, May 5, 2017.

165. "The Kelly-Nash Political Machine," *Fortune*, August 1936, p. 50.

166. John Rawls, *Political Liberalism* (New York, NY: Columbia University Press, 2005), p. xxv.

167. "Kelly-Nash," *Fortune*, August 1936, p. 50.

168. Ibid.

169. Ibid.

170. Deepa Fernandes, "A brother and sister flee gang violence in El Salvador and start over the US," *Public Radio International*, March 8, 2017.

171. Fernandes, "A brother and sister flee gang violence," March 8, 2017.

172. Luigi Barzini, *The Italians* (New York: Atheneum, 1965): p. 339.

CHAPTER 7. AT A CROSSROADS: CAN GUATEMALA PREVAIL IN FIGHT AGAINST VIOLENCE?

1. Research assistance provided by Carolyn Scorpio and Luciana Jhon.

2. José Elías, "La matanza de 27 campesinos conmociona a Guatemala," *El País*, May 16, 2011.

3. "Zetas asesinan a 27 jornaleros en Petén," *Prensa Libre*, May 16, 2011.

4. Hannah Stone and Miriam Wells, "Zetas to Face Trial for 2011 Farm Massacre in Guatemala," *InSight Crime*, March 1, 2013, www.insightcrime.org/news-briefs/zetas-to-face-trial-for-2011-farm-massacre-in-guatemala, accessed July 2017.

5. "Intentional homicide count and rate per 100,000 population, by country/terri tory (2000–2012)," *United Nations Office on Drugs and Crime*, www.unodc.org/gsh/en/data.html, last accessed July 2017.

6. Adriana Beltrán, "Will the Rebellion for the Rule of Law Prevail in Guatemala?" in *Fragile States in the Americas*, ed. Jonathan D. Rosen and Hanna S. Kassab (New York: Lexington Books, 2016), p. 39.

7. *International Narcotics Control Strategy Report: Volume 1 Drug and Chemical Control* (Washington, DC: U.S. Department of State, 2016), 169, www.state.gov/documents/organization/253655.pdf, accessed July 2017.

8. Ibid., p. 167.

9. Ibid, p. 62.

10. Ibid, p. 168.

11. *Corridor of Violence: The Guatemala-Honduras Border* (Brussels: International Crisis Group, June 4, 2014), 4.

12. "Lorenzanas," *InSight Crime*, March 9, 2017, www.insightcrime.org/guatemala-organized-crime-news/los-lorenzana, accessed July 2017.

13. Julie Lopez, "Guatemala's Crossroads: The Democratization of Violence and Second Chances," in *Organized Crime in Central America: The Northern Triangle*, ed. Cynthia J. Arnson and Eric L. Olson (Washington, DC: Woodrow Wilson International Center for Scholars, November 2011), p. 153.

14. "Global Study on Homicide: 2013," (Vienna: United Nations Office on Drugs and Crime, 2014).

15. "Trafficking in Persons 2016 Report," *U.S. Department of State*, www.state.gov/j/tip/rls/tiprpt/countries/2016/258775.htm, accessed July 2017.

16. "Human Trafficking for Sexual Exploitation Purposes in Guatemala," (Guatemala: Comisión Internacional contra la Impunidad en Guatemala and UNICEF, 2016), pp, 67–68, www.cicig.org/uploads/documents/2016/Trata_Ing_978_9929_40_829_6.pdf.

17. For a detailed account of the CIACS, see: Susan C. Peacock and Adriana Beltrán, *Hidden Powers in Post-Conflict Guatemala* (Washington, DC: Washington Office on Latin America, 2003).

18. Steven S. Dudley, "Drug Trafficking Organizations in Central America: Transportistas, Mexican Cartels, and Maras," in *Organized Crime in Central America: The Northern Triangle*, ed. Cynthia J. Arnson and Eric L. Olson (Washington, DC: Woodrow Wilson International Center for Scholars, November 2011), p. 76.

19. Steven Dudley, "Drug Trafficking Organizations in Central America: Transportistas, Mexican Cartels, and Maras," p. 34; and *Guatemala: Squeezed Between Crime and Impunity* (Brussels: International Crisis Group, June 22, 2010), p. 16.

20. For more information, see: *Financiamiento de la política en Guatemala* (Guatemala: Comisión Internacional contra la Impunidad en Guatemala, July 2015).

21. *Financiamiento de la política en Guatemala*, p. 41.

22. Kevin Casas-Zamora, "U.S.-Central America Security Cooperation: Testimony before the U.S. Senate Caucus on International Narcotics Control," *Brookings Institution*, May 25 2011, www.brookings.edu/research/testimony/2011/05/25-us-central-america-security-cooperation-casaszamora, accessed July 2017.

23. Sarah Garland, *Gangs in Garden City: How Immigration, Segregation, and Youth Violence are Changing America's Suburbs* (New York: Nation Books, 2009), p. 98.

24. *Guatemala: Squeezed Between Crime and Impunity*, p. 12.

25. *Transnational Organized Crime in Central America and the Caribbean, A Threat Assessment* (Vienna: United Nations Office on Drugs and Crime, September 2012), p. 29.

26. Clare Ribando Seelke, *Gangs in Central America* (Washington, DC: Congressional Research Service, 2016), p. 3.

27. Nicholas Phillips, *CARSI in Guatemala: Progress, Failure, and Uncertainty* (Washington, DC: Woodrow Wilson International Center for Scholars, 2014), p. 10.

28. For a detailed map of gangs operating in the capital, see: Kyra Gurney, "Mapping MS13, Barrio 18 Territory in Guatemala City," *InSight Crime*, September 10, 2014, www.insightcrime.org/news-briefs/ms13-gang-barrio-18-guatemala-city-map, accessed July 2017.

29. Anthony W. Fontes, *Beyond the Maras: Violence and Survival in Urban Central America* (Washington, DC: Woodrow Wilson International Center for Scholars, December 2014), p. 2.

30. "Closed Doors: Mexico's Failure to Protect Central American Refugee and Migrant Children," *Human Rights Watch*, March 31, 2016, www.hrw.org/report/2016/03/31/closed-doors/mexicos-failure-protect-central-american-refugee-and-migrant-children, accessed July 2017.

31. Clare Ribando Seelke, *Gangs in Central America*, p. 3.

32. Kyra Gurney, "Guatemala Extortion Generates $61 Mn a Year: Govt," *InSight Crime*, July 18, 2014, www.insightcrime.org/news-briefs/guatemala-extortion-generates-61-mn-a-year-govt, accessed July 2017.

33. Kyra Gurney, "700 Extortion-Related Murders in Guatemala through July 2014: NGO," *InSight Crime*, August 15, 2014, www.insightcrime.org/news-briefs/guatemala-700-homicides-extortion-2014, accessed July 2017.

34. Manuel Rodríguez, "GAM: 35 mil denuncias por denuncias por extorsiones en siete años," *La Hora*, February 26, 2015.

35. "Víctimas de hechos delictivos cometidos por año y sexo, según tipo de causa," *Instituto Nacional de Estadistica Guatemala,* www.ine.gob.gt/index.php/estadisticas-continuas/hechos-delictivos, accessed July 14, 2017,

36. *Guatemala En La Encrucijada, Panorama de Una Violencia Transformada* (Geneva: Geneva Declaration on Armed Violence and Development, 2011), pp. 65–66.

37. Interview with Professor Mark Ungar, July 25, 2017.

38. *Transnational Organized Crime in Central America and the Caribbean, A Threat Assessment*, p. 61.

39. Interview with Professor Mark Ungar, July 25, 2017. This is based on his interview with ATF in San Salvador on January 19, 2016.

40. *Guatemala En La Encrucijada, Panorama de Una Violencia Transformada* (Geneva: Geneva Declaration on Armed Violence and Development, 2011), pp. 65–66.

41. During the internal armed conflict the entire state apparatus was placed under the control and oversight of the military. In its report, the Historical Clarification Commission (CEH) noted that the control of the military reached its highest expression in 1982 when the military junta issued a decree which granted it the power to

appoint the head and magistrates of the supreme court and all other courts, as well as the Comptroller general, who at the time also acted as Attorney General.

42. Claudia Paz y Paz Bailey, *Transforming Justice in Guatemala: Strategies and Challenges Investigating Violent Deaths 2011–2014* (Washington, DC: Georgetown University and Open Society Foundations, 2016).

43. Ibid, p. 67

44. Ibid, p. 34.

45. Ibid.

46. Ibid, p. 36.

47. Ibid, p. 10

48. Congress selects three candidates from the list of six to serve in the Public Ministry Council, which acts as an advisory body to the Attorney General and has the power to appoint staff and confirm or amend directives, including disciplinary measures, from the Attorney General. For more information, see: Mirte Postema, *The selection process of the Attorney General in Guatemala: increased regulation does not mean less arbitrariness* (Washington, DC: Due Process of Law Foundation, August 1, 2014), p. 2.

49. Steven Dudley, "Backroom Justice—The War for Guatemala's Courts," *InSight Crime*, September 2014, www.insightcrime.org/investigations/the-war-for-guatemala-s-courts, accessed July 2017.

50. *Protect and Serve? The Status of Police Reform in Central America* (Washington, DC: Washington Office on Latin America, June 2009), p. 5.

51. The Criminal Investigation Service (*Servicio de Investigación Criminal*, SIC) was comprised of a large number of former members of the Department of Criminal Investigation (*Departamento de Investigación Criminal*, DIC) of the National Police, who were assigned to transferred to the new unit after having passed a three-month basic training course and subsequently a one-month specialized course.

52. Patrick Gavigan, "Organized Crime, Illicit Power Structures and Guatemala's Threatened Peace Process," *International Peacekeeping* 16 (2009): p.66.

53. *Police Reform in Guatemala: Obstacles and Opportunities* (Brussels: International Crisis Group, July 20, 2012), p. 5.

54. Adriana Beltrán, "Will the Rebellion for the Rule of Law Prevail in Guatemala?" p. 44.

55. *Guatemala: Squeezed Between Crime and Impunity*, p. 12.

56. Adriana Beltrán, "Will the Rebellion for the Rule of Law Prevail in Guatemala?" p. 44.

57. Ibid., p. 45.

58. "Informe revela insalubridad, hacinamiento y mal estado de sedes policiales," *La Hora*, June 19, 2017.

59. *Annual report of the United Nations High Commissioner for Human Rights on the activities of his office in Guatemala* (New York, NY: United Nations, January 11, 2017), p. 8.

60. "Urge ampliar la infraestructura carcelaria, con planificación y control," *El Centro de Investigaciones Económicas Nacionales*, August 6, 2014, www.cien.org

.gt/index.php/urge-ampliar-la-infraestructura-carcelaria-con-planificacion-y-control, accessed July 2017.

61. Berlin, Daniel, Erin Brizius, Micah Bump, Daren Garshelis, Niloufar Khonsari, Erika Pinheiro, Kate Rhudy, Rebecca Shaeffer, Sarah Sherman-Stokes, and Thomas Smith, *Between the Border and the Street: A Comparative Look at Gang Reduction Policies and Migration in the United States and Guatemala* (Washington, DC: Georgetown Law Center, 2007), pp. 9–10.

62. *Mafia of the Poor: Gang Violence and Extortion in Central America* (Brussels: International Crisis Group, April 6, 2017), p. 7.

63. A 2013 report by the Center for Legal Action in Human Rights (CALDH) found that between 2005 and 2012, prosecutors investigated a total of 6,805 cases of extrajudicial executions, but only 22 of these resulted in convictions. The report also revealed a 50 percent increase in cases of extrajudicial killings from 2011–2012, the first year of the Pérez Molina administration. For more information, see: Bargent, James. "Extrajudicial Killings on the Rise in Guatemala." *InSight Crime*, July 4, 2013. www.insightcrime.org/news-briefs/extrajudicial-killings-on-the-rise-in-guatemala, accessed July 2017.

64. Stone, Hannah. "Can Guatemala's Military President Reform the Police?" *InSight Crime*, August 6, 2012. www.insightcrime.com/news-analysis/can-guatemalas-military-president-reform-the-police, accessed July 2017.

65. Adriana Beltrán, "Will the Rebellion for the Rule of Law Prevail in Guatemala?"

66. Mariela Castañon, "Se Invierten Q108 Millones En Los Escuadrones de Seguridad; ¿Más Ejército, Menos Violencia?" *La Hora*. June 17, 2013.

67. *Report of the United Nations High Commissioner for Human Rights on the activities of his office in Guatemala* (New York, NY: United Nations, January 12, 2015), 11, www.insightcrime.com/images/2015/March-2015/UNGuatemalaReport.pdf.

68. During the Portillo administration, the Guatemalan congress signed Accord 40–2000, which permitted the Guatemalan military to support the police in public security operations. His successor Oscar Berger (2004–2008) reduced the size of the military by 43 percent during his first year of government. Yet in 2006, under pressure to respond to rising crime rates, 3,000 former soldiers were tapped to make up a special citizen security team. They had retired only a few months earlier during the series of layoffs to reduce the size of the military. According to press reports, the former soldiers were sent out on the street patrols after receiving a 45 day basic police training course.

69. Susan Fitzpatrick-Behrens, "Guatemala's New Civil Conflict: The Case of Ramiro Choc," *NACLA*, nacla.org/news/guatemala%E2%80%99s-new-civil-conflict-case-ramiro-choc accessed July 12, 2017; and *Police Reform in Guatemala: Challenges and Opportunities*, p. 8; Ronan Graham, "More Military Spending in Central America Giving Rise to Old and New Fears," *InSight Crime*, October 24, 2011, www.insightcrime.org/news-analysis/more-military-spending-in-central-america-giving-rise-to-old-and-new-fears, accessed July 2017.

70. *Report of the United Nations High Commissioner for Human Rights on the activities of his office in Guatemala* (2015), p. 11.

71. "Monitoreo Final de PNC Reportó 258 Homicidios Menos En El País," *Ministerio de Gobernación de Guatemala*, January 1, 2017, mingob.gob.gt/monitoreo-final-de-pnc-reporto-258-homicidios-menos-en-el-pais/; Adriana Beltrán, "Guatemala: A Glimmer of Hope for Violence Reduction in the Region," *Washington Office on Latin America*, January 9, 2017, www.wola.org/analysis/guatemala-glimmer-hope-violence-reduction-region/, accessed July 2017. The downward trend is also seen in autopsies performed by INACIF, from a rate of 50.2 per 100,000 inhabitants in 2009 to 33.2 in 2016. The number of autopsies is higher as it includes cases associated with criminal acts under investigation, suicides, and firearms accidents, which are not recorded in the PNC figures. Nonetheless, the sustained drop in the INACIF data suggests that the reduction is real and not the result of changes or manipulation of police records.

72. Claudia Paz y Paz assumed the position of Attorney General in December 2010. The first woman to hold the position, her appointment was also unprecedented due to her civil society, academic, and human rights background. CICIG statements connecting him to parallel power structures resulted in the revocation of the appointment of Attorney General Conrado Arnulfo Reyes, and enabled the election of Paz y Paz.

73. For more information see: Paz y Paz Bailey, *Transforming Justice in Guatemala: Strategies and Challenges Investigating Violent Deaths 2011–2014.*

74. Paz y Paz Bailey, *Transforming Justice in Guatemala: Strategies and Challenges Investigating Violent Deaths 2011–2014.*

75. Police Reform in Guatemala: Obstacles and Opportunities, p. 13.

76. Nicholas Phillips, *CARSI in Guatemala: Progress, Failure, and Uncertainty*, p. 4.

77. "Sexto Informe de Labores de La Comisión Internacional Contra La Impunidad En Guatemala (CICIG)" (Guatemala: Comisión Internacional contra la Impunidad en Guatemala, August 2013) p. 6.

78. The smartphone app *Denuncia MP Extorsiones* (Denounce MP Extortions) uses and automatically updates the public prosecutor's database of phone numbers detected as belonging to extortion rings. Users are alerted when an incoming call is from a number registered in its database. The app also gives users the option to report extortion cases direction to the Public Prosecutor's Office, as well the capacity to record calls and save the number. For more information, see: *Mafia of the Poor: Gang Violence and Extortion in Central America*, p. 20.

79. The three operations carried out in 2016 were "Rescue of the South" in May, in which 72 alleged members of the Barrio 18 were captured in the departments of Guatemala, Retalhuleu, Escuintla, Santa Rosa, and Izabal; "Rescuing Guatemala" in July, in which 11 alleged gang members were arrested in 7 departments throughout the country, and "Guatemala is Ours" in December, a two-day operation resulting in the arrests of 112 individuals. For more information, see: Byron Vásquez y Glenda Sánchez, "Capturan a 72 pandilleros que cobraron Q3 millones por extorsión," *Prensa Libre*, May 2, 2016, www.prensalibre.com/guatemala/justicia/despliegan-operativo-nacional-en-contra-de-extorsionistas; Henry Pocasangre, "Operativos dejan 744 capturados por extorsión," *Prensa Libre*, December 30, 2016, www.prensalibre.com/

guatemala/justicia/operativos-dejan-744-capturados-por-extorsion; and Claudia Palma y José Manuel Patzán, "Redada masiva deja 112 arrestos," *Prensa Libre*, December 8, 2016, www.prensalibre.com/guatemala/justicia/redada-masiva-deja-112-arrestos; and *Mafia of the Poor: Gang Violence and Extortion in Central America*, 20.

80. In April 2015, the CICIG and Public Prosecutor's Office revealed a massive customs fraud ring within the country's tax agency called "La Línea" implicating then-Vice President Roxana Baldetti, who resigned in May. In August of the same year, investigators presented evidence of Pérez Molina's involvement leading to his resignation and arrest in September. Since then, both have been implicated in a number of other corruption cases, including the "Cooptación del Estado" case, in which the Public Prosecutor's Office and CICIG revealed that the former president's party, Partido Patriota, was essentially set up as a mafia-style organization to co-opt the Guatemalan state and illegally enrich party members and associated businesses. For more information see: www.cicig.org/.

81. Política Criminal Democrática del Estado de Guatemala 2015–2035, (Guatemala: Ministerio Público de Guatemala, April 2016), p. 12.

82. "Ministro Rivas Presenta Plan Para Reducción de Homicidios y Delitos Patrimoniales," *Ministerio de Gobernación de Guatemala*, June 13, 2016, mingob.gob.gt/ministro-rivas-presenta-plan-para-reduccion-de-homicidios-y-delitos-patrimoniales/, accessed July 2017.

83. Adriana Beltrán, "Guatemala: A Glimmer of Hope for Violence Reduction in the Region."

84. According to police statistics, the largest drop in violent deaths in 2016 occurred in the departments of Escuintla (19 percent), Santa Rosa (34 percent), and Chiquimula (20 percent). For more information, see: Adriana Beltrán, "Guatemala: A Glimmer of Hope for Violence Reduction in the Region."

85. Among first actions undertaken by the International Commission against Impunity in Guatemala (CICIG) during its first years was the promotion of a set of legislative reforms to provide better investigative tools and enhance criminal prosecutions and sentencing, including the use of wiretaps, the figure of confidential informant, the implementation of a witness protection program, and the creation of the courts for high risk crimes. With the support of the CICIG, the special methods of investigation unit and the bureau of crime analysis were created, staffed and trained. The CICIG also helped establish and train a special prosecutor's office that coordinates investigative activities with the CICIG.

86. For more information, see: "The CICIG: An Innovative Instrument for Fighting Criminal Organizations and Strengthening the Rule of Law," (Washington, DC: Washington Office on Latin America, June 2015), www.wola.org/wp-content/uploads/2015/07/WOLA_CICIG_ENG_FNL_extra-page.pdf, accessed July 2017; and Adriana Beltrán, *"Will the Rebellion for the Rule of Law Prevail in Guatemala?"*

87. Adriana Beltrán, "Guatemala: A Glimmer of Hope for Violence Reduction in the Region."

88. Data received from the Guatemalan Public Prosecutor's Office through information request in July 2017.

89. "Guatemala," *International Displacement Monitoring Centre*, www.internal-displacement.org/countries/guatemala, July 2017.

90. "CICIG proposes wealth tax to fund justice and security," *The Economist*, November 19, 2015, country.eiu.com/article.aspx?articleid=253696009&Country=Guatemala&topic=Politics&subtopic=Forecast&subsubtopic=Political+stability&u=1&pid=985598882&oid=985598882&uid=1, accessed July 2017.

91. "Crutch to Catalyst? The International Commission against Impunity in Guatemala," (Brussels, International Crisis Group, January 29, 2016), p. 13, www.crisisgroup.org/latin-america-caribbean/central-america/guatemala/crutch-catalyst-international-commission-against-impunity-guatemala, accessed July 2017.

92. "CICIG Proposes Wealth Tax to Fund Justice and Security."

93. "The World Bank in Guatemala," *The World Bank*, www.worldbank.org/en/country/guatemala/overview, accessed August 1, 2017.

94. "Guatemala: Nutrition Profile," *United States Agency for International Development*, www.usaid.gov/what-we-do/global-health/nutrition/countries/guatemala-nutrition-profile, accessed July 14, 2017.

95. Ibid.

96. Adriana Beltrán. "Children and Families Fleeing Violence in Central America," *Washington Office on Latin America*, February 21, 2017, www.wola.org/analysis/people-leaving-central-americas-northern-triangle/, accessed July 2017.

97. *Guatemala Social Sector Expenditure and Institutional Review* (Washington, DC: World Bank, August 25, 2016), p. 10.

CHAPTER 8. VIOLENCE IN MEXICO: AN EXAMINATION OF THE MAJOR TRENDS AND CHALLENGES

1. For more, see: Ted Galen Carpenter, *The Fire Next Door: Mexico's Drug Violence and the Danger to America* (Washington, DC: CATO Institute, 2012).

2. For more, see: Ted Galen Carpenter, *The Fire Next Door: Mexico's Drug Violence and the Danger to America*.

3. Diana Villiers Negroponte, "Mexico's Energy Reforms Become Law," *Brookings*, August 14, 2014.

4. United Nations Office on Drugs and Crime (UNODC), *Global Study on Homicide: 2013* (New York, NY: UNODC, 2013).

5. Ibid.

6. "The world's most dangerous cities," *The Economist*, March 31, 2017, http://www.economist.com/blogs/graphicdetail/2017/03/daily-chart-23, accessed April 2017.

7. Ibid

8. Ibid.

9. David Vicenteño, "Cinco cárteles pelean Guerrero; es la entidad más disputada por el narco," *Excelsior*, September 23, 2015; see also, Luis Alonso Pérez, "Mexico's Jalisco Cartel–New Generation: From Extinction to World Domination," *InSight Crime*, December 26, 2016, http://www.insightcrime.org/news-analysis/mexico-cartel-jalisco-new-generation-extinction-world-domination, accessed April 2017.

10. For more on drug trafficking organizations, see: Nathan P. Jones, *Mexico's Illicit Drug Networks and The State Reaction* (Washington, DC: Georgetown University Press, 2016).

11. For more on corruption, see: Stephen D. Morris and Joseph L. Klesner, "Corruption and trust: Theoretical considerations and evidence from Mexico," *Comparative Political Studies* 43, no. 10 (2010): pp. 1258–1285; Peter Andreas, "The political economy of narco-corruption in Mexico" *Current history* 97 (1998): p. 160; Louise Shelley, "Corruption and organized crime in Mexico in the post-PRI transition," *Journal of Contemporary Criminal Justice* 17, no. 3 (2001): pp. 213–231; Stephen D. Morris, *Political corruption in Mexico: The impact of democratization* (Boulder, CO: Lynne Rienner Publishers, 2009).

12. For more on Mexican politics, see: Emily Edmonds-Poli and David A. Shirk, *Contemporary Mexican Politics* (Lanham, MD: Rowman & Littlefield, 2016, third edition); David A Shirk, *Mexico's New Politics: the PAN and Democratic Change* (Boulder, CO: Lynne Rienner Publishers, 2005).

13. Jonathan D. Rosen and Roberto Zepeda, *Organized Crime, Drug Trafficking, and Violence in Mexico: The Transition from Felipe Calderón to Enrique Peña Nieto* (Lanham, MD: Lexington Books, 2016).

14. "Corruption Perceptions Index 2014: Results," *Transparency International*, http://www.transparency.org/cpi2014/results, accessed September 2016.

15. For more on the police, see: Diane E. Davis, "Undermining the rule of law: Democratization and the dark side of police reform in Mexico," *Latin American Politics and* Society 48, no. 1 (2006): pp. 55–86; Benjamin Reames, "Police forces in Mexico: A profile," *Center for US-Mexican Studies* (2003); Nelson Arteaga Botello and Adrián López Rivera, "'Everything in This Job Is Money': Inside the Mexican Police," *World Policy Journal* 17, no. 3 (2000): pp. 61–70; Guillermo Zepeda Lecuona, "Mexican Police and the Criminal Justice System," *Police and Public Security in Mexico* (2009): pp. 39–64; Wayne A. Cornelius and David A. Shirk, eds., *Reforming the administration of justice in Mexico* (Notre Dame, IN: University of Notre Dame Press, 2007).

16. Mimi Yagoub, "Most Mexicans Think Police Controlled by Org. Crime: Poll," *Insight Crime*, January 10, 2017, http://www.insightcrime.org/news-briefs/most-mexicans-think-police-controlled-by-org-crime-poll, accessed April 2017.

17. Ibid.

18. James Bargent, "Mexico Impunity Levels Reach 99%: Study," InSight Crime, February 4, 2016, http://www.insightcrime.org/news-briefs/mexico-impunity-levels-reach-99-study, accessed April 2016.

19. Maureen Mayer and Ximena Suarez Enriquez, *WOLA report: Mexico's new judiciary system* (Washington, DC: Washington Office of Latin America, 2016).

20. "Mexico suffering from 'serious crisis of violence and impunity,' report says," *The Guardian*, March 2, 2016.

21. For more on neoliberalism, see: John Gledhill, *Neoliberalism, transnationalization, and rural poverty: a case study of Michoacán, Mexico* (Boulder, CO: Westview Press, 1995); Kathleen McAfee and Elizabeth N. Shapiro, "Payments for ecosystem services in Mexico: nature, neoliberalism, social movements, and the state,"

Annals of the Association of American Geographers 100, no. 3 (2010): pp. 579–599; Richard Snyder, "After neoliberalism: the politics of reregulation in Mexico," *World Politics* 51, no. 02 (1999): pp. 173–204; Richard Snyder, "After the state withdraws: Neoliberalism and subnational authoritarian regimes in Mexico," *Subnational politics and democratization in Mexico* (1999): pp. 295–341.

22. Ninis is a Spanish acronym used to describe the young population who are neither studying nor working. This share of the population is aged between 15 and 24 years old. More than 20 million people in Latin America are in this condition.

23. Rafael de Hoyos, Halsey Rogers, and Miguel Székely, *Out of School and Out of Work: Risk and Opportunities for Latin America's Ninis* (Washington, DC: World Bank, 2016).

24. Rubén Aguilar and Jorge Castañeda, *El narco: la guerra fallida* (México: Punto de Lectura, 2009).

25. For more on this topic, see: Jorge Chabat, "La respuesta del gobierno de Calderón al desafío del narcotráfico: entre lo malo y lo peor," *Centro de Investigación y Docencia Ecónomicas (CIDE)*, División de Estudios Internacionales, 2010.

26. Peter Watt and Roberto Zepeda. *Drug War Mexico: Politics, Neoliberalism and Violence in the new Narcoeconomy*. (London: Zed Books, 2012), p. 2.

27. Clare Ribando Seelke and Kristin Finklea, *U.S.–Mexican Security Cooperation: The Mérida Initiative and Beyond* (Washington, DC: Congressional Research Service, 2016).

28. "Merida Initiative at a Glance: The Four Pillars," *US Embassy*, http://www.usembassy-mexico.gov/eng/merida/emerida_factsheet_fourpillarscooperation.html, accessed September 2016; see also Jorge Chabat, "La Iniciativa Mérida y la relación México-Estados Unidos: En busca de la confianza perdida," *Centro de Investigación y Docencia Ecónomicas (CIDE)*, División de Estudios Internacionales, 2010.

29. For more, see: Bruce M. Bagley and Jonathan D. Rosen, eds., *Drug Trafficking, Organized Crime, and Violence in the Americas Today* (Gainesville, FL: University Press of Florida, 2015).

30. Bruce Bagley, *Drug Trafficking and Organized Crime in the Americas: Major Trends in the Twenty-First Century* (Washington, DC: Woodrow Wilson International Center for Scholars, 2012), p. 9.

31. Jesus Murillo Karam quoted in Patrick Corcoran, "Mexico Has 80 Drug Cartels: Attorney General," *InSight Crime*, December 20, 2012. http://www.insightcrime.org/news-analysis/mexico-has-80-drug-cartels-attorney-general, accessed September 2016, 1.

32. Ted Galen Carpenter, *The Fire Next Door: Mexico's Drug Violence and the Danger to America* (Washington, DC: CATO Institute, 2012); Ioan Grillo, *El Narco: Inside Mexico's Criminal Insurgency* (New York, N.Y.: Bloomsbury Press, 2012).

33. Peter Watt and Roberto Zepeda, *Drug War Mexico: Politics, Neoliberalism and Violence in the New Narcoeconomy* (London, U.K.: Zed Books, 2012); see also Nathan P. Jones, *Mexico's Illicit Drug Networks and the State Reaction* (Washington, DC: Georgetown University Press, 2016).

34. For more on this topic, see: Marcos Pablo Moloeznik, "The Militarization of Public Security and the Role of the Military in Mexico," *Police and Public Security*

in Mexico (2009): pp. 65–92; Angel Gustavo. López-Montiel, "The military, political power, and police relations in Mexico City," *Latin American Perspectives* 27, no. 2 (2000): pp. 79–94; Shannon O'Neil, "The real war in Mexico: How democracy can defeat the drug cartels," *Foreign Affairs* (2009): pp. 63–77.

35. David A. Shirk, *Drug Violence in Mexico: Data and Analysis from 2001–2009* (San Diego, CA: Trans-Border Institute: Joan B. Kroc School of Peace Studies, 2010). 4.

36. David A. Shirk, *Drug Violence in Mexico: Data and Analysis from 2001–2009*, 7.

37. Rafael López and M. del Pozo, "27 ejecutados al día," *Milenio*, December 1, 2012.

38. Notimex, "Segob da a conocer lista de 26,000 desaparecidos," *El Financiero*, December 12, 2014.

39. Veronica Macias, "Han encontrado 246 narcofosas, en tres años," *El Economista*, June 11, 2014; see also "Narcofosas en 13 estados: el saldo del horror," *El Informador*, April 6, 2014.

40. Jim O'Neil, "Building Better Global Economic BRICs," Global Economics Paper No. 66. November 30, 2001.

41. Matthew Boesler, "The Economist Who Invented The BRICs Just Invented A Whole New Group Of Countries: The MINTs," *Business Insider*, November 13, 2013.

42. Consejo Nacional de Población (CONAPO), *Proyecciones de la población 2010–2030.* (CONAPO, México, 2014).

43. INEGI, Encuesta Nacional de Ocupación y Empleo Trimestral 2015 (third trimester), www.inegi.gob.mx, consulted in October 2016.

44. For more, see: Mexico, *The World Bank*, http://www.worldbank.org/en/country/mexico, accessed April 2017.

45. Daron Acemoglu and James Robinson, *Why Nations Fail. The Origins of Power, Prosperity and Poverty* (New York, NY: Crown, 2012).

46. Ibid.

47. "Mexico Peace Index 2017, mapping the evolution of peace and its drivers," *Institute for Economics and Peace*, http://visionofhumanity.org/report/mexico-peace-index-2017/, accessed March 2017.

48. Kate Linthicum, "Even before Trump's visit, Peña Nieto was Mexico's least popular president ever. Too late to change that?" *Los Angeles Times*, September 2, 2016, p. 2–3.

49. David Bacon, "Why Are Mexican Teachers Being Jailed for Protesting Education Reform?" *The Nation*, June 17, 2016; Diana Villiers Negroponte, "Mexico's Energy Reforms Become Law," *The Brookings Institution*, August 14, 2014, https://www.brookings.edu/articles/mexicos-energy-reforms-become-law/, accessed September 2016.

50. Jonathan D. Rosen and Roberto Zepeda, *Organized Crime, Drug Trafficking, and Violence in Mexico: The Transition from Felipe Calderón to Enrique Peña Nieto.*

51. "Dramático repunte de homicidios dolosos en México," *La Opción de Chihuahua*, April 01, 2017.

52. Kirk Semple, "Mexico grapples with a surge in violence," *New York Times*, December 13, 2016.

53. Ibid.

54. Zorayda Gallegos, "With 'El Chapo' Guzmán gone, war erupts in Mexican state of Sinaloa," *El País*, March 7, 2017.

55. Azam Ahmed, "How El Chapo Was Finally Captured Again," *New York Times*, January 16, 2016.

56. Hannah Stone, "The Disappeared of Iguala, Mexico: A Crime Foretold," *InSight Crime*, November 20, 2014, http://www.insightcrime.org/news-analysis/mexico-disappeared-iguala-crime-foretold-students, accessed September 2016, 2.

57. Maureen Meyer quoted in "On the Eve of the 2nd Anniversary of the 43 Students' Disappearance, the Mexican Government Still Holds on to Already Disproven 'Historic Truth,'" *Washington Office on Latin America*, September 22, 2016, https://www.wola.org/2016/09/eve-2nd-anniversary-43-students-disappearance-mexican-government-still-holds-already-disproven-historic-truth/, accessed September 2016.

58. Joseph S. Nye, Jr., *Soft Power: The Means to Success in World Politics* (New York, NY: PublicAffairs, 2004).

59. Azam Ahmed, "Police Sex Abuse Case Is Bad News for Mexico's Leader," *New York Times,* September 22, 2016.

60. Maria Patricia Romero Hernández quoted in "The Women of Atenco," http://www.nytimes.com/interactive/2016/09/22/world/americas/women-of-atenco.html, accessed September 2016.

61. Georgina Edith Rosales Gutiérrez quoted in "The Women of Atenco."

62. For more, see: Ioan Grillo, "After Vigilante War, Drug Trafficking Returns to Michoacan, Mexico," *InSight Crime*, October 13, 2014, http://www.insightcrime.org/news-analysis/vigilante-war-drug-trafficking-michoacan-mexico, accessed April 2017; Salvador Maldonado Aranda, "Drogas, violencia y militarización en el México rural: el caso de Michoacán," *Revista mexicana de sociología* 74, no. 1 (2012): pp. 5–39.

63. Jacobo García, "La corrupción de los gobernadores sacude México y cerca a Peña Nieto," *El País*, April 12, 2017.

64. Eric Martin, "Mexican President's Support Plumbs New Low as Gasoline Soars," *Bloomberg,* January 18, 2017.

65. Silvia Inclán Oseguera, "Judicial Reform in Mexico: Political Insurance or the Search for Political Legitimacy?" *Political Research Quarterly* 62, no. 4 (2009): pp. 753–766.

66. Jonathan D. Rosen and Marten W. Brienen, eds., *Prisons in the Americas in the Twenty-First Century: A Human Dumping Ground* (Lanham, MD: Lexington Books, 201); see also: Ishaan Tharoor, "The amazing luxuries found inside a Mexican prison," *The Washington Post*, February 16, 2016; Monica Cruz, "Two Years Inside a Mexican Prison," *The Atlantic*, August 12, 2013.

67. International Labour Organization (ILO), *Informal employment in Mexico: Current situation, policies and Challenges* (Lima, Peru: ILO, 2014).

68. "Los Ninis: Mexico's Lost Generation," *Pulitzer Center on Crisis Reporting*, September 15, 2011; José Manuel Salazar-Xirinachs, "Generation Ni/Ni: Latin America's Lost Youth," *Americas Quarterly*, Spring 2012.

69. "Los ninis de México: 7.5 milliones de jóvenes," *El Universal*, January 22, 2016.

70. For more on *mano dura,* see: Sonja Wolf, Mano dura: The Politics of Gang Control in El Salvador (Austin, TX; The University of Texas Press, 2017)

71. For more, see: Roberto Zepeda and Jonathan D. Rosen, eds., *Cooperation and Drug Policies in the Americas: Trends in the Twenty-First Century* (Lanham, MD: Lexington Books, 2014); Marten W. Brienen and Jonathan D. Rosen, eds., *New Approaches to Drug Policies: A Time for Change* (New York, NY: Palgrave Macmillan, 2015).

72. Kevin Johnson, "Heroin 'apocalypse' shadows New Hampshire primary," *USA Today*, February 8, 2016, 2.

CHAPTER 9. VIOLENCE IN HAITI: HISTORY, REFORMS, AND CURRENT TRENDS

1. "Hispaniola," Yale University, gsp.yale.edu/case-studies/colonial-genocides-project/hispaniola, accessed November 2017.

2. For more, see "Haiti," *The Clinton Foundation*, www.clintonfoundation.org/our-work/clinton-foundation-haiti/programs/growing-haitian-coffee-sector, accessed November 2017.

3. C. L. R. James, *The Black Jacobins* (New York: The Dial Press, 1938).

4. For more on this topic, see: Laurent Dubois, *Haiti: The Aftershocks of History* (New York, NY: Metropolitan Books, 2012).

5. Peter Granitz, "Hollande Promises to Pay 'moral Debt' to Former Colony Haiti," *Reuters*, May 12, 2015.

6. "Haiti Overview," *World Bank*, www.worldbank.org/en/country/haiti/overview, accessed October 2017.

7. Ibid.

8. Mike LaSusa, "Haiti Political Instability Complicates Efforts to Confront Crime," *InSight Crime*, March 17, 2016, www.insightcrime.org/news/brief/haiti-political-instability-complicates-efforts-to-confront-crime/, accessed November 2017.

9. OSAC, *Haiti 2017 Crime & Safety Report* (Washington, DC: OSAC, 2017).

10. Patrick Lemoine, Fort-Dimanche: Dungeon of Death (Freeport, NY: Fordi9, 2011).

11. Paul Christopher Johnson, "Secretism and the Apotheosis of Duvalier," *Journal of the American Academy of Religion* 74, no. 2 (2006): pp. 420–445.

12. "Haiti: Bureau of Democracy, Human Rights, and Labor, *U.S. Department of State*, February 28, 2005, www.state.gov/j/drl/rls/hrrpt/2004/41764.htm, accessed October 2017.

13. "Security Council Boosts Force Levels for Military, Police Components of United Nations Stabilization Mission in Haiti," *UN Press*, January 19, 2010, www.un.org/press/en/2010/sc9847.doc.htm, November 2017.

14. Timothy Donais, "Back to Square One: The politics of police reform in Haiti, *Civil Wars* 7, no. 3 (2005): pp. 270–287.

15. "Haiti Corruption," *Transparency International*, www.transparency.org/country#HTI, accessed September 2017; see also The World Bank, *The World Bank's Country Policy and Institutional Assessment: An Evaluation* (Washington, DC: The World Bank, 2010).

16. OSAC, *Haiti 2014 Crime and Safety Report* (Washington, DC: OSAC, 2014).

17. Ibid.

18. Jared Wadley, "U-M report: Violent crime escalates in Haiti as confidence in police erodes," *University of Michigan News*, March 9, 2012.

19. OSAC, *Haiti 2017 Crime & Safety Report* (Washington, DC: OSAC, 2017).

20. "World Report Haiti," *Human Rights Watch*. January 20, 2010, www.hrw.org/world-report/2010/country-chapters/haiti, accessed April 2017.

21. "Actes de provocation, de violence et de barbarie: le RNDDH tire la sonnette d'alarme," *RNDDH*, January 21, 2016 rnddh.org/content/uploads/2016/01/1-Violences-manifestations-21Jan16.pdf, accessed November 2017.

22. United States Department of State: Bureau for International Narcotics and Law Enforcement Affairs, *Money Laundering and Financial Crimes Country Database* (Washington, DC: INL, 2013).

23. Roberto Perito and Greg Maly, "Haiti's Drug Problems," *United States Institute of Peace*, June 1, 2007.

24. Thompson, Ginger, "A New Scourge Afflicts Haiti: Kidnappings," *New York Times*, June 6, 2005.

25. Small Arms Survey, *Small Arms Survey: Global Gangs* (Cambridge: Cambridge University Press, 2010).

26. Athena R. Kolbe, "Revisiting Haitis Gangs and Organized Violence," *HASOW*, (2013): pp. 2–35.

27. Ibid.

28. Small Arms Survey, *Small Arms Survey: Global Gangs.*

29. Athena R. Kolbe, "Revisiting Haitis Gangs and Organized Violence."

30. "Haiti: UN pushes on with anti-gang crackdown; 59 suspects arrested so far," *UN News Centre*, February 23, 2007, www.un.org/apps/news/story.asp?NewsID=21659&Cr=haiti, accessed November 2017; "Dozens of additional UN Police start work in Haiti to help local officers," *UN News Centre*, February 5, 2010, www.un.org/apps/news/story.asp?NewsID=21659&Cr=haiti&Cr1#.Umk_-RbvwzZ, accessed November 2016.

31. Johnston, Jake, "Recent Murders in Port-au-Prince Are a Bad Omen for Haiti's Election," *VICE News*, October 20, 2015, news.vice.com/article/recent-murders-in-port-au-prince-are-a-bad-omen-for-haitis-election, accessed November 22, 2017; Michael Deibert, "Could the Gangs of Port-au-Prince Form a Pact to Revitalise Haiti's Capital?" *The Guardian*, July 14, 2015.

32. Joseph Guyler Delva, "Violent street protests break out in Haiti over tax hikes," *Reuters*, September 12, 2017.

33. "Haiti Travel Warning." U.S. Department of State. September 12, 2017. Accessed September 27, 2017. travel.state.gov/content/passports/en/alertswarnings/haiti-travel-warning.html

34. Ibid.

35. "Haiti–FLASH: Violence to Arcahaie, several victims, many damages," *Haiti Libre*, August 26, 2008.

36. Jacqueline Charles, "Violent protest erupt in Haiti over budget passed on the eve of Hurricane Irma," *Miami Herald*, September 12, 2017. Accessed November 1, 2017; Samuel Maxime, "Massive Protests against President Jovenel Moise's Budget of Tax Hikes," *Haiti Sentinel*, September 20, 2017.

37. Ibid.

38. "A Police Woman Murdered in Haiti," *Belpolitik*, October 31, 2017.

39. OSAC, *Haiti 2017 Crime & Safety Report* (Washington, DC: OSAC, 2017).

40. "Haiti–Security: Crime, the Prime Minister tries to reassure" *Haiti Libre*, December 6, 2017.

41. Associated Press, "UN Mission Says Vigilantes Have Impunity in Haiti," *VOA News*, January 17, 2017.

42. "An end to mob justice in Haiti," *United Nations Human Rights Office of the High Commissioner*, May 8, 2013, www.ohchr.org/EN/NewsEvents/Pages/LynchingInHaiti.aspx, August 2017.

43. For more on this topic, see: Felipe Puerta, "Over 400 Vigilante Killings Have Gone Unpunished in Haiti: UN," *InSight Crime*, January 18, 2017, www.insight crime.org/news/brief/hundreds-vigilante-killings-left-unpunished-in-haiti-un-report/, accessed November 2017.

44. Ibid.

45. Ibid.

46. Manuel Roig-Franzia, "Many of Haiti's most-wanted on the loose after earthquake," *The Washington Post*, April 9, 2010.

47. "Peace brief 2010," *US Institute of Peace*, www.eisf.eu/resources/item/?d=4097, accessed November 2017.

48. Ibid, p. 2

49. Athena R. Kolbe, Royce A. Hutson, Harry Shannon, Eileen Trzcinski, Bart Miles, Naomi Levitz, Marie Puccio, Leah James, Jean Roger Noel, and Robert Muggah, "Mortality, crime and access to basic needs before and after the Haiti earthquake: a random survey of Port-au-Prince households," *Medicine, conflict and survival* 26, no. 4 (2010): pp. 281–297.

50. Philip Sherwell and Patrick Sawer, "Haiti earthquake: looting and gun-fights break out," *Telegraph*, January 16, 2010.

51. "Haiti: Cholera Outbreak–Oct 2010," ReliefWeb, reliefweb.int/disaster/ep -2010-000210-hti, accessed October 2017.

52. Jessica Desvarieux, "At the Heart of Haiti's Cholera Riots, Anger at the U.N.," *Time*, November 22, 2010.

53. James North, "Haitians Are Rising Up Against the Stolen Elections," *The Nation*, November 13, 2015.

54. Joseph Guyler Delva, "Deadly attack on Haiti police headquarters as tensions escalate," *Reuters*, May 16, 2016.

55. For more on this topic, see: "Haitians must lead on human rights," *United Nations Human Rights Office of the High Commissioner*, www.ohchr.org/EN/News Events/Pages/DHCInHaiti.aspx, accessed November 2017.

56. CICAD, *Hemispheric Drug Strategy* (Washington, DC: CICAD, 2010).

57. Julienne Gage, "How Haiti Successfully Curbed Kidnappings," *InSight Crime*, March 11, 2014, www.insightcrime.org/news/analysis/how-haiti-success fully-curbed-kidnappings/, November 2017.

58. "Top UN peacekeeping officials hail success of community violence reduction programmes," *UN News Centre*, November 16, 2016, www.un.org/apps/news/story .asp?NewsID=55572#.Wh0B0VLMzLY, accessed November 2017.

59. Carrie Kahn, "U.N. Peacekeepers Withdraw From Haiti, After 13 Years There," *NPR*, November 13, 2017.

60. Jacqueline Charles, "Haiti opens army recruitment," *The Miami Herald*, July 17, 2017.

61. Miriam Jordan "Trump Administration Ends Temporary Protection for Haitians." *The New York Times*, November 20, 2017.

62. Karen DeYoung and Nick Miroff, "Trump administration to end provisional residency protection for 60,000 Haitians." *The Washington Post*. November 21, 2017.

63. Hurricane Matthew: Haiti south '90% destroyed,'" *BBC*, October 8, 2016.

CHAPTER 10. TRANSNATIONAL ORGANIZED CRIME AND VIOLENCE IN THE AMERICAS

1. "Por cuarto año consecutivo, San Pedro Sula es la ciudad más violenta del mundo," *Seguridad, Justicia, y Paz*, January 19, 2015.

2. Rafael Ernesto Gochez, "Niños migrantes," *La Prensa Grafica*, April 11, 2015.

3. Frank Newport, "Democrats, Republicans Agree on Four Top Issues for Campaign," *Gallup*, February 1, 2016.

4. Dudley Althaus and Steven Dudley, "Mexico's Security Dilemma: The Rise of Michoacan's Militias," *Insight Crime,* April 30, 2014, www.insightcrime.org/investi gations/mexico-security-rise-militias-michoacan, accessed April 2017.

5. "Mexico's Cartels and the Economics of Cocaine," *Stratfor*, January 3, 2013, www.stratfor.com/weekly/mexicos-cartels-and-economics-cocaine, accessed April 2017.

6. Peter Shadboldt, "Philippines raid reveals Mexican drug cartel presence in Asia," *CNN*, February 25, 2014.

7. See, for example, Samuel Logan, "A Profile of Los Zetas: Mexico's Second Most Powerful Drug Cartel," Combatting Terorism Center, U.S. Military Academy, February 16, 2012.

8. R. Evan Ellis, "The Struggle Against Organized Crime in Guatemala," *Latin America Goes Global*, November 10, 2016, latinamericagoesglobal.org/2016/11/ struggle-organized-crime-guatemala/, accessed April 2017.

9. David Gagne, "Alleged Head of Honduras Drug Cartel in US Custody," *Insight Crime*, February 3, 2015, www.insightcrime.org/news-analysis/alleged-head-of -honduras-drug-cartel-in-us-custody, accessed April 2017.

10. "Leaders of Honduran Drug Cartel Face Federal Drug and Money Laundering Charges in the Eastern District of Virginia," Federal Bureau of Investigation Offi-

cial Website, December 19, 2014, www.fbi.gov/washingtondc/press-releases/2014/leaders-of-honduran-drug-cartel-face-federal-drug-and-money-laundering-charges-in-the-eastern-district-of-virginia, accessed April 2017.

11. R. Evan Ellis, "Honduras: A Pariah State, or Innovative Solutions to Organized Crime Deserving U.S. Support?" U.S. Army War College Strategic Studies Institute, June 2016.

12. R. Evan Ellis, "Transformación Militar en el Contexto del Crimen Organizado Transnacional en América Latina: Los Casos De Mexico, El Salvador, Honduras Y Perú," Colombian Army Transformation Command, August 2016, issuu.com/ejercitonacionaldecolombia/docs/revista_digital_transformaci__n_mil, accessed April 2017.

13. R. Evan Ellis, "Honduras: A Pariah State, or Innovative Solutions to Organized Crime Deserving U.S. Support?" U.S. Army War College Strategic Studies Institute, June 2016.

14. "Decreto 228/2016," *Boletín Oficial de la República de Argentina, January 21, 2016,* www.boletinoficial.gob.ar/#!DetalleNorma/140329/20160122, accessed April 2017.

15. R. Evan Ellis, "Argentina at the Crossroads—Again," *Military Review*, March–April 2017.

16. "Police use shipping containers to separate Brazil prison gangs," *Yahoo*, January 21, 2017.

17. Alejandro Dominguez, "Estrategias en Michoacán comenzaron en 2006 y siguen," *Milenio*, January 13, 2014.

18. "La Procuraduría General de la República ubica 9 cárteles; controlan 43 pandillas," *Excelsior*, September 16, 2014.

19. Phil Gast, Catherine E. Shoichet, and Evan Perez, "Extradited 'El Chapo' Guzman arrives in US; hearing set for Friday," *CNN*, January 20, 2017.

20. "Violent new drug cartel alarming authorities in Mexico," *CBS News*, May 2, 2015.

21. "As cartels renew battle, violence in border city of Ciudad Juarez spikes again," *Fox News*, November 4, 2016.

22. "Report: 'El Chapo' Guzman's Sons Wounded in Cartel Attack," *ABC News*, February 9, 2017.

23. Andre Valencia, "Cartel Jalisco Nueva Generación va por 'territorios' de Los Zetas en Tamaulipas ante caída del Z42," *Blog del Narco*, March 2015, www.blogdelnarco.mx/2015/03/cartel-jalisco-nueva-generacion-va-por.html, accessed April 2017.

24. "Fearing deportations, Mexico warns its citizens in the U.S.," *Los Angeles Times,* February 10, 2017.

25. U.N. Office on Drugs and Crime (UNODC), *Transnational Organized Crime in Central America and the Caribbean: A Threat Assessment, September 2012* (New York, NY: UNODC, 2012).

26. "El Salvador con más homicidios en C.A.," *La Prensa Grafica*, January 3, 2016.

27. Ibid.

28. Interview with personnel at the Office of the Technical Secretary of the Guatemalan National Security Council, Guatemala City, November 2, 2016.

29. Ismael Gordón Guerrel, "Informe de Fiscalía reporta unas 204 pandillas en Panamá," *La Estrella de Panama*, April 7, 2016.

30. Ibid.

31. "Principal narcotraficante do Panamá é capturado, diz polícia," *Globo*, September 6, 2016.

32. See Alessandro Solis Lerici, "Detrás de la economía de las maras salvadoreñas," *Nacion*, January 15, 2017.

33. Interview with Salvadoran security official, San Salvador, El Salvador, May 2016.

34. Interview with Salvadoran security official, San Salvador, El Salvador, May 2016.

35. "Operación 'Sultán.'"

36. R. Evan Ellis, "The Struggle Against Organized Crime in Guatemala," *Latin America Goes Global*, November 10, 2016.

37. "Venezuela: 5 Dead as Anti-Government Protests Intensify," *NBC News*, April 14, 2017.

38. Hugo Prieto, "Chaos Looms Over Venezuela," *New York Times*, May 3, 2017.

39. "Venezuela: Murder Rate for Year May Be World's Worst, Report Says," *New York Times*.

40. "Caracas, Venezuela, la ciudad más violenta del mundo del 2015," *Seguridad, Justicia y Paz*, January 25, 2016.

41. R. Evan Ellis and Roman D. Ortiz, "Un acuerdo entre interrogantes," *Foreign Affairs Latinoamérica*, Vol. 17: No. 1 (2017): pp. 93–100.

42. David Gagne, "Who Are the Urabeños Leaders Indicted by the U.S.?" *Insight Crime*, June 24, 2015, www.insightcrime.org/news-analysis/us-indicts-17-leaders-of-colombia-urabenos, accessed May 2017.

43. John Marulanda, "Asunto de Dignidad," March 30, 2017, jmarulanda.com/2017/03/30/asunto-de-dignidad/, accessed April 2017.

44. William Neumann, "Defying U.S., Colombia Halts Aerial Spraying of Crops Used to Make Cocaine," *New York Times*, May 14, 2015.

45. "Colombia's coca production soars to highest level in two decades, US says," *The Guardian*, March 14, 2017.

46. Interview with Colombian security professional, Bogotá, Colombia, May 2017.

47. "Colombia accepts role in 1980s killings of leftist politicians," *Reuters*, September 15, 2016.

48. Manuel Rodriguez, "Ex-agente de la DEA: Reverol es líder en el Cártel de los Soles," *Noticias Venezuela*, August 2, 2016.

49. "El impresionante éxodo de venezolanos a Colombia," *Semana*, July 23, 2017.

50. Antonia Maria Delgado, "Identifican a Diosdado Cabello como jefe del Cartel de los Soles," *El Nuevo Herald*, January 26, 2015, www.elnuevoherald.com/noticias/mundo/america-latina/venezuela-es/article8206548.html.

51. "Venezuela gives 'hero's welcome' to freed general Carvajal," *BBC*, July 28, 2014.

52. Loren Riesenfeld, "Peru Shoots Down Narco Plane Heading to Bolivia," *Insight Crime*, March 2, 2015, www.InsightCrime.org/news-briefs/peru-shoots-down-narco-plane-heading-to-bolivia, accessed April 2017.

53. R. Evan Ellis, "The Evolving Transnational Crime-Terrorism Nexus in Peru and its Strategic Relevance for the U.S. and the Region," *PRISM*, Vol. 5, No. 4 (2015): pp. 189–205.

54. R. Evan Ellis, "The evolution of transnational organized crime in Peru," *Latin America Goes Global,* May 4, 2017, latinamericagoesglobal.org/2017/05/evolution-transnational-organized-crime-peru/, accessed April 2017.

55. "Mafias del Callao se reorganizan tras caída de 'Caracol,'" *El Comercio*, May 7, 2016.

56. Ricardo Muga M., "In Chile, Cocaine Consumption is on the Rise," *Santiago Times*, April 25, 2010.

57. "Bolivia presenta amparo para liberar a detenidos en Chile," *Los Tiempos*, April 11, 2017.

58. Truth and Reconciliation Commission, *Final Report*, August 28, 2003, www.cverdad.org.pe/ingles/ifinal/index.php, accessed April 2017.

59. R. Evan Ellis, "New Developments in Organized Crime in Peru," *The Cipher Brief*, May 20, 2016.

60. Lloyd Belton, "Report Spotlights Drug Traffic at Santos Port, Brazil's Drug Policies," *Insight Crime*, July 20, 2016, www.InsightCrime.org/news-analysis/report-spotlights-drug-trafficking-at-santos-port-brazil-drug-policies, accessed April 2017.

61. Stephanie Nolan, "Crack cocaine is king in Brazil: What Sao Paulo is doing about it," *The Globe and Mail*, April 26, 2014.

62. Stephanie Nolan, "Crack cocaine is king in Brazil: What Sao Paulo is doing about it," *The Globe and Mail*, April 26, 2014.

63. "A lethal location," *The Economist*, September 17, 2016.

64. Pablo Ferri and Jose Luis Pardo, "Paraguay's Marijuana Trade: The Bitter Green Smell of the Red Land," *Insight Crime*, August 4, 2014, www.insightcrime.org/news-analysis/inside-paraguay-marijuana-trade-to-brazil, accessed April 2017.

65. David Gagne, "Lucrative Cocaine Trade Fuels Gang Presence in Brazil's Amazon," *Insight Crime*, January 13, 2017, www.insightcrime.com/news-briefs/lucrative-cocaine-trade-fuels-gang-presence-brazil-amazon, accessed May 2017.

66. "Economia Subterranea."

67. Aaron Daugherty, "Murder Draws Attention to Paraguay-Uruguay Marijuana Trade," *Insight Crime*, February 11, 2016, www.insightcrime.org/news-briefs/murder-draws-attention-to-paraguay-uruguay-marijuana-trade, accessed April 2017.

68. "Narcos brasileños usan Uruguay de trampolín," *El Pais*, January 24, 2014, www.elpais.com.uy/informacion/narcos-brasilenos-uruguay-trampolin-crimen.html.

69. Francisco Leali, "Polícia Federal aponta elo entre facção brasileira e Hezbollah," *O Globo*, September 11, 2014.

70. Bruno Ribeiro, "PCC envia dinheiro do tráfico para Estados Unidos e China," *O Estado de S. Paulo*, January 15, 2015.

71. "Brazilian army moves to stem prison violence," *The Guardian*, January 28, 2017.

72. For a detailed analysis, see R. Evan Ellis, "Chinese Organized Crime in Latin America," *Prism*, Vol. 4, No. 1, (2012): pp. 67–77.

73. Cecilia Di Lodovico, "Tres bandas de la mafia china operan en la Argentina y pelean por el poder," *Perfil,* February 26, 2017.

74. Elyssa Pachico, "Latin America's Weak Points in Fighting Money Laundering," *Insight Crime*, March 4, 2016, www.insightcrime.org/news-analysis/latin-america-weak-points-in-fighting-money-laundering, accessed April 2017.

CHAPTER 11. UNITED STATES SECURITY POLICY IN LATIN AMERICA AND THE CARIBBEAN

1. Sections of this chapter are from Eric L. Golnick, "United States Defense Policy in Latin America and the Caribbean," in *Fragile States in the Americas*, eds. Jonathan D. Rosen and Hanna S. Kassab (Lanham, MD: Lexington Books, 2017), pp. 301–322.

2. Mark P. Sullivan, *Latin America and the Caribbean: Key Issues for the 114th Congress* (Washington, DC: Congressional Research Service, 2015), p. 1.

3. Ibid, p. 1.

4. Carol Morello and Anne Gearan, "Senators sharply question State Department budget cuts," *The Washington Post*, June 13, 2017.

5. Ibid, p. 1.

6. Ibid, p. 1.

7. Ibid, p. 1.

8. Frank Mora, "The Top Seven Myths of U.S. Defense Policy," *Military Review* (2010): p. 2.

9. Ibid., p. 3.

10. Alex Daugherty, "The Trump whisperer: Marco Rubio has the president's ear on Latin America," *The Miami Herald*, June 26, 2017.

11. Ibid.

12. Christopher Sabatini, "Will Latin America miss U.S. hegemony?" *Journal of International Affairs*, Vol. 66, No. 2 (2013): pp. 1–15, esp. p. 1.

13. Ibid., p. 2.

14. Ibid., p. 3.

15. Mark T. Gilderhus, "The Monroe Doctrine: Meanings and Implications. *Presidential Studies Quarterly*," Vol. 36, No. 1, (2006): pp. 5–16.

16. Frederick S. Rudesheim, Michael L. Burgoyne, "Beyond Cocaine Cowboys," *Military Review*, Vol. 92, Issue 3, (May/Jun 2014): p. 34.

17. Ibid., p. 34.

18. Mark P. Sullivan, *Latin America and the Caribbean: Key Issues for the 114th Congress*, p. 6.

19. Ibid., p. 6.

20. Ibid., p. 6.

21. U.S. Department of State, Secretary of State John Kerry, "Remarks on U.S. Policy in the Western Hemisphere," November 18, 2013. www.state.gov/secretary/remarks/2013/11/217680.htm.

22. Abraham F. Lowenthal, "Obama and the Americas," *Foreign Affairs*, Vol. 89, No. 4 (2010): pp. 110–124, esp. p. 110.

23. Lois Beckett, "How Jeff Sessions and Donald Trump have restarted the war on drugs," *The Guardian*, August 21, 2017.

24. "Merriam-Webster Dictionary: Policy" www.merriam-webster.com/dictionary/policy.

25. "Presidential Policy Directive 1." Fas.org/irp/offdocs/ppd/ppd-1.pdf.

26. "National Security Council." www.whitehouse.gov/administration/eop/nsc/.

27. "Presidential Policy Directive 1." Fas.org/irp/offdocs/ppd/ppd-1.pdf.

28. Craig Deare, "Time to Improve U.S. Defense Structure for the Western Hemisphere," *Joint Forces Quarterly*, Vol. 53, No. 2. (2009): p. 42.

29. Ibid, p. 38.

30. "A U.S. Embassy at Work." www.state.gov/r/pa/ei/rls/dos/129183.htm.

31. "Bureau of Western Hemisphere Affairs," U.S. Department of State, www.state.gov/p/wha/index.htm, accessed September 2016.

32. "Department of Defense Directive 5105.75." www.samm.dsca.mil/glossary/senior-defense-official-sdo-and-defense-attach%C3%A9-datt.

33. Ibid.

34. "United States Southern Command." www.southcom.mil/Pages/Default.aspx.

35. Kathleen J. McInnis and Nathan J. Lucas, *What Is Building Partner Capacity?" Issues for Congress* (Washington, DC: Congressional Research Service, 2015), p. 1.

36. Ibid., p., 5.

37. Ibid., p. 8.

38. Ibid., p. 9.

39. Mark P. Sullivan, *Latin America and the Caribbean: Key Issues for the 114th Congress*, p. 15.

40. "Countering Transnational Organized Crime."www.southcom.mil/ourmissions/Pages/Countering%20Transnational%20Organized%20Crime.aspx.

41. "Joint Interagency Taskforce South," www.jiatfs.southcom.mil/.

42. Frank Mora, "The Top Seven Myths of U.S. Defense Policy," p. 3.

43. Ibid., p. 3.

44. Office of the President of the United States, *2015 National Drug Control Strategy* (Washington, DC: 2015).

45. "Countering Transnational Organize Crime," Unites States Southern Command, www.southcom.mil/ourmissions/Pages/Countering%20Transnational%20Organized%20Crime, accessed April 2016.

46. Office of the President of the United States, *2015 National Drug Control Strategy* (Washington, DC: 2015).

47. Don Winslow. "President Trump's War on Drugs Is Catastrophic," *Time Magazine*, June 20, 2017.

48. Mark P. Sullivan, *Latin America and the Caribbean: Key Issues for the 114th Congress*, p. 26.

49. Ibid., p. 26.

50. Craig Deare, "Time to Improve U.S. Defense Structure for the Western Hemisphere," *Joint Forces Quarterly*, Vol. 53, No. 2 (2009): p. 35.

51. Mark P. Sullivan, *Latin America and the Caribbean: Key Issues for the 114th Congress*, p. 26.

52. Ibid., p. 6.

53. "U.S.-Venezuela Relations Fact Sheet." Department of State, www.state.gov/r/pa/ei/bgn/35766.htm, accessed April 2016.

54. "Contingency Response," United States Southern Command, www.southcom.mil/ourmissions/Pages/Contingency-Response-Disaster-Relief-Humanitarian-Assistance-.aspx, accessed April 2016.

55. Mark P. Sullivan, *Latin America and the Caribbean: Key Issues for the 114th Congress*, p. 20.

56. "U.S. Army South plays a vital role in mass migration exercise" U.S. Army, www.army.mil/article/144159/U_S__Army_South_plays_a_vital_role_in_mass_migration_exercise/, April 2016.

57. John Kelly, *United States Southern Command Posture Statement before the 114th Congress* (Washington, DC: US Southern Command, 2015).

58. "Global Peace Operations Initiative (GPOI): State-DoD Partnership," U.S. Department of State, www.state.gov/t/pm/ppa/gpoi/c47008.htm, accessed April 2016.

59. The White House, *2015 National Security Strategy* (Washington, DC: The White House, 2015).

60. Ralph Espach, "Security Planning and policies to meet the Challenges of Climate Change," Center for Naval Analyses, 2010,oai.dtic.mil/oai/oai?verb=getRecord&metadataPrefix=html&identifier=ADA570771, accessed April 2016, p. 1.

61. Rene Marsh, "Trump administration dismisses climate change advisory panel," *CNN*, August 21, 2017.

62. Department of the Army, Department of the Navy, Department of the Navy, Department of the Airforce, and United States Coast Guard, *Joint Publication 1: Doctrine for the Armed Forces of the United States* (Washington, DC: Department of the Army, 2013).

63. For more on this topic, see: Paul Rexton Kan, *Drug Trafficking and International Security* (Lanham, MD: Rowman & Littlefield, 2016).

64. Craig Deare, "Time to Improve U.S. Defense Structure for the Western Hemisphere," *Joint Forces Quarterly*, Vol. 53, No. 2 (2009): p., 36.

65. Ibid., p. 38.

66. Nina M. Serafino, June S. Beittel, Lauren Ploch Blanchard, and Liana Rosen, *"Leahy Law" Human Rights Provisions and security Assistance: Issue Overview* (Washington, DC: Congressional Research Service, 2014), p. 1.

67. Ibid, p. 1.

68. Ibid, p. 1.

69. Ryan Dube, "Peru Looks to Restart Aerial Interdiction Program, Antidrug Chief Says," *Wall Street Journal*, July, 11 2014.

70. Gustavo Palencia, "Honduras approves shooting down suspected drug planes." *Reuters News*. January 17, 2014.

71. Adam Isacson, "Latin America's Dangerous Shift to Aerial Shootdown Policies in War on Drugs," *World Politics Review*, February 4, 2014.

72. Craig Deare, "Time to Improve U.S. Defense Structure for the Western Hemisphere," p. 34.

73. Cynthia Watson, Cynthia, "China's Use of The Military Instrument in Latin America: Not Yet The Biggest Stick," *Journal of International Affairs*, Vol. 66 Issue 2, (Spring/Summer2013): pp. 101–111, esp. p. 102.

74. Ibid., p.102.

75. Ibid., p. 102.

76. George A. Walborn II, "The Americas in Balance," *FAOA Journal of International Affairs*, Vol. 18, No. 1 (Spring2015 2015): pp. 12–20., esp. p. 15.

77. Stephen Blank and Younkyoo Kim, "Russia and Latin America," *Problems of Post-Communism,* Vol. 62 Issue 3, (2015): pp. 159–173, esp. p. 169.

78. Mark P. Sullivan, *Latin America and the Caribbean: Key Issues for the 114th Congress*, p. 20.

79. Ibid, p. 20.

80. Ibid., p. 33.

81. Ibid., p. 34.

82. The White House, *2015 National Security Strategy* (Washington, DC: The White House, 2015).

83. *Testimony of Roberta Jacobson, Assistant Secretary of State, Bureau of Western Hemisphere Affairs, Before the Subcommittee on Western Hemisphere Affairs* (Washington, DC: United States House of Representatives, November 2014).

84. Mark P. Sullivan, *Latin America and the Caribbean: Key Issues for the 114th Congress*, p. 35.

85. Ibid., p. 35.

86. "Fact Sheet: Peace Colombia—A New Ear of Partnership between the United States and Colombia," United States White House. www.whitehouse.gov/the-press-office/2016/02/04/fact-sheet-peace-colombia-new-era-partnership-between-united-states-and, accessed April 2106.

87. The White House, *2015 National Security Strategy.*

88. "Fact Sheet: Peace Colombia—A New Ear of Partnership between the United States and Colombia," United States White House.

89. Nicholas Casey, "Colombia's Congress Approves Peace Accord With FARC," *New York Times*, November 30, 2016.

90. "U.S. Relations with Brazil," U.S. Department of State, Bureau of Western Hemisphere Affairs, July 29, 2015. www.state.gov/r/pa/ei/bgn/35640.htm, accessed April 2016.

91. Peter J. Meyer, *Brazil Background and U.S. Relations* (Washington, DC: Congressional Research Service, 2016), p. 9.

92. Ibid., p. 22.

93. Martine Powers, "Caribbean nationals join forces with ISIS," *The Miami Herald*, October 15, 2015.

94. Mark P. Sullivan, *Latin America and the Caribbean: Key Issues for the 114th Congress*, p. 32.

95. Ibid., p. 32.
96. Ibid., p. 32.
97. Ibid., p. 32.
98. Ibid., p. 32.
99. Dianne E. Rennack and Mark. P. Sullivan, *Cuba Sanctions: Legislative Restrictions Limiting the Normalization of Relations* (Washington, DC: Congressional Research Service, 2015), p. 2.
100. Matthew Taylor, "Open Questions about Latin American Relations During the Trump Administration," *Council on Foreign Relations*, June 25, 2017, www.cfr.org/blog/open-questions-about-latin-american-relations-during-trump-administration, accessed September 2017.
101. Frank Mora, "The Top Seven Myths of U.S. Defense Policy," p. 4.

Bibliography

Bagley, Bruce M. and Rosen, Jonathan D. eds., *Drug Trafficking, Organized Crime, and Violence in the Americas Today*. Gainesville, FL: University Press of Florida, 2015.

June S. Beittel. *Colombia: Background, U.S. Relations, and Congressional Interest*. Washington, D.C.: Congressional Research Service, 2012.

Edmonds-Poli, Emily and Shirk, David A. *Contemporary Mexican Politics*. Lanham, MD: Rowman & Littlefield, 2016, third edition.

Feldmann, Andreas E. and Hinojosa, Victor J. "Terrorism in Colombia: Logic and Sources of a Multidimensional and Ubiquitous Phenomenon," *Terrorism and Political Violence* 21 (2009): pp. 42–61.

Goldstein, Daniel and Williams Castro, Fatima. "Creative Violence: How Marginal People Make News in Bolivia," *Journal of Latin American Anthropology* 11/2 (2006): p. 394.

Goldstein, Daniel M. *The Spectacular City: Violence and Performance in Urban Bolivia*. Durham, NC: Duke University Press, 2004.

Isacson, Adam. "Latin America's Dangerous Shift to Aerial Shootdown Policies in War on Drugs," *World Politics Review*, February 4, 2014.

Kessler, Gabriel. *El Sentimiento de Inseguridad. Sociología del Temor al Delito*. Buenos Aires: Siglo XXI Editores, 2009.

Klein, Herbert S. *Bolivia: The Evolution of a Multi-Ethnic Society*. New York, NY: Oxford University Press, 1992.

Lagos, Maria. *Autonomy and Power: The Dynamics of Class and Culture in Rural Bolivia*. Philadelphia: University of Pennsylvania Press, 1994. Latin American Public Opinion Project (LAPOP), *The Political Culture of Democracy in the Americas, 2014: Democratic Governance Across 10 Years of the Americas Barometer*. Nashville, TN: Vanderbilt University, 2014.

David A Shirk. *Mexico's New Politics: the PAN and Democratic Change*. Boulder, CO: Lynne Rienner Publishers, 2005.

Ribando Seelke, Clare and Finklea, Kristin. *U.S.-Mexican Security Cooperation: The Mérida Initiative and Beyond.* Washington, D.C.: Congressional Research Service, 2016.

Rosen, Jonathan D. and Zepeda, Roberto. *Organized Crime, Drug Trafficking, and Violence in Mexico: The Transition from Felipe Calderón to Enrique Peña Nieto.* Lanham, MD: Lexington Books, 2016.

Jonathan D. Rosen. *The Losing War: Plan Colombia and Beyond.* Albany, NY: State University of New York Press, 2014.

Snodgrass Godoy, Angelina. "When Justice is Criminal: Lynchings in Ciontemporary Latin America." *Theory and Society* 33 (2004): p. 621.

United Nations Office on Drugs and Crime, *Global Study on Homicides, 2013*. Vienna: United Nations Office on Drugs and Crime, 2013.

Zilberg, Elana. "Fools Banished from the Kingdom: Remapping Geographies of Gang Violence between the Americas (Los Angeles and San Salvador)," *America Quarterly*, V. 56, N. 3 (September 2004): p. 762.

Index

About the Contributors

Acácio Augusto is professor at the International Relations undergraduate course of the National University of São Paulo (UNIFESP). He has a PhD in social sciences (political science) from the Pontifical Catholic University of São Paulo, Brazil. Augusto is researcher at Nu-Sol/PUC-SP and author of *Política e polícia: cuidados, controles e penalização de jovens* [*Politics and Police: cares, controls, and penalization of youngsters*] (2013).

Adriana Beltrán has championed the promotion of a comprehensive, rights-based approach to tackling insecurity, violence, and the growing influence of organized crime in Central America for 15 years. As head of the Citizen Security Program for the Washington Office on Latin America (WOLA), a US-based research and advocacy organization, she promotes policies that identify and address the root causes of violence and improve the effectiveness and accountability of police and judicial systems. Beltrán's long-time advocacy for a UN-sponsored commission to investigate and prosecute organized criminal networks linked to the state helped establish the International Commission against Impunity in Guatemala (CICIG) in 2007. She has written and co-authored various reports and articles on police reform, organized crime, and violence in Latin America, including *Protect and Serve? The Status of Police Reform*, and *Hidden Powers in Post-Conflict Guatemala*, a groundbreaking study documenting the rise and impact of criminal networks since the end of the civil war in that country. Beltrán has testified before Congress and is a frequent commentator in the media—including the *Washington Post*, the *New York Times*, and leading outlets in Latin America. She holds a Master's Degree in International Public Policy from Johns Hopkins School for Advanced International Studies (SAIS).

Marten Brienen is lecturer in the Department of Political Science at Oklahoma State University. Dr. Brienen taught in both the African and Latin American Studies programs at the University of Miami from 2004 to 2013. From 2011 to 2013, he served as the director of the Latin American Studies program at the University of Miami. While he has worked on a variety of subjects, the fundamental principle that binds them together is his ongoing interest in the struggle between marginalized populations and the interests of states in the process of national construction in Africa and Latin America. From that perspective, he has in recent years focused primarily on energy security, drug trafficking, and complex emergencies. His recent publications include: Marten W. Brienen and Jonathan D. Rosen, eds., *New Approaches to Drug Policies*: A *Time for Change* (New York, NY: Palgrave Macmillan, 2015); Jonathan D. Rosen and Marten W. Brienen, eds., *Prisons in the Americas in the Twenty-First Century: A Human Dumping Ground* (Lanham, MD: Lexington Books, 2015).

Sebastián A. Cutrona is professor at Universidad Nacional de La Rioja, Argentina. He earned his PhD in international studies from the University of Miami. In addition to Fulbright, the organization that funded his studies in the U.S., Dr. Cutrona has held scholarships from Santander Bank, the Latin American Studies Association, the United Nations Conference on Trade and Development, among others. His most recent book, published by Routledge, is *Challenging the U.S.-Led War on Drugs: Argentina in Comparative Perspective.* Dr. Cutrona has taught drug trafficking and organized crime at the University of Miami, Universidad Nacional de Cordoba, and Universidad de San Andrés in Argentina. His research interests mainly consist in Latin American politics, organized crime, and drug trafficking.

R. Evan Ellis is research professor of Latin American studies at the US Army War College Strategic Studies Institute with a focus on the region's relationships with China and other non-Western Hemisphere actors, as well as transnational organized crime and populism in the region. Dr. Ellis has published over 170 works, including the 2009 book *China in Latin America: The Whats and Wherefores*, the 2013 book *The Strategic Dimension of Chinese Engagement with Latin America*, and the 2014 book, *China on the Ground in Latin America.* Dr. Ellis has presented his work in a broad range of business and government forums in twenthy-six countries and four continents. He has given testimony on Latin America security issues to the US Congress on various occasions, has discussed his work regarding China and other external actors in Latin America on a broad range of radio and television programs, and is cited regularly in the print media in both the US and Latin America for his work in this area. Dr. Ellis holds a PhD in political science with a specialization in comparative politics.

Eric L. Golnick is the co-founder and CEO of Veteran and First Responder Healthcare, a national mental health and substance abuse treatment company specifically for veterans, first responders and their families. Eric graduated with honors from the University of Miami in 2009. He attended US Navy Officer Candidate School shortly after and was commissioned as a Naval Officer in the summer of 2009. In his first position with the Navy, Eric served onboard two U.S Navy warships as a project manager for over 300 million dollars of equipment while supervising over 100 sailors. He was involved in multiple operations and exercises throughout Asia including a position with the Commander of US Naval forces in Japan. In this position, Eric helped plan and conduct emergency disaster relief operations during the 2011 earthquake, tsunami, and nuclear meltdown at the Fukushima nuclear power plant. After finishing his time in the Navy, Eric returned to Florida and earned a Master's degree in public and international administration from the University of Miami. While achieving this degree, Eric simultaneously took a position as a senior foreign policy analyst at the Department of Defense dealing with US military operations in Latin America. Eric worked directly with the president's National Security Council, the Office of the Secretary of Defense, the Joint Chiefs of Staff, and the US Congress on many topics regarding US foreign policy.

Victor J. Hinojosa joined the Baylor University faculty in 2003 and the Honors program in 2007. He earned a BA in economics with a minor in philosophy from Baylor University and an MA and PhD in political science from the University of Notre Dame. Dr. Hinojosa's primary research is in Latin American Politics and US-Latin American relations. He also has research interests in religion and politics, both empirically (how religion shapes political attitudes) and normatively (how Christians should think about international relations). His book, *Domestic Politics and International Narcotics Control*, was published by Routledge in 2007. His articles have appeared in *Political Science Quarterly*, the *Journal for the Scientific Study of Religion*, and the *Mennonite Quarterly Review*. His current book project explores the use of terrorism in Colombia's internal conflict.

Mariana Kalil has a PhD in International Relations from the University of Brasília (UnB), is vice-chair at the Global South Caucus (GSC) of the International Studies Association (ISA), and is lecturer at the Institute for Strategic Studies (INEST), Fluminense National University (UFF).

Hanna S. Kassab is visiting assistant professor at Northern Michigan University. He is the author of *Weak States in International Relations Theory: The Cases of Armenia, St. Kitts and Nevis, Lebanon, and Cambodia* and *The Power of Emotion in Politics, Philosophy and Ideology* both published by Palgrave. He is also the co-editor and author of *Reconceptualizing Security in the Americas in the Twenty-First Century* and the *Obama Doctrine and the Americas*, published by Lexington Books. He has published articles on International Relations Theory, national security, politics of the far-right and nationalism, acts of political suicide, and foreign policy. His most recent books are: Hanna Samir Kassab, *Prioritization Theory and Defensive Foreign Policy: Systemic Vulnerabilities in International Politics* (New York, NY: Palgrave Macmillan, 2017); Jonathan, D. Rosen and Hanna S. Kassab, *U.S.-Cuba Relations: Charting a New Path* (Lanham, MD: Lexington Books, 2016).

Barnett S. Koven is senior researcher at the University of Maryland's National Consortium for the Study of Terrorism and Responses to Terrorism (START), a US Department of Homeland Security Center of Excellence. He is also an affiliated scholar at the Jack D. Gordon Institute for Public Policy at Florida International University. Dr. Koven received his PhD, MPhil, and MA in political science at the George Washington University, as well as a BA in international affairs and Latin American and hemispheric studies. His dissertation examined under what conditions development assistance reduces or exacerbates insurgent violence, both where it is implemented and in geographically proximate areas. In addition to his dissertation research, Koven also works on other issues pertaining to counterinsurgency, counterterrorism, countering violent extremism, counter-narcotics, gray zone conflict, security cooperation, organized criminal violence, weapons availability and conflict onset, post-conflict reconstruction and the material and nonmaterial sources of military power. A complete list of journal articles, book chapters and policy publications can be found on his personal website: barnettkoven.weebly.com.

Cynthia McClintock is professor of political science and international affairs at George Washington University (GWU) and director of GWU's Latin American and Hemispheric Studies program. She holds a BA degree from Harvard University and a PhD from the Massachusetts Institute of Technology. Dr. McClintock was president of the Latin American Studies Association in 1994–95. In addition, she was a member of the Council of the American Political Science Association in 1998–2000, and served as the chair of its Comparative Democratization Section in 2003–2005. During 2006–2007,

Dr. McClintock was a fellow at the Woodrow Wilson International Center for Scholars. Based on her research at the Center, she is writing a book on the implications for democracy of runoff versus plurality rules for the election of the president in Latin America. Professor McClintock has received fellowships from the US Institute of Peace, Fulbright, and the Social Science Research Council as well as from the Woodrow Wilson International Center for Scholars. She has testified before the Subcommittee on Western Hemisphere Affairs of the US House of Representatives and has appeared on a variety of television and radio programs, including the "News Hour with Jim Lehrer," CNN International, CNN Spanish, National Public Radio, and the Diane Rehm Show.

Bradford R. McGuinn holds a PhD in international studies, with concentration in Middle Eastern studies, from the University of Miami. Dr. McGuinn is senior lecturer with the Department of Political Science and associate director of the Master of Arts in International Administration program at the University of Miami. His fields of research and teaching include international security, Middle Eastern studies, civil-military relations and political violence. For many years Dr. McGuinn has lectured to groups in the United States military and law enforcement community on questions of violence and insurgency. He has contributed book chapters dealing with security questions in the Middle East, Latin America, and the Caucasus.

Christa L. Remington is a nonprofit consultant and an adjunct instructor at Florida International University (FIU). Dr. Remington holds a Bachelor's degree in sociology/anthropology, a master's degree in public administration, and a PhD degree in public affairs from the Steven J. Green School of International and Public Affairs, Florida International University. Her research focuses on cultural competence, program effectiveness, and post-disaster response and recovery. She has done field work at international NGO headquarters, hospitals, IDP camps, and prisons in Haiti. She currently serves as the project director for The Mission Haiti Inc., a non-profit organization that focuses on education and community building in rural western Haiti.

Thiago Rodrigues is full professor of international relations at the Institute of Strategic Studies of the Fluminense National University (UFF), in Rio de Janeiro, Brazil. He has a PhD in international relations from the Pontifical Catholic University of São Paulo, Brazil, and the Institut des Hautes Études de l'Amérique Latine of the Sorbonne Nouvelle University, Paris. He is a researcher and member of Nu-Sol/PUC-SP and associate researcher of the Regional Coordinator of Economic and Social Research (CRIES), Buenos

Aires, Argentina. Dr. Rodrigues is Director of Institutional Relations at the Brazilian Association for Defense Studies (ABED) and Communications' Director of the Global South Caucus/International Studies Association (ISA). In addition, he is an associated editor for the journal *International Political Sociology* (IPS). He has published several articles and books in Portuguese, Spanish and English, including *Política e Drogas nas Américas: uma genealogia do narcotráfico* [Politics and Drugs in the Americas: a genealogy of drug-trafficking] (2017) and, in co-authorship, *Drug Policies and the Politics of Drugs in the Americas* (2016).

Jonathan D. Rosen is assistant professor of criminal justice at Holy Family University. Dr. Rosen earned his Master's in political science from Columbia University and received his PhD in international studies from the University of Miami. His recent publications include: Jonathan D. Rosen, *The Losing War: Plan Colombia and Beyond* (Albany, NY: State University of New York Press, 2014); Roberto Zepeda and Jonathan D. Rosen, eds., *Cooperation and Drug Policies in the Americas: Trends in the Twenty-First Century* (Lanham, MD: Lexington Books, 2014); Bruce M. Bagley and Jonathan D. Rosen, eds., *Drug Trafficking, Organized Crime, and Violence in the Americas Today* (Gainesville, FL: University Press of Florida, 2015); Jonathan D. Rosen and Marten W. Brienen, eds., *Prisons in the Americas in the Twenty-First Century: A Human Dumping Ground* (Lanham, MD: Lexington Books, 2015); Marten W. Brienen and Jonathan D. Rosen, eds., *New Approaches to Drug Policies*: A *Time for Change* (New York, NY: Palgrave Macmillan, 2015); and Bruce M. Bagley and Jonathan D. Rosen, eds., *Colombia's Political Economy at the Outset of the Twenty-First Century: From Uribe to Santos and Beyond* (Lanham, MD: Lexington Books, 2015).

Roberto Zepeda is researcher at the Centro de Investigaciones sobre América del Norte (CISAN) at the Universidad Nacional Autónoma de México (UNAM). Previously, he was research professor at the Institute of International Studies at the Universidad del Mar, in Huatulco, Mexico. Dr. Zepeda holds a PhD in politics from the University of Sheffield as well as a Master's in international studies at the University of Sinaloa (UAS), focusing on North America. He has taught politics at UNAM in Mexico City, and in the Department of Politics at the University of Sheffield. His most recent publications include: Roberto Zepeda, "Collateral Effects of Migration in the Americas: Security Implications," in *Reconceptualizing Security in the Americas in the Twenty-First Century*, eds. Bruce M. Bagley, Jonathan D. Rosen, and Hanna S. Kassab (Lanham, MD: Lexington Books, 2015). Peter Watt and Roberto Zepeda, *Drug War Mexico: Politics, Neoliberalism, and*

Violence in the New Narcoeconomy (London: Zed Books, 2012); Roberto Zepeda, "Disminución de la tasa de trabajadores sindicalizados en México durante el periodo neoliberal," *Revista Mexicana de Ciencias Políticas*, LI (207): 57–81, 2009. He is a member of the National System of Researchers (SNI, level 2) in Mexico since 2014. He has published nine book chapters, eighteen articles in academic journals, and five books, focused primarily on neoliberalism, migration, labor unions, and drug trafficking.